CENSUS OF INDIA, 1931

Owing to the antiquity and rarity of this book, certain pages are regrettably absent, and readability is compromised due to the blurring of the original text. If you possess any insights regarding the availability of these missing sections, kindly inform us. Your assistance is crucial in ensuring the completion of this significant work for the benefit of future generations.

CENSUS OF INDIA, 1931

THE ANDAMAN
AND
NICOBAR ISLAND

BY
M. C. C. BONINGTON

IN 28 VOLS. (IN 52 BINDINGS)
VOL. II
PART I - REPORT
PART II TABLES

GYAN

Published by

Gyan Publishing House
5, Ansari Road
Daryaganj, New Delhi-110002
Phone: 011-47034999, 9811692060
E-mail: books@gyanbooks.com

Distribution Network
gyanbooks.com
India, USA, Canada, UK, Australia

© Publisher

All rights reserved. No part of this work may be reproduced, stored, adapted, or transmitted in any form or by any means, electronic, mechanical, photocopying, micro-filming, recording or otherwise, or translated in any language, without the prior written permission of the copyright owner and the publisher.

ISBN: 978-81-212-7123-3 (Set)
978-81-212-7607-8 (PB)
First Published, 1933

2nd Impression 2024

Printed at: Gyan Press, Delhi.

The book is sold subject to the condition that it shall not, by way of trade or otherwise, be lent, resold, hired out, or otherwise circulated without the prior publisher's written consent.

CENSUS OF INDIA 1931 (VOL. II, PART. I & II)
Author: M. C. C. BONINGTON

CENSUS OF INDIA, 1931

VOLUME II

THE ANDAMAN AND NICOBAR ISLANDS

Part I—REPORT
Part II—TABLES

By
M. C. C. BONINGTON,
Superintendent of Census Operations.

CALCUTTA : GOVERNMENT OF INDIA
CENTRAL PUBLICATION BRANCH
1932

Government of India Publications are obtainable from the Government of India Central Publication Branch, 3, Government Place, West, Calcutta, and from the following Agents :—

EUROPE.

OFFICE OF THE HIGH COMMISSIONER FOR INDIA, INDIA HOUSE, ALDWYCH, LONDON, W. C. 2.

And at all Booksellers.

INDIA AND CEYLON : Provincial Book Depôts.

MADRAS :—Superintendent, Government Press, Mount Road, Madras.
BOMBAY :—Superintendent, Government Printing and Stationery, Queen's Road, Bombay.
SIND :—Library attached to the Office of the Commissioner in Sind, Karachi.
BENGAL :—Bengal Secretariat Book Depôt, Writers' Buildings, Room No. 1, Ground Floor Calcutta.
UNITED PROVINCES OF AGRA AND OUDH :—Superintendent of Government Press, United Provinces of Agra and Oudh, Allahabad.
PUNJAB :—Superintendent, Government Printing, Punjab, Lahore.
BURMA :—Superintendent, Government Printing, Burma, Rangoon.
CENTRAL PROVINCES AND BERAR :— Superintendent, Government Printing, Central Provinces, Nagpur.
ASSAM :—Superintendent, Assam Secretariat Press, Shillong.
BIHAR AND ORISSA :—Superintendent, Government Printing, Bihar and Orissa, P. O. Gulzarbagh, Patna.
NORTH-WEST FRONTIER PROVINCE :—Manager, Government Printing and Stationery, Peshawar.

Thacker, Spink & Co., Ltd., Calcutta and Simla.
W. Newman & Co., Ltd., Calcutta.
S. K. Lahiri & Co., Calcutta.
The Indian School Supply Depôt, 309, Bow Bazar Street, Calcutta.
Butterworth & Co. (India), Ltd., Calcutta.
M. C. Sarcar & Sons, 15, College Square, Calcutta.
Standard Literature Company, Limited, Calcutta.
Association Press, Calcutta.
Chukervertty, Chatterjee & Co., Ltd., 13, College Square, Calcutta.
The Book Company, Calcutta.
James Murray & Co., 12, Government Place, Calcutta. (For Meteorological Publications only.)
Ray Chaudhury & Co., 68-5, Ashutosh Mukherji Road, Calcutta.
Scientific Publishing Co., 9, Taltola Lane, Calcutta.
Chatterjee & Co., 3-1, Bacharam Chatterjee Lane, Calcutta.
Standard Law Book Society, 8-2, Hastings Street, Calcutta.
The Hindu Library, 3, Nandalal Mallick Lane, Calcutta.
Kamala Book Depôt, Ltd., 15, College Square, Calcutta.
* Bengal Flying Club, Dum Dum Cantt.
Kali Charan & Co., Municipal Market, Calcutta.
N. M. Roy Chowdhury Co., 11, College Sqr., Calcutta.
B. C. Basak, Esq., Proprietor, Albert Library, Dacca.
Higginbothams, Madras.
Rochouse & Sons, Madras.
G. A. Nateson & Co., Publishers, George Town, Madras.
P. Varadachary & Co., Madras.
City Book Co., Madras.
Law Publishing Co., Mylapore, Madras.
The Booklover's Resort, Taikad, Trivandrum, South India.
E. M. Gopalakrishna Kone, Pudumandapam, Madura.
Central Book Depôt, Madura.
Vijapur & Co., Vizagapatam.
Thacker & Co., Ltd., Bombay.
D. B. Taraporevala Sons & Co., Bombay.
Ram Chandra Govind & Sons, Kalbadevi Road, Bombay.
N. M. Tripathi & Co., Booksellers, Princess Street, Kalbadevi Road, Bombay.
New and Secondhand Bookshop, Kalbadevi Road, Bombay.
J. M. Pandia & Co., Bombay.
A. H. Wheeler & Co., Allahabad, Calcutta and Bombay.
Bombay Book Depôt, Girgaon, Bombay.
Bennett, Coleman & Co., Ltd., The Times of India Press, Bombay.
The Popular Book Depôt, Bombay.
The Manager, Oriental Book Supplying Agency, 15, Shukrawar, Poona City.
Rama Krishna Bros., Opposite Bishrambag, Poona City.
S. P. Bookstall, 21, Budhwar, Poona.
Mangaldas & Sons, Booksellers and Publishers, Bhaga Talao, Surat.
The Standard Book and Stationery Co., 32-33, Arbab Road, Peshawar.
The Students Own Book Depôt, Dharwar.
Shri Shankar Karnataka Pustaka Bhandara, Malamuddi, Dharwar.
The Standard Bookstall, Karachi, Quetta, Delhi, Murree and Rawalpindi.
Frontier Book and Stationery Co., Rawalpindi.
*Hossenbhoy Karimji & Sons, Karachi.
The English Bookstall, Karachi.
Bose & Co., Karachi.
The Standard Bookstall, Quetta.
U. P. Malhotra & Co., Quetta.
J. Ray & Sons, 43, K. & L., Edwardes Road, Rawalpindi, Murree and Lahore.
The Standard Book Depôt, Lahore, Nainital, Mussoorie, Dalhousie, Ambala Cantonment and Delhi.
The North India Christian Tract and Book Society, 18, Clive Road, Allahabad.
Ram Narain Lal, Katra, Allahabad.
"The Leader", Allahabad.
The Indian Army Book Depôt, Dayalbagh, Agra.
The English Book Depôt, Taj Road, Agra.
Gaya Prasad & Sons, Agra.
Narain & Co., Meston Road, Cawnpore.
The Indian Army Book Depôt, Jullundur City, Daryaganj, Delhi.
Manager, Newal Kishore Press, Lucknow.
The Upper India Publishing House, Ltd., Literature Palace, Ammuddaula Park, Lucknow.
Rai Sahib M. Gulab Singh & Sons, Mufid-i-Am Press, Lahore and Allahabad.
Rama Krishna & Sons, Booksellers, Anarkali, Lahore.
Students Popular Depôt, Anarkali, Lahore.
The Standard Bookstall, Lahore.
The Proprietor, Punjab Sanskrit Book Depôt, Saidmitha Street, Lahore.
The Insurance Publicity Co., Ltd., Lahore.
The Punjab Religious Book Society, Lahore.
The Commercial Book Co., Lahore.
The University Book Agency, Kachari Road, Lahore.
Manager of the Imperial Book Depôt, 63, Chandney Chawk Street, Delhi.
J. M. Jaina & Bros., Delhi.
Fono Book Agency, New Delhi and Simla.
Oxford Book and Stationery Company, Delhi, Lahore, Simla, Meerut and Calcutta.
Supdt., American Baptist Mission Press, Rangoon.
Burma Book Club, Ltd., Rangoon.
S. C. Talukdar, Proprietor, Students & Co., Cooch Behar.
The Manager, The Indian Book Shop, Benares City.
Nandkishore & Bros., Chowk, Benares City.
The Srivilliputtur Co-operative Trading Union, Ltd., Srivilliputtur (S. I. R.).
Raghunath Prasad & Sons, Patna City.
The Students' Emporium, Patna.
K. L. Mathur & Bros., Guzri, Patna City.
Kamala Book Stores, Bankipore, Patna.
G. Banerjea & Bros., Ranchi.
M. C. Kothari, Raipura Road, Baroda.
B. Parikh & Co., Baroda.
The Hyderabad Book Depôt, Chaderghat, Hyderabad (Deccan).
S. Krishnaswamy & Co., Teppakulam P. O. Trichinopoly Fort.
Karnataka Publishing House, Bangalore City.
Bheema Sons, Fort, Bangalore City.
Superintendent, Bangalore Press, Lake View, Mysore Road, Bangalore City.

AGENT IN PALESTINE :—Steimatzky, Jerusalem.

*Agent for publications on Aviation only.

Part I
REPORT.

TABLE OF CONTENTS.

PART I—REPORT.

PART II—TABLES.

INTRODUCTION.

Census of the Settlement.—The organisation for the Census of the settlement was not found to be a difficult problem owing to the comparatively small population. Except in one or two stray cases there was generally a sense of ready co-operation and interest especially by the local-born population who did most of the enumeration. The local Government had however, issued a notification to the effect that Government servants, if required, should render all possible assistance in taking of the Census.

Staff and Organisation.—An officer with a separate office establishment, consisting of a clerk on Rs. 75 per mensem and 4 sorters, was appointed. The previous censuses were taken by the ordinary office staff of the settlement offices. In 1911 and 1921 the Deputy Commissioner wrote the Census Report and in 1901 the Chief Commissioner wrote the report. The brevity of the 1921 Census Report showed that it was desirable to appoint an officer on special duty.

The Census Operations of the settlement of Port Blair were carried out by responsible Gazetted officers of the settlement to whom general instructions were given by the Superintendent of Census Operations. The three Tahsildars were appointed as Charge Superintendents. Personal instructions were given by them to the Supervisors and Enumerators appointed for the Census work who were mostly clerks of the settlement offices. All the enumerators and supervisors rendered much assistance during the Census without claiming any remuneration or allowance.

The convict population who were in convict stations were enumerated under the supervision of the jailors of the respective stations, and those in service and in villages were enumerated by the enumerators of the respective blocks. It was however found that all convicts did not record themselves as convicts, an omission which was brought to light when comparing the total of persons returned as convicts with the actual number of convicts on the roll in the Deputy Commissioner's office. All the forest camps and forest boats under the Divisional Forest Officer, South Andaman, were enumerated under the supervision of the Divisional Forest Officer, South Andaman. The enumeration of the whole of North Andaman which is a forest settlement was carried out under the supervision of the Divisional Forest Officer, North Andaman. All the ships crews and fishing boats and persons living on boats were enumerated by the Port Officer. Patients in different hospitals were enumerated under the supervision of the sub-assistant surgeons of the respective hospitals.

The preliminary Census was carried out from 6th February 1931 to 9th February 1931. As a large number of office clerks were employed on Census work the local Government at the request of the Superintendent of Census Operations granted two days holidays to all offices.

Mr. N. M. Ananthapadmanabhan, Census Clerk, was appointed as touring officer and he toured throughout the settlement during preliminary and final enumerations inspecting and instructing the enumerators and supervisors. The preliminary and final enumerations were creditably completed entirely under his supervision in Port Blair in the absence of the Superintendent of Census Operations who had gone to the Nicobars for the enumeration there.

Financial.—Except the pay of a whole-time officer for 9 months* and his office establishment the cost of the Census work was not excessive as Travelling allowance or other allowances to enumerating staff were not necessary. The settlement and Public Works Department lorries were placed

**Note by Census Commissioner for India.*—From October 1931 to April 1932 Mr. Bonington's services as Superintendent of Census Operations for the Andaman and Nicobar Islands were generously given by him without any remuneration.

J. H. H.

at the disposal of the Superintendent of Census Operations for the preliminary and final enumeration to facilitate the visits of Census officials to the outlying villages scattered about the settlement and only petrol charges were paid out of the Census grant. The total cost of the Census of the Andamans and Nicobars amounted to Rs. 5,901-15-6 during 1930-31 as under.

	Rs.	A.	P.
A. 1.—Pay of Officers	4,500	0	0
A. 2.—Pay of Establishment	578	12	0
A. 3.—Allowances and Honoraria	490	6	0
A. 4.—Contingencies	135	0	6
Total A.—Superintendence	5,704	2	6
B. 1.—Allowances and Honoraria	68	0	0
B. 2.—Contingencies	129	13	0
Total B.—Enumeration	197	13	0

An amount of Rs. 11,710-0-0 has been provided for the Census work during the year 1931-32 as under.

	Rs.	A.	P.
A. 1.—Pay of Officers	9,000	0	0
A. 2.—Pay of Establishment	1,070	0	0
A. 3.—Allowances and Honoraria	700	0	0
A. 4.—Contingencies	200	0	0
Total A.—Superintendence	10,970	0	0
B. 1.—Pay of Establishment	343	0	0
B. 2.—Allowances and Honoraria	147	0	0
Total B.—Enumeration	490	0	0
E.—Printing and other stationery charges	250	0	0

An expenditure of Rs. 700 is anticipated during the year 1932-33 as under.

	Rs.	A.	P.
A. 2.—Pay of Establishment	250	0	0
A. 3.—Allowances and Honoraria	100	0	0
A. 4.—Contingencies	100	0	0
Total A.—Superintendence	450	0	0
E.—Printing and other stationery charges	250	0	0

The Census of the Nicobars.

Census enumeration of Kar Nikobar was entirely done by the Assistant Commissioner with the help of several youths from the Mission School and the Census of the Central group was taken by the Tahsildar. The Census Superintendent visited the remaining islands and took the Census with the assistance of the Tahsildar, Nankauri, on a special 10 days' trip of the Station Steamer.

The Census of the aborigines was taken by the Superintendent on a special trip in the S. L. Akbar lasting about a fortnight. It was however not possible to enumerate more than a part of the population of Little Andaman as many septs were absent in the interior at the time of the Census and landing on the east coast was not possible owing to the weather conditions.

Mr. C. J. Bonington, Honorary Assistant Superintendent of Census, camped about a month on Chaura Island and collected anthropological and ethnological data. Dr. T. V. Damodaram Naidu accompanied him to give medical assistance and to take anthropometrical data. The assistance of the latter officer has been of great value especially in connection with the treatment of yaws. The Senior Medical Officer, Major D'Souza, also specially visited the islands in the latter connection.

Mr. C. J. Bonington has been of the greatest assistance in compiling this report especially with the chapters in the History and Cultural Anthropology of the Nicobarese. He spent several months in these islands. He also wrote the note on Bhantus in co-operation with Staff Captain Sheard of the Salvation Army. I am also indebted to the Reverend Stevenson who wrote the note on the Religion of the Nicobars. Dr. J. H. Hutton, Census Commissioner for India, and Colonel M. L. Ferrar, late Chief Commissioner of the Andaman and Nicobar Islands, have kindly gone through the report and I am indebted to them for their valuable advice.

CENSUS OF INDIA
1931

Part I-A.—REPORT ON THE ANDAMANS.

CHAPTER I.

Geography and Oceanography.

The Andamans, some 204 large and small islands, lie in the Bay of Bengal, 590 miles from the Hooghly mouth, 120 miles from Cape Negrais in Burma, and 340 miles from the northern extremity of Sumatra, within a parallelogram formed by the 10th and 14th degrees of north latitude and 92nd and 94th degrees of east longitude. The extreme length of the island group is 219 miles, with an extreme width of 32 miles, covering a land area of 2,508 square miles.

A study of the contours and physiological factors exhibited indicates that the Andamans and Nicobars form a continuous range of lofty submarine mountains extending from Cape Negrais in Burma to Achin Head in Sumatra, which Colonel R. B. Seymour Sewell in his "Geographic and Oceanographic Research in Indian Waters" (J. A. S. B., Volume IX, No. 1) proves is interrupted in places by channels of various depths formed prior to the triassic period which marks the evolution of mammalia, eliminating the theory advanced by Kurz that the islands have within this period been connected with Burma. Colonel Sewell dates the Andaman-Nicobar ridge to the late cretaceous period considerably prior to the triassic, and holds that these main channels, *viz.*, Preparis channel (100 fathoms), Ten Degrees channel (400 fathoms) and the channel between Sumatra and the Nicobars (about 750 fathoms) were fractures of this period.

Boden Kloss in "The Andamans and Nicobars" (1903), having made a thorough study of the mammalian and avian fauna, holds that there has never been any surface connection with the continent. Thus Colonel Sewell's valuable work disposes of the theory current in the last century of connection with the mainland since the triassic period.

It was further opined by Kurz in 1866 and Oldham in 1884 that the Andamans were the residue above water of submarine subsidence which was still continuing. Sir R. Temple supported this theory in his Census Report, 1901. The writer's observations spread over some thirty years, lead him to believe that rising and subsidence in various parts still continue, but are purely of a local and superficial character. They are readily visible in the tidal forests, for instance, as certain species of mangrove will only grow at certain tide levels. When small areas suddenly die out without reproducing their own species, the cause may be traced to either a local rise or subsidence of the soil or to conditions being changed by the formation of a new beach during a cyclone. Examples of the latter are found on North Reef Island as well as at Bumila Creek, Little Andaman, where a fresh-water *jhil* of considerable extent has formed and consequently mangrove forests have died. It is these local changes that were mistaken by Kurz for a sign of continuous subsidence of the islands. That the islands have risen from the sea bed is shown by the coral formation on the North East of Havelock, Little Andaman and Katchal as well as Chaura, Kar Nikobar, and Bompoka where coral formations are found at considerable heights. On Chaura, for instance, the hill at the end of the island (359) feet is covered with coral. At Kar Nikobar, within the memory of the people, part of the island rose and another subsided during an earthquake.

CHAPTER II.

Soil and Configuration.

The Andamans consist of a mass of hills enclosing very narrow valleys, the whole covered by dense tropical jungle. Throughout South and Middle Andaman there are two main ranges of steep hills of sandstone formation, from which spurs run in all directions. On the east the hills rise to considerable height, the chief being Mount Diavolo behind Cuthbert Bay, 1,678 feet, in Middle Andaman; in South Andaman, Koiob, 1,505 feet, Mount Harriet 1,193 feet and the Cholunga Range 1,063 feet; in North Andaman, Saddle Peak 2,400 feet; in Rutland Island, Ford's Peak 1,422 feet. Intrusive rock of serpentine appears here and there throughout the group, especially at the Cinque Islands, Rutland Island and Saddle Peak in North Andaman. Between the chief mountain ranges, which follow the east and west coast lines, undulating ground is found which often consists of impermeable blue clay beds, indurated shales and conglomerates containing pebbles of quartz and jasper beds; sandstone hills and knolls crop up irregularly. Such areas are usually waterless in the dry season.

The geological formation of Ritchie's Archipelago is quite different from that of South Andaman. Havelock Island is surrounded for the most part by white clayey limestone cliffs up to 540 feet high (Mt. Yoto). These surround a basin in the centre of the island, which is drained by the Golugma Creek. This basin is undulating and the underlying rock is a fine grained calcareous sandstone. Peel and Wilson Islands are nearly all gently undulating or flat. The latter has a hill 708 feet in the west corner. On the two last named islands, the geological formation is similar to that of Havelock.

There is about a square mile of level ground at the north end of Havelock of coral and sand formation particularly suitable for a coconut plantation, which on this soil would come into bearing after five or six years.

Several square miles of level ground suitable for wet cultivation are found in the Betapur valley in Middle Andaman.

CHAPTER III.

The Forests.

All the islands are densely wooded except perhaps a few of the higher peaks, parts of the Cinque Islands and 50 square miles or thereabouts which have been cleared in what is now the settlement of Port Blair. The forests are divided into two main types, *i.e.*, evergreen and deciduous, the type depending entirely on the underlying soil and rock formation, which determines the presence or absence of water near the surface during the dry weather, and this is probably the real factor governing the distribution of the two types of forests.

In the deciduous forests, which exist mainly on the lower and more gentle slopes of the hills, the principal tree is *Pterocarpus dalbergioides* (Padauk) and associated with it are *Canarium euphyllum* (Dhup), *Sterculia campanulata* (Papita), *Albizzia lebbek* (Koko), *Bombax insigne* (Didu), *Lagerstroemia hypoleuca* (Pyinma), *Terminalia Manii* (Black Chuglam), *Terminalia bialata* (White Chuglam), and *Terminalia procera* (Badam), which are the principal timber trees. Besides these there are many other species of minor importance from a timber or revenue-producing point of view.

The moist valleys along fresh water streams and also the steeper hills are taken up by evergreen forests. Various species of *Dipterocarpus* (Gurjan) are the most conspicuous and with it are associated *Sterculia campanulata*, *Myritsica irya* (Nutmeg), *Calophyllum spectabile* (Lalchini), *Artocarpus chaplasha* (Taungpeing) and several others of minor importance.

Mangrove forests are found on the estuaries of the many creeks in belts varying from a few yards to over a mile in width. Some of these growing near high tide limits are covered with high trees (*Bruguiera gymnorhiza*) up to 5 feet in girth, which form more or less pure forests, the yield varying perhaps from 50 to 100 tons to the acre or even more.

There are a number of excellent harbours and for the greater part the islands are cut up by many small tidal creeks which make the working of the forests comparatively easy and the average drag seldom exceeds a mile. At the same time exploitation requires some experience of local conditions and foresight as the coastal areas are exposed to the open seas and advantage has to be taken of the various seasons of the year to work different tracts. Camps have also often to be shifted because the areas are waterless in the dry weather and elephant fodder is sometimes scarce.

Government have worked these forests by departmental agency almost from the beginning of the establishment of the settlement. A start was made with portable forest saw mills and hand sawing in the forest of sleepers and Padauk poles for the Indian Telegraph Department; later a saw mill was erected by the Public Works Department at Chatham with an average out-turn of 100 tons monthly. In 1915 this mill was closed and a new mill was bought by the Forest Department from the Bombay Burma Trading Company with a possible monthly output of 750 tons in squares and scantlings. A second mill, an American Circular mill, was erected in Chatham in 1927. An American Band mill was opened on North Andaman in 1925. The total capacity of the Andaman mills is about 20,000 tons annually. Extraction has been mainly by elephants but of late years with the advent of the match log trade buffaloes have also been used successfully.

Mechanical extraction by means of a skidder was tried in 1930. Unfortunately it had to be closed down temporarily owing to the general trade depression. It was proved however that it was as economical as elephant power, if not more so in selected areas so long as mature timbers of all species are taken out, but the difficulty of marketing all species has still to be solved.

The net revenue obtained from the forests from 1869 to 1930 amounts to Rs. 45,65,764 which includes a capital asset of Rs. 21,39,983. During the same period some 650 thousand tons of timber excluding poles and firewood have been removed so that Government has obtained a profit of approximately Rs. 7 a ton on an average. An inside knowledge of departmental working however reveals the fact that nearly all the profit has been obtained on about one-third of the total output, *i.e.*, on Padauk and of late on soft wood logs which are consumed by the match trade and a limited number of squares of other species. The remaining timber mainly scantlings have often been sold at a loss.

In 1918 a new division was formed on North Andaman with headquarters at Stewart Sound. It was originally intended to confine exploitation mainly to Padauk, but in order to establish a more regular and systematic working of the forest exploitation of other species, so-called hard woods which form the bulk of the stand of these forests, was eventually decided on. An American band mill was erected for the purpose at Stewart Sound. Except when a considerable quantity of Padauk was extracted, the new division has never been a financial success, and the extraction camps and the mill were closed down in 1931, as owing to the world trade depression a market could not be found for the output of both divisions. The division is never likely to be a financial success unless either exploitation be confined to the more valuable species, as was originally intended, or market conditions improve and the out-turn is considerably increased. The out-turn of the mill would at least have to be doubled to bring down over-heads. In order to achieve this a better sales organisation and expert management would be necessary and both of these are difficult to organize under Government agency for various reasons as experience has proved. These problems are recognised and are receiving attention. It might prove satisfactory to lease out the forest to private enterprise.

The Timber Stand of the Forests.

Of the 2,508 square miles forming the total land area of the Andamans about 1,500 square miles are estimated to contain forests other than mangrove. Recent enumeration of all species shows that the stand of mature timber of all species varies from 8 to 30 tons per acre, and averages 15 tons to the acre. It is therefore roughly estimated that the forests contain some 14 to 15 million tons of mature timber ripe for the axe. *All these timbers however cannot* be sold at present because there is no market demand for them, moreover *only* about two-thirds of the whole forest area is accessible for working, the remainder being either exposed to long stretches of a weather-beaten open coasts or effectively occupied by savage tribes. Eliminating such areas the estimated stand of the principal species for which there is a demand is as follows :—the first column giving the total amount of mature timber available and the second column the exploitable amount per annum accepting a felling rotation of 30 years in the first instance :—

	Tons.	Tons.
Padauk	5,00,000	16,666
Dhup	5,00,000	16,666
Papita	5,00,000	16,666
Gurjan	6,00,000	20,000
White Chuglam	1,50,000	5,000
Badam	4,00,000	13,333
Koko	50,000	1,666
Didu	80,000	2,666
Taungpeing	50,000	1,666
	28,30,000	94,329

The estimate though rough is conservative and it may safely be taken that about a hundred thousand tons per annum can be removed and can probably be marketed. This is only a little more than twice the amount which has been taken out in recent years. Besides there are other species for which a market is sure to be found in the near future, especially soft wood packing case timber which could not be dealt with in the local mills because the plant is not suitable for it. If the Government obtain a royalty on an average of seven lakhs of rupees annually, four lakhs of rupees may be counted on as not return after allowing for maintenance of establishment and sylvicultural works. This is an estimate of the revenue obtainable if the forests are leased to a private firm. The forests are therefore a valuable asset of the Andamans.

CHAPTER IV.

History.

The history of the Andamans has been described in detail by both Sir R. Temple and Mr. R. F. Lowis, but a short summary follows of the history of the settlement to make the report self-contained.

(*a*) *Early History.*—Owing to their central position along the trade routes of India, Burma and the Far East, many mentions of the islands are found in ancient history. Their excellent harbours served both as a refuge in the monsoons as well as a place to replenish water supply. Like the Nicobars the islands are mentioned by Claudius Ptolemy (2nd Century) as

Agmatae* while the Arab travellers of the 9th Century mention them as Angamanain, by the Chinese Buddhist Monk I'Tsing (672), Marco Polo (1286), Friar Odoric (1322) and Nicolo Corti (1430). The earliest mention of the islands and their inhabitants has been seen by some in the Ramayana of Hindu Mythology which is regarded as indicating the inhabitants of the Andaman by its references to the 'Hanuman' or 'monkey peoples', the aboriginal antagonists of the Aryan immigrants in India. According to Temple (Census Report, 1901) the Malays refer to them as 'Handuman' a corrupt form of 'Hanuman' which has been carried down to them in story and tradition. Malays for many centuries used the islands for piratical purposes and for a trade in Andamanese slaves. These slaves found their way to the courts of Siam, Cambodia, and Indo-China for many a century, thus naturally bringing about the deepest distrust and hostility on the part of the aborigines to all visitors to the islands.

(b) *History of the Settlement.*—Owing to the activities of Malay pirates, the massacres of shipwrecked crews, and the desire to found a penal colony in 1788, Lord Cornwallis sent Lt. Colebrook and Lt. Blair to survey the islands and write a report as to their suitability for colonization. In 1789 the first settlement was established on Chatham Island at Port Cornwallis, now Port Blair, consisting of a free colony. In 1792 the settlement was transferred to north-east harbour, now Port Cornwallis, which owing to its vastly superior harbour, was excellent for the fleet. This however proved to be very unhealthy, and a high mortality rate caused the settlement at Port Cornwallis to be abolished. The idea of making the settlement a penal colony was first entertained when it moved to the northern harbour. The settlement was cleared but no mention of it was made for several years beyond having a station ship in the islands to show that the Government had not relinquished their claim.

For the next 60 years the islands have scant notice in the records. In 1824 the British Fleet was appointed to rendezvous at Port Cornwallis before the first Burmese War. In 1825 J. E. Alexander (*Travels from India to England*) gives an interesting account of a landing at Little Andaman. In 1837, Dr. Helfer, a Russian geologist, was murdered while searching for gold north of Port Cornwallis. In 1844, occurred the queerly coincidental wrecks of the transports "Runneymede" and "Briton", bound for Calcutta with troops from Sidney and Gravesend respectively, in the same storm off the Archipelago. The vessels were driven up on to the mangrove within a quarter of a mile of one another. Various attacks were made on the troops by Andamanese of the Aka-Balawa tribe.

Second Establishment of the Settlement.—The wrecks and visits of various vessels to the islands involved their crews in affrays with the Andamanese which ended in a general massacre. To prevent this as well as to establish a penal colony, necessitated by the Mutiny, Government ordered a comprehensive report to be submitted on the islands by a special selected committee. In 1857 Port Blair was selected as the best site for the establishment of a Penal Settlement.

Dr. J. P. Walker.—In March 1858 Dr. J. P. Walker arrived in the Andamans with 200 convicts and a guard of 50 men of the Old Naval Brigade. At the end of 3 months this number was increased to 773, but only 481 remained as 292 or 37 per cent. had either escaped, died in hospital or been hanged. Dr. Walker was a very strict disciplinarian and had to resort to severe measures to deter the convicts from escape.

**Note by Census Commissioner for India.*—"Agmatæ" is a variant reading probably to be preferred to the more usual "Aginnatæ"; an obvious emendation on the variant readings is "Agmnatæ", which brings us very close to the Arabic dual Angamanain for Great and Little Andaman though in point of fact it is the islanders not the islands whom Ptolemy describes as *Agmnatae*. Yule however suggests a similar identification for the island next mentioned by Ptolemy—*Agathou daimonos*, for which he would ingeniously read *Agdaimonos Nesos*, getting thus still nearer to our "Andaman". Apparently the Agmnatæ islanders are to be regarded as inhabiting both *Agdaimonos Nesos* and the adjoining five *Barussae* islands, which Yule identifies with the Nicobars under their name of *Lankha Balus* (*vide infra*, page 64).

J. H. H.

Attacks by the Andamanese were frequent and of a serious nature, and culminated in the Battle of Aberdeen on the 14th May 1859. Fortunately the settlement had been warned by an escaped convict Dudh Nath Tewari who had for several years been living with the aborigines, and the authorities were able to make preparations for the impending attack or the consequences might have been serious. Dudh Nath was among the Aka-Bea-da and not the Jarawa as stated in von Eickstedt's publication. He was granted his release for his timely services.

Colonel J. C. Haughton (October 1859).—Captain J. C. Haughton of the Moulmein Commission succeeded Dr. Walker. He adopted a more humane method of treatment of convicts and much endeared himself to them. He managed to establish friendly relations with the Andamanese, who began to visit the settlement. In 1861 the administration of the islands was transferred from the control of the Government of India to that of the Chief Commissioner of Burma. Mr. Haughton is still known to the local-born population as Jān Hāton.

Colonel Tytler (1862).—Colonel Tytler continued Colonel Haughton's humane methods. At this period some 149 acres had been cleared and cultivated.

Lord Napier of Magdala visited the islands in 1863, and wrote a memorandum suggesting certain reforms. He also secured a grant from Government for the formation of the Andaman Home. There were some 3,000 convicts in the settlement by 1864.

During Colonel Ford's tenure (1864), the number of convicts in the settlement increased from 3,294 to 6,965. The area under cultivation increased from 149 to 353 acres while a further 724 acres were cleared.

In 1863 General Man, who had been deputed ten years earlier to annex the settlement, assumed charge. Having previously occupied important positions in the Straits Settlement, he decided to introduce the penal system current there, which was founded by Sir Stamford Raffles in 1823. In 1869 a branch penal settlement was established in the Nicobars which continued till 1888. The number of convicts increased to 8,873, and 3,000 acres of land had been cleared and 876 been brought under cultivation. The health of the settlement improved, showing a reduction of the death rate from 10·16 per cent. to 1·2 per cent. In 1869 the settlement was re-transferred to the control of the Government of India.

General Stewart (1871) (Afterwards Field Marshal Sir D. Stewart).—The Viceroy of India, Lord Mayo, who took a keen personal interest in the settlement, drew up a scheme of reforms for General Stewart to carry out. "He directed that special attention be paid to cultivation, produce of the self-supporters, cattle-raising, timber, and produce from the Andamanese, as well as the codifying of General Man's rules into regulations". (Sir Richard Temple, Census Report, 1901, page 360.) On the 8th February 1872 Lord Mayo was murdered by a convict at Hope Town while on a visit to the Andamans. In 1872 the administration was raised to the rank of a Chief Commissionership. The Andaman Regulation of 1874 was drafted, placing the settlement judicially under the Government of India, instead of under the High Court of Calcutta, and life-term convicts could be released after 20—25 years of penal servitude, provided it had been accompanied by good conduct.

During General A. C. Barwell's tenure (1875) the Andaman and Nicobar Regulation III of 1876 came into force.

Colonel T. Cadell, V. C. (1879).—Colonel Cadell held the appointment for thirteen years which are marked by great economical developments of the settlement and its resources. In 1883 the Forest Department was established. In 1890 the Lyall-Lethbridge Commission included the proposal of separate confinements for a short period for convicts, and further confinement in an associated jail for a period of three years. The Cellular Jail was built as a result of these proposals but the Associated Jail was not built because it was found that it would be difficult to find sufficient intramural work for the convicts ; moreover, the incarceration of a large number of convicts would denude the settlement of the necessary labour for carrying out current public works in the colony. Actually also the two sites on the Minie Bay and Pahargaon hills were found too small.

Colonel Horsford (1892).—Colonel Horsford held the post for two years, when in 1894 he was attacked and nearly murdered by a convict. He pursued the reforms suggested by the Lyall-Lethbridge Commission.

During *Sir Richard Temple's* period of office from 1894 to 1903 the old Penal Settlement was at its zenith. The Cellular Jail was completed during this period and the Phœnix Bay Dockyard and workshops were considerably enlarged, while the reclamation of the South Point-Aberdeen swamp, which was started during this time but completed only in about 1918, had the most far reaching effects on the health of the future colony.

It was during *Colonel Douglas's* period of office from 1913 to 1920 that the Jails Committee formed its report and suggested abolishing the Andamans as a penal colony. During his term of office a forest colony was started in the North Andaman Division which has steadily grown but unfortunately had to be temporarily closed down in 1931 owing to the General Trade depression. Foreseeing the closing of the penal settlement in the near future several thousand acres of coconut plantations were planted up, which now yield an annual revenue of about Rs. 12,000 per annum.

Enquiries were also made during this period into the total indebtedness of the Nicobarese to traders, and further credit was prohibited. As a result of this enquiry a period of years was allowed during which traders might collect what they could, after which all remaining debts were to be wiped out.

During *Colonel Beadon's* tenure from 1920-23 orders were received to close the Penal Settlement. With the exception of some 1,400 Mappilla rebellion prisoners and some Punjabis no more convicts were received. Unmarried women convicts were returned to India, also certain categories of men convicts. The Government coconut plantations were made over to private lessees, barracks were closed down and some curtailment of staff made. The convict strength fell from 11,532 to 8,823. Colonel Beadon contemplated various changes which could not be carried out for want of funds, but at least a beginning was made in the abolition of some of the rigours of discipline and in shortening the probationary stages of convict sentences.

Colonel Ferrar held charge from 1923—1931. During this period very large changes were introduced and the plans for an immediate abandonment of the settlement gave way to a scheme for colonization and development through the agency of an enlarged population which was to be created by the settlement in Port Blair of ex-convicts and their families. All troublesome habituals or violent criminals were repatriated. The recruitment of convicts was placed on a voluntary instead of a compulsory basis and volunteers to be accepted had to be youngish men free from pronounced criminal taint. The old period of 10 years on probation as a labouring convict was abolished and after a few months in the Cellular Jail all convicts found themselves placed on a wages basis and freed from the necessity to wear convict dress and from other regulations which became progressively obsolete as the moral standard and general outlook of the convicts changed. Any convict wishing to import his wife and family could do so and during the period comparatively large homogeneous communities of Mappillas, Burmans, Bhantus and Sikhs were formed. The spending of their wages by five thousand or more *talabdars*, as the wage-earning convicts who work for Government are now termed, has given a great stimulus to local trade and improved the local standards of living. At the same time the lot of the free man was improved. New Regulations, III of 1926 and others later, have introduced security of land tenure for all classes of agriculturists, have abolished landing permits and restricted the obligation to obtain annual residential licenses. These measures have had a visible effect on the land, and on the urban and rural population. Everywhere the ephemeral huts of former times are giving way to well constructed two storied houses of sawn timber and iron roofs, with staircases, glazed windows and other amenities. A modern agricultural department has been started, co-operative societies organized and other social movements have received an impetus. Some of the more conspicuous public works have been the new deep water jetty at Chatham, connected with the main land by a causeway wide enough to take two motor lorries abreast, also Ross Island has received an up-to-date electric power plant. The most outstanding of all has been the filling of almost all the important malarial swamps round the harbour by dredgers of which special mention is made elsewhere. These changes have been mentioned here in some detail as they shed light on the changes that have occurred in the population, of which the chief points are the increase in the proportion that the free population bears to the convict, and the great increase in women and children. An interesting fact which shows what the outside world thinks of prospects in the Andamans is the building and equipping of a match factory by private enterprise at a cost of three and a half lakhs of rupees. This commercial venture, it is expected, will lead to others.

CHAPTER V.

The Aborigines.

The Negrito race is surmised to have been the earliest people to inhabit the continent of South Eastern Asia and of this race the Andamanese and the Semangs of the Malay Peninsula represent to-day perhaps the purest type. In the Philippines the Aetas are of the same origin but less pure in type, while traces of their race inbred with other tribes are represented in Malaya and are perhaps to be found in Assam and in the hills of Southern India. The chief characteristic of these peoples, a characteristic which is the key-note of Andamanese life, is, that they are naturally, "collectors of food, and not cultivators.... The social units is the family, and they move in family groups, where game, fish and wild yams are easiest to obtain." The many anthropological similarities of customs, religion, weapons, treatment of the dead, etc., point clearly to the definite relationship of the Andamanese to the aboriginal race inhabiting South Eastern Asia which is mentioned in Hindu Mythology.

It is only owing to their unique position and complete isolation from the rest of the continent that their survival can be accounted for.

The Andamanese are of two types :—(*a*) The coast tribes of South Andaman and all the tribes of Middle and North Andaman. (*b*) The Önges of Little Andaman, including the Jarawas of South Andaman and the Sentinelese of North Sentinel Island.

The difference between these two types is distinct, both in features, mode of dress, structure of bows, and language. Sir R. Temple in his Census Report, 1901, divided the first group into two sections. The Yerewa or northern section containing the Chariar, Kora, Tabo, Yere, and Kede tribes. The southern or Bojigngiji section containing the Juwai, Kol, Bea, Balawa, and Bojigyab tribes. This first group is however no longer an actuality.* Its members have lost all cohesion since some of the clans have entirely died out, while the remaining individuals marry irrespective of tribe, with however no contact with the Önge-Jarawa group, who keep to themselves.

Fortunately valuable historical, anthropological and ethnological data of this group have been recorded by Man, Temple, Portman and Brown, so no further mention need be made of them.

The Southern group or Önge-Jarawa group is the only one which is still intact. These inhabit the whole of South Andaman, Rutland, Little Andaman and North Sentinel. In addition there was a fourth clan of Jarawas on Rutland of which nothing has been seen since 1907. In that year a boy of the clan was reported to be staying with the Önges, but he escaped before he was seen by the authorities. A small communal hut belonging to those people however was seen. The hut was of the same type as that built by the Önges but quite different to the Jarawa communal huts ; nevertheless the Önges

*See Chapter V (*a*). The Andaman Home.

called them Jarawas and did not claim any relationship with them. This is interesting, in view of the fact that the fourth clan of the Southern group has not been again recorded, though Portman mentions that the Rutland Jarawas were distinct from the South Andaman Jarawas.

Portman further opines that the Jarawas and Önges, were originally one people consisting of *eremtaga, i.e.,* forest dwellers and *aryoto,* or coast dwellers and these tribes were the first to come in contact with Blair's settlers from 1789—7996 and that contact with civilization reduced the group so considerably that they could no longer hold their own against the Aka-Beas. Thus the Önges, coast-dwellers, retreated to Rutland and Little Andaman, while the Jarawas, forest dwellers, retreated to the interior of South Andaman. This theory is possible but it is doubtful whether the separation took place as recently as 1789-96, for though there are many points of similarity between the Önges and Jarawas which entirely separate them from the other Andamanese of Great Andaman, there are nevertheless distinct differences in dialect, custom, wearing apparel, house construction, etc., which makes one believe that they have been separated for more than a hundred years.

Cultural Differences, Bows.—The Jarawa, Önge, and Sentinel islanders bow is a curved long bow, while that of the remaining Southern tribes is S shaped and the North Andaman bow though also S shaped is somewhat different from that of the Southern Andamanese and is invariably inverted when unstrung. The Jarawa bow though considerably longer, broader and heavier is similar to the Önge bow. The Jarawa and Sentinelese bows have similar patterns marked on them, while the Önge bow has no special markings.

Baskets.—The Önge-Jarawa baskets have a pointed bottom and are coarsely woven while the rest of the Andamanese make a basket with a "kink" in the bottom and finely woven. A basket found on North Sentinel in 1927 was of very fine workmanship.

Wearing Apparel.—The Önge-Jarawas do not wear the bustle *(bod)* on their posteriors as the coastal Great Andamanese do. They do not wear leaves in the front as the Bojigngiji, but long tassels of fibre ; the Jarawas and Sentinel islanders wear a short tassel and have also been found quite naked.

Canoes.—The outrigger canoe of the Önges differs from those of the two Northern groups ; the prow from which the turtle are harpooned is according to Portman of recent origin and copied from the Great Andaman pattern. The Sentinelese have a different type of canoe altogether turning upwards and cut off short at both ends, which is not a good sea boat and could only be used on the shallow reefs surrounding the island. The Jarawas have no canoe but build rafts for crossing the straits.

Huts.—The Jarawas and Önges construct large communal huts though differing in shape. The Önges sleep on raised cane platforms in the huts, while the Jarawas and Sentinelese sleep on the ground. The remaining groups have no communal huts now but ordinary thatched lean-to shelters.

Remains of Ancestors.—The Önge, Jarawas, and Sentinelese have never been found to carry the complete skulls of their relations about with them, but part of the jaw-bone and other small bones. The other groups preserve the entire skull. It has however been found that the Sentinelese bury their infants in their huts placing a Nautilus shell and other smaller shells over the grave. The same has been recorded of the other groups.

Dancing.—The Jarawas and Önges do not use specially scooped out pieces of board for beating the time upon when they assemble for dancing, although a Jarawa woman has been seen using a hollow tree to dance on. The dances of the Önges and Jarawas are quite distinct from one another. The Jarawas usually dance in their communal huts where they always keep a large number of bundles of small leaf branchlets for the purpose. The Coastal Great Andamanese usually use similar bunches of leaves with which to strike the ground in their turtle dance, hopping all the time on both feet in a bent down attitude with the knees thrown forward. The Önges dance in the open, men and women standing opposite each other bending their knees forward at the same time lifting their heels. Such dances have a sexual inspiration.

Arrows.—The Onges and Sentinelese use multiple-headed arrows for shooting fish and birds. In the case of the Sentinelese, they use arrows barbed with small splinters of pigeon-bone. Specimens taken at North Sentinel showed they had been mainly used in shooting pigeon as they had a large number of small feathers adhering to the prongs. Perhaps part of their diet consists of such meat, for the number of pig so small an island must be limited. On a visit to the island a few pig were however seen.

Marriage.—The Önges marry while young, the girls being ten or eleven years old and not even developed. This is not to be wondered at for Önge children seem to know all about sex matters which is perhaps due to their living together in communal huts as well as to the actions exhibited in their dances. With the Önges there seems to be no elaborate ceremony as with other Andamanese. Men on a casual visit from distant villages are very often given a young girl* by an elder merely placing the man's hand on the girl's wrist, no word being spoken. The girl is quite docile and goes along but should the man let go, she will escape into the jungle and he has to go home without her. Nothing is known about the Jarawas.

Greeting.—The Önges unlike the Andamanese are completely silent when they meet. The residents of a village when meeting friends sit on the sand and the visitors sit on their laps; thus they embrace each other for several minutes without saying a word and pass on from one person to the next until all have been embraced, both men and women. Nothing is known about the Jarawas or Sentinelese.

From general observation of the customs of the clans of the outer group, the Önges of Little Andaman and the Jarawas of South Andaman may be classed as closely related. They are known to understand each other, whereas none of the friendly Great Andaman tribes understand either the Önges or the Jarawas.

The Jarawas of South Andaman and the Sentinelese are apparently very closely allied; possibly the latter are Jarawas, who while crossing Macpherson Straits on a raft were drifted out to sea by the tide and landed on North Sentinel Island.

Portman also mentions the existence of an *eremtaga* clan of Önges on Little Andaman. This information was derived from some Andamanese who were left on Little Andaman for a short time. They had told him of men coming from the south who had larger bows than the Önges, and of similar length to the Jarawa bow. A considerable portion of Little Andaman both in the Northern and Southern parts of the island has been surveyed by the writer, but no indication of a separate *eremtaga* clan was found. Its existence is therefore doubtful. Possibly the people belonged to a neighbouring sept, which had larger bows, for it happens that particular septs make larger bows when they are at enmity with another sept. On the other hand the island has not been completely explored, and the existence of an inland sept may still be found.

Conclusion.—Von Eickstedt, a German anthropologist who recently visited the Andamans, was also of the opinion that the Önge-Jarawas and the remaining Andamanese represented two different layers of the primitive Negrito race. He further mentioned that he noticed among the Önges of Little Andaman somatic influences of Arab and other alien origin, whereas the Great Andamanese possessed a considerable mixture of Burmese and other elements. These elements he opined were due to shipwrecks. Von Eickstedt's views and opinions require confirmation. It is however of interest to note that Portman found hereditary syphilis to be present among the race. Dr. Hutton suggests that Portman mistook yaws for syphilis, but the writer has not noticed among the Önges the distinctive features of this disease which is frequent in the Nicobars. Further investigation is necessary to confirm either view.

Of those Great Andamanese that the German anthropologist saw, a very considerable number must have been half-breeds who differ from the pure-blooded Negrito both in facial features and in stature. The most

*It is probable that these marriages have been arranged on previous visits.

noticeable difference between the hybrid and the pure Negrito lies in the hair, which is distinctly frizzly like that of the Papuan whereas the pure Negrito hair is curly and short, growing in what appear to be at first sight separate and as it were insulated tufts. This is especially remarkable in a few half-bred civilized women (of whom one is at school in Rangoon) who have allowed their hair to grow long, while those who retain their primitive life keep it short. It is this feature of the hair and height of stature mainly which does not seem noticeable among the Önges in the somatic strain, so named, of von Eickstedt. Among the Great Andamanese, only one instance came to notice of a girl with undoubted Burmese features, but with the hair and skin of an Andamanese, while one Önge was seen with frizzly hair.

Dr. Hutton has suggested the aquiline nose noticed by von Eickstedt among the Andamanese may be the result not of an Arab mixture but of Papuan strain since the aquiline nose arising from a glabial depression is a typical Papuan feature. Since both Papuans and Negritos are branches of the Oceanic Negro family, an early connection between the two is not impossible and the hair in that case would probably conform to the negroid type. In connection with von Eickstedt's remarks of difference in features among the Önges leading him to suspect somatic influences, it may be mentioned that similar differences were noticeable among the Andamanese when these tribes were still pure and numerous. These differences exist also among the Jarawas.

CHAPTER V(*a*).

The Andaman Home.

The primary object in the foundation of a settlement in the Andamans was to conciliate the aborigines. The policy adopted towards the Andamanese was, under an order by the Governor-General in Council "to adhere strictly to a conciliating line of conduct," and "to absolutely prohibit any aggression upon them and not to allow force on any account to be resorted to unless it be absolutely necessary to repel their attacks". Prior to the appointment of Colonel Tytler (1862) as Superintendent, relations with the Andamanese were of an extremely precarious nature, and there was much bloodshed on both sides, involving the indiscriminate massacre of runaway convicts. The only solution to the problem was to bring the Andamanese into the settlement, thus ensuring friendly relations and extending them to the outlying tribes by a policy of kindness and tact.

Through the efforts of the Rev. H. Corbyn, Chaplain at Port Blair, friendly relations were established in 1863, and a few Andamanese, 28 in number, were induced to visit the settlement. These established themselves in a collection of huts on Ross Island and the enclosure came to be known as the Andaman Home. A ticket of leave convict was placed in direct supervision of the Home under Mr. Corbyn, the Government of India granting an allowance of Rs. 100 per mensem for its upkeep.

While in charge of the Andamanese Mr. Corbyn greatly extended relations with the tribes of the mainland and the Labyrinth. In 1863 Lord Napier of Magdala while inspecting the islands suggested that an allowance of Rs. 200 per mensem should be granted to the Andaman Home owing to its enlargement and that full approbation should be given to Mr. Corbyn by Government for his services.

The aims of Mr. Corbyn's policy was to civilize the Andamanese in the Home. He attempted to teach them English and to use his own words "daily employed them in work with native convicts cleaning sites, etc." The immediate results were that illness broke out among the Andamanese and many escaped. The remainder were put under restraint with convict guards in attendance. The impossibility was only too clearly indicated of striving to keep a primitive nomadic people to a civilized and settled life, a measure solely attainable under conditions of restraint akin to slavery.

In 1864 Colonel Ford succeeded Colonel Tytler and disagreed with Mr. Corbyn in his policy of administration of the Andaman Home. Mr. Corbyn resigned, and Mr. J. N. Homfray assumed charge of the Home.

Mr. Homfray was in charge of the Andaman Home for some ten years and during the course of his charge brought many of the outlying tribes into contact with the settlement, relations extending as far north as Interview Island. Attacks were becoming unknown. The Home was now transferred from Ross to the mainland, where it became more popular as there was no longer a feeling of restraint ; as many as 100 Andamanese would be in residence together. In 1867 Homfray placed the number of Andamanese of Great Andaman at 3,000. He considered that the race was becoming extinct, as Dr. Mouat in 1858 had computed the number at 5,000. Conditions at the Home also appeared to be unnatural, for though 2 births were recorded per mensem, all the children died within a week of birth. The Andamanese proved to be of great use to the settlement in capturing runaways. They also realised profits for the extra expenditure incurred by the Home by working in boats, looking after gardens which they rented from Government, tending cattle, rearing pigs and poultry and selling forest produce.

Their employment as boatmen they did not however relish as it necessitated considerable restraint, numbers deserting as a consequence.

In 1874 Mr. Tuson succeeded Mr. Homfray and a system was developed of establishing homes for the Andamanese at various strategical points around the settlement, under the care of convicts, which allowed for the maintenance of friendly relations with the outlying Andamanese as well as controlling the movements of runaways. In 1875 Mr. Man succeeded Mr. Tuson in the charge of the Home for a period of some four years. It was then noticed for the first time that the Andamanese were suffering from syphilis owing to their intimacy with convicts, the petty officer in charge of the Home being the chief offender. During the course of his charge Mr. Man visited and for the first time persuaded the inhabitants of North Andaman to come to the settlement. In 1877 however a severe outbreak of measles occurred in the Homes, to which many Andamanese succumbed. The epidemic spread to the North and Middle Andaman tribes. This together with syphilis caused great ravages among the aborigines ; indeed by the latter disease scarcely a household on Great Andaman was uninfected.

In 1879 M. V. Portman assumed charge over the Home. He was much struck by the decrease in the numbers of the Andamanese and the ravages caused by syphilis on North Andaman ; some 134 cases of syphilis were admitted into hospital during the year, and it was noticed that hereditary syphilis was beginning to appear.

With the exception of a break of a few years Mr. Portman was in charge of the Home till 1900. He took a great interest in the Andamanese and was always in touch with them as he established a home for them in his compound, employing them as his own boatmen and servants in his house, which was much appreciated by the Andamanese.

In 1863 an orphanage was founded by the Rev. Mr. Corbyn for young Andamanese, who were to be educated and later employed as servants. A convict was placed in charge of them and their school education consisted of " English reading and writing, Urdu translation and elementary arithmetic ".

That the young Andamanese resented the conditions of restraint under which they were put, can be vouched for by the fact the orphanage was continually empty as its inmates had run away.

To quote the Rev. Mr. Chard's report " Little success attends the projects of cultivating in Andamanese boys in the orphanage a taste for settled life, or for a livelihood gained by farming, cultivation or domestic services ", etc., As a result of the complete lack of success the orphanage was finally closed down in 1888.

In 1882 the sick and death rate being very high, the Home was transferred to Haddo. A hospital was later attached to all other Homes, proving of a great help to the inmates. In 1885 Portman wrote " It is sad to see the ravages which syphilis is working among them, and their numbers are becoming less year by year ". The death rates were far in advance of the births and the hospital was always full. In 1896, eleven years later, he noted that " quite two-thirds of Great Andaman being now depopulated, the extinction of this branch of the race cannot be far off ". In Middle Andaman and Stewart Sound many deaths occurred and " Bodies were said to have been seen lying in the huts, there being no one left to bury them ".

Under Portman the balance in the funds of the Home greatly increased as he initiated the Trepang Fishery and took over the collection of edible bird's nests. This accumulation of the balance of the fund was in later years to be the actual Home Fund, and the Government allowance was withdrawn.

Isolated cases of crime involving violence occasionally appeared but these were only signs of the highly strung temperament of the aborigines and they occurred very rarely. The delinquents were usually flogged and confined to the settlement for a stated period.

Births at the Home decreased considerably year by year and invariably involved the death of the child within a few weeks of birth. It was found wiser to send all Andamenese women in the Home to be confined in the jungle among their own people as there appeared to be a greater chance of the children surviving.

The most creditable achievement in Portman's work was his successful conciliation of the Önges of Little Andaman, a full account of which is found in the chapter on Önges. On the retirement of Portman from the Andamans in 1900, the Andaman Home came under the administrative charge of the Deputy Commissioner, special officers being placed in executive charge. In 1901 the Census took place, and the Andamanese of Great Andaman were first enumerated, the Aka-Tabo tribe being discovered on North Andaman. The Andamanese had then decreased by some 90 per cent. since Homfray's estimation of their number.

In 1903 the present writer took over executive charge of the Home from Mr. C. G. Rogers. A daily average of 140 Andamanese were maintained at the Homes. Steps were taken to remove the Andamanese as far as possible from all contact with the settlement. By 1911, the number of Andamanese of the friendly Tribes of Great Andaman had dwindled to 209 and the end of the race appeared in sight. Owing to the hereditary syphilis the birth rate was excessively low.

The reorganisation of the settlement which involved the abolition of the Andaman Commission, reducing the five Assistants to two, left no one available specially to look after the Andamanese. Moreover neither of these two deputed officers of the Indian Police could spare the time to take the special interest in the aborigines which was given them by specially selected officers of the previous organisation.

In 1931, the present writer again took over charge of the Home and the Census showed that only 90 remained and of these the majority suffer from hereditary syphilis while the men are completely sterile. There are however a few healthy half-bred children, the result of unions between Andamanese women and the convicts. The opening up of the forest camps at Stewart Sound certainly hastened the extinction of the Andamanese in those parts owing to contagious diseases having been introduced among them, especially influenza.

At the beginning of this year the writer after a medical inspection by the Senior Medical Officer, Port Blair and Lady Doctor followed by necessary treatment transferred the few remaining Andamanese from the vicinity of the Settlement to Ritchie's Archipelago, where, away from all contact with Port Blair, it is hoped that the few derelicts of the once numerous aboriginal race will be less exposed to contact with civilization. Unfortunately the move has come too late and it is doubtful whether there will be any pure bred Andamanese of the coastal tribes left in another generation. The death rate is high, an average of one dying every month so far, but those who succumbed had been in poor health for many years and with one or two exceptions those who remain are fairly healthy.

It must be borne in mind that the Andaman Home was established with the object of maintaining a place within the settlement where the Andamanese could be kept separate from the convict population and at the same time Government could establish close contact with them so as to befriend and conciliate them. This would have been impossible without some such institution as the Home, as is only too apparent in the case of the Önges who, with the exception of one or two septs of the North East coast of the Little Andaman who regularly visit Port Blair, could not really be trusted even at the present day were shipwrecked mariners to land on their coast, although they may be quite friendly when officials visit them to leave presents. To protect shipwrecked mariners against massacre by the aborigines was one of the main objects of establishing the settlement. Yet the only places on the Andaman coast where they would be given any assistance even to-day are those parts inhabited by the friendly tribes of Great Andaman while more than half of the west coast of Great Andaman, inhabited by Jarawas, and the coast of North Sentinel are probably as unsafe to-day as they were 100 years ago, and every unarmed stranger would be killed. Only recently a shipwrecked crew landed on the Andamans, fortunately on a part of the coast inhabited by friendly Andamanese and they were eventually, after several months' great hardship, brought to Port Blair.

It is difficult but necessary to place a just value on the successful efforts of our predecessors towards establishing friendly relations with the Andamanese through the Home, in order to meet the criticism published by von Eickstedt that the Andaman Home was the door of death to the Andamanese race. There can be no doubt that had our predecessors had the experience which has been now gained, a different policy would have been pursued but it must be borne in mind that in order to befriend a savage, contact with civilization must be established and once this is done the dying out of a primitive race like the Negrito is apt to follow in due course as local history and general experience elsewhere only too clearly shows. It seems to be unavoidable that individuals should get infected by diseases such as syphilis, measles, influenza, etc., and once infection starts it overruns the whole tribe because those infected cannot be segregated or brought in for treatment owing to their nomadic habits, natural dislike of any civilized treatment and disregard for those seriously ill, who are usually left exposed outside their crude shelters.

Well-meaning officials made attempts to civilize the Andamanese; if they had succeeded, which I have already pointed out to be contrary to experience, the race might have been preserved longer, because it would have experienced the benefits of civilization in the form of medical treatment; this is evident in the case of a few Andamanese who were taken on as domestic servants. The main obstacles were that very few people take the necessary personal interest in and patience with a savage race to train them, and the Andamanese themselves were difficult to wean from their nomadic habits.

At the time of writing there is one half-bred Andamanese girl in the Bishop's Home in Rangoon reading in the eighth standard. It is her desire to become a Hospital nurse. There is also a Jarawa boy at the Roman Catholic Mission school in Ranchi. This boy was found by Captain West's party. He was for some years under the care of the medical authorities and was sent to Ranchi with some Oraons in order to keep him away from the influence of convicts. He has always shown an antipathy towards the coast Andamanese. The boy is now about 7 years of age and quite strong and healthy. He is very reserved with the missionaries but happy in the Oraon family with which he lives. Sometimes he shows a violent temperament and in those fits he eats earth. He insists on getting meat and fish daily. He is now attending school and is reported to be progressing well. It is hoped that some day he will return to the Andamans as a forester.

CHAPTER V (*b*).

Record of Relations with Jarawas.

Contact was first made with the Jarawa in 1790, during the foundation of the first settlement. They then occupied the south side of the harbour and curiously enough were more disposed to friendly relations with the settlement than with the Aka-bea-da who occupied the north side. Both Lts. Colebrooke 1789-90 and Blair, 1789-96 make mention of them in their diaries, the former securing a small vocabulary of their language. Lt. Blair was apt to confuse them with the Aka-bea-da and changed his first favourable opinion of them. Major Syme in his *Embassy to Ava* in 1794 gives a short but distorted account of them.

On the foundation of the second settlement in 1858, the Jarawa, owing to their decimation by disease introduced by Lt. Blair's men, had been ousted from the vicinity of the harbour by the Aka-bea-da. The partiality shown by the Administration to the Aka-bea-da, provoked the Jarawa, who grew to fear the settlement as much as they did the Andamanese tribe.

In 1863 Mr. Corbyn undertook an expedition into the mainland and the behaviour of the Andamanese gave him the first intimation of the presence of a hostile tribe in the interior. The year 1872 marks the first recorded Jarawa raid on the settlement, and from then to the present day, scarcely a year has passed without raids being made on the settlement to obtain iron implements, etc., etc.

It is a deep rooted psychological fact in the strain of every primitive people that their territorial divisions are sacred to themselves alone, and any attempt at invasion is invariably met with the fiercest hostility. The isolation of the Andamanese into their various communities is due to "constitutional peculiarities of jealousy". Each tribe has its own special territory for hunting, and regards all incursions as a serious trespass and a necessary occasion of inter-tribal warfare. Examples of this were recently found in Little Andaman in the neighbourhood of Jackson creek, where inter-sept warfare took place. Hence the attitude of the Jarawa must be regarded as natural in his sphere of outlook, as the clearing of the jungle on a large scale at the time of the foundation of the settlement probably aroused great resentment.

In 1921 and subsequent years the Jarawas began to come into the settlement and waylaid people on the roads and in the fields. In three years 21 convict settlers were killed and the menace grew so grave that a punitive expedition was decided on in 1925. The services of Captain West, M. C., and a platoon of 30 Kachin Military Police were placed at the disposal of the Chief Commissioner for the purpose.

Captain West divided his party into a number of patrols which started operations simultaneously at Alipur, Jatang, Middle Strait, Ike Bay, and the Northern extremity of South Andaman. These patrols came into contact with the Jarawa on eight occasions during the four months they were out. The principal attack by Jarawas on one of the patrols was at Ike Bay. Some 40 Jarawa participated in the attack and the shouts of a man among them in Burmese proved the presence of a runaway. During the course of operations thirty-seven Jarawa were claimed to have been shot and were seen to have dropped, but only six were actually found dead. The results showed that the most effective form of punitive expedition against the Jarawa is "Organizing and keeping in action a number of small mobile parties of practiced game trackers and hunters". This expedition did not however stop Jarawa raids. Like the Bushman of South Africa, the Jarawa is implacable and will continue to fight to extermination. A few months later Jarawas killed a man at Hobdaypur. Burman Bush Police were sent after them immediately and 2 Jarawa were killed on that occasion. A party of five Jarawa again attacked Ferrarganj village and badly wounded 2 Bhantus. A police party found these attackers several days later twenty miles north of Ferrarganj. The Jarawa fled leaving their complete personal weapons, implements and property and also property of the wounded Bhantus.

In 1929, a forest camp at Bajalunta in the Middle Andaman was attacked. Fortunately convict Bush Police were present and the Jarawa were shot on this occasion. The forest camps were removed to Baratang, an island separated from the mainland by Homfray and Middle Straits, which could be protected by boat patrols. The Jarawa have lived on the island for several months in the dry season, in close proximity to the camps but no raids have taken place during the last two years, probably because the Jarawa have found the men in the vicinity to be invariably armed, whereas it is their present custom to attack only unarmed parties.

CHAPTER V (*c*).

History of our Relations with the Önges.

The early history of relations with the Önges of Little Andaman presents a series of fruitless attempts at conciliation. For many years the Önges proved a source of much worry to the Settlement, owing to the precarious position in which any visiting or shipwrecked crews were placed in landing on Little Andaman.

In 1867, the Captain and seven of the crew of the ship *Assam Valley* who went ashore to cut a spar, were never seen again. The *Kwantung* under Mr. Homfray was sent out to discover the whereabouts of the missing men, but failed in its quest owing to the hostile attacks of the Önges and the very heavy surf. The I. G. S. *Aracan* was next fitted out as a punitive expedition and discovered the remains of the Europeans who had obviously been murdered. The party were often attacked by the Önges and owing to their ammunition getting wet, and the difficulties of landing and taking off in an extremely heavy surf, were placed in a dangerous position. However the great bravery of several individuals resulted in the party being safely extricated, five men receiving the Victoria Cross for their brave actions. It was further estimated that some seventy Önges were killed.

In 1873 General Stewart visited the island, the Önges keeping out of sight, having no doubt profited by the experience gained in their former lesson. On his return to Port Blair however General Stewart discovered that five of the crew of the junk *Quangoon* trading between Moulmein and the Straits had been attacked and murdered while searching for water. A party sent out as a punitive expedition discovered their remains, and being attacked drove the Önges off with great loss to them. They also burnt down a few communal huts, several canoes being found hanging up, in one, one particularly large one. One Önge was captured and taken to Port Blair but he died soon after without his language being found out or understood.

An attempt of the Chief Commissioner to land in 1874, met with the same ill success. In 1878 it was found that the Önges visited Macpherson Straits and the Cinque islands, canoes being seen in Portman Bay. In 1880 while on a trip to the Nicobars, Colonel Cadell and Portman visited Jackson Creek, Little Andaman, to be attacked by a great number of Önges. On the return trip however, a few showed signs of friendship in fact they embraced the Andamanese sent ashore. This was the first demonstration of friendship on the part of the Önges, and numerous presents were left behind to still further encourage the peaceful intentions already shown. However another group of Önges seen still further up the coast attacked the party sent to meet them forcing them to take to the sea.

The objective of the settlement was now if possible to capture a few Önges and by humane treatment conciliate them, loading them with presents on their release and return to the tribe.

In 1885 occurred an event on South Cinque which led to the conciliation and subsequent friendliness of these aborigines. An old Önge, who was taken to be a Jarawa, was captured. Finding traces of a large party there, an expedition was fitted out for their capture. 8 men, 6 women and 10 children were subsequently taken. Of these some eleven individuals were brought to Port Blair, the rest being given their canoes and released. By kind treatment and donation of many presents the mistrust of the captured Önges was overcome and they soon became very friendly. A Jarawa boy who had lately been captured could talk to the Önges and it was at first thought the captured party were Jarawas but their subsequent recognition of Little Andaman on their way back to the Cinque Islands dispelled this theory. The years 1886 and 1887 mark the definite conciliation of the tribe, the credit for which lies with Mr. Portman. He made many trips to Little Andaman and on one occasion stayed there two and a half months, successfully accomplishing a coastline survey. The Önges everywhere showed great friendliness to the party and never once was it attacked. Portman says that while there he noticed hereditary syphilis prevalent among them. He also noticed cases of scurvy and elephantiasis.

In 1905 the writer of this report brought 3 Önges to Port Blair where they stayed for 3 or 4 months enabling a vocabulary of some 350 words and some of the grammar to be recorded. Since that time relations have always been friendly. Parties have regularly landed on Little Andaman and presents have been freely distributed. With the exception of isolated cases they have shown no signs of their former animosity. Occasionally a few individuals visit Rutland and come in contact with the Settlement, but this is avoided as much as possible.

In September 1930 three Önges from Hut Bay were persuaded to accompany the writer to Port Blair *via* the Nicobars. They showed no alarm until they were frightened by the Nicobarese at Kar Nikobar. One man ran into the jungle and has never since been seen. As a small canoe disappeared at the same time, it was suspected that he tried to return to Little Andaman.

The other two men could thereafter only be kept on board by restraint. During the night one successfully eluded the police and Andamanese guards and jumped overboard at sea, and must have been drowned. The third man also tried to jump over board on several occasions and had to be locked up until taken back to Little Andaman. Their whole behaviour after first being frightened showed a very highly strung temperament. On subsequent visits it became apparent that news of the incident had spread all round the island, but the people were friendly and recognized that the officials were not to blame.

It appears, however, that the wives of the two missing men were subsequently put to death by order of the headman of their sept. They are said to have been drowned by the other women of their own sept.

Tribal Distribution.—Portman while at Little Andaman identified six Önge septs. The other six mentioned below are those which were found among the Önges who came to Rutland and the inhabitants of the west coast of Little Andaman.

1. Ekdi.
2. Palalankwe.
3. Tokynia.
4. Tambebui.
5. Titaije.
6. Tobechelebe.
7. Totamadale.
8. Quingandange.
9. Quananame.
10. Yantige.
11. Tugalange.
12. Chetamale.

N.B.—There may be several unknown septs, in the interior, but nothing definite has ever been found.

Cultural Anthropology.—Little is really known about the cultural anthropology of the Önges, no doubt on account of their comparative isolation and natural timidity. The few superficial cultural differences have already been remarked on, but a vast field of research awaits the anthropologist of the future*. Portman was able to collate a vocabulary of some hundred words of their language, but their psychology, morals, superstitions, religious beliefs, or mythology have not yet been discovered and as a result are excluded from the following resumé of their cultural developments.

Government and Tribal Communities.—Little Andaman is divided between various septs, the names of which are found under the heading "Tribal Distribution". Each sept possesses a stretch of territory or hunting ground which has definitely recognized boundaries. Any intrusion on to this hunting ground is regarded as a sufficient occasion for the outbreak of inter-sept warfare, even though the different septs may be related by marriage.

Habitation.—Each sept occupies a large circular communal hut which is generally built on the sea-shore, but it is not unusual, when the coast is exposed to the full force of the monsoon or in the season for collecting fruit and honey for all its occupants to take to the jungle. These huts are ingeniously made, with a frame of circular cane-work rising to a point. Over this thatching is neatly bound. Around the hut are a series of small raised cane platforms used for sleeping purposes. Trophies of the chase by way of ornament are suspended from the roof of the hut. Buckets made of logs and sometimes of giant bamboo are found suspended in the huts as well as nets and baskets. The bamboos are collected on the shore, having drifted there from Burma.

Tribal Government.—There is a nominal chief, but to use Man's words while describing the Andamanese system of internal government "Communism modified by authority" holds sway; a feature common to most primitive tribes. The elders of the sept undoubtedly possess an authority almost equal to that of the chief.

Marriage.—Marriage is usually exogamous, sometimes the wife goes and lives with the sept of the husband and at other times the husband joins the sept of the wife. One or two cases are on record where man and wife are both of the same sept. The Önges marry quite young being perhaps only ten or eleven years old and not fully developed. The writer has on several occasions witnessed a marriage. The ceremony was very simple and consisted in an elder of the sept taking the wrist of his daughter and place it in the hands of the young man of the visiting sept. The girl then became his wife and he was free to take her away provided the girl did not release herself and runaway in the interior, in which case she was free to go back to her sept. This actually happened in the writer's presence, much to the annoyance of the would-be husband. Consummation of the marriage and pregnancy likewise appear to take place before the bride attains maturity, and a woman may be a grandmother when she is 30 years old or younger. The average age attained by the healthy is perhaps not much more than 40 years, and persons known to the writer 30 years ago as children have within his knowledge declined and died when they were about 40 years old.

Divorce.—To leave a wife appears to be a breach of tribal morality. The writer came across a case where a man deserted his wife and went to live with another sept. On his return to his own sept to live with his former wife he was much scolded by an old woman of the sept and was told to go away again.

Death and Burial.—Nothing is known about the burial ceremony. They preserve the jaw-bones of deceased relatives which is not unlike the Great Andamanese custom.

Ornaments and Attire.—The Önges possess no broad tasselled belts as common among friendly tribes of Great Andamanese, and their women-folk wear a tassel of yellow fibre in front in the place of the leaf worn by the women of the Great Andaman coastal tribes. The yellow dried skin of a dendrobium orchid is used for decorative purposes, while white clay is smeared by both sexes on their faces and body sometimes in ornamental patterns.

* Provided, that is, that the Önge survives long enough.

J. H. H.

Greeting.—The Önges are completely silent when they meet. The residents of a sept meeting friends sit on the sands and the visitors sit on their laps, thus they embrace each other for about a minute without saying a word and pass on from one person to the next until all have been embraced, both men and women.

Food.—Portman mentions the staple food of the Önge to be the seed of the mangrove boiled, as he always found it in their huts. Artocarpus fruit is eaten after roasting it on hot stones. Since their acquisition of dogs they have been able to obtain more readily the wild pig which have always formed their staple food. They are fond of turtle but not all know the art of using the harpoon. Turtle are much appreciated as presents. Their eggs are to be found on the long stretches of sandy beaches and are often seen in the huts hanging up in nets. The women catch fish almost daily in hand nets and these are dried and stored. Portman argues that this is probably due to alien influence which " they must have been in contact with at some previous period ".

Canoes.—The canoe-culture of the Önges is on a much lower standard than that of the Great Andaman tribes possessing neither the technique or the finish. The canoe is of the outrigger type like that of Great Andaman, from which it has been copied, since formerly, as recorded by Portman, their canoe had no prow.

Bows.—The Önge bow resembles the European type of long bow but is much smaller and flatter. It is generally made of *Mimusops littoralis* and the string is made of fibre.

Arrows.—For shooting fish and birds a multiple-headed arrow is used, similar to that used on North Sentinel. The Sentinelese arrow is however barbed with small pieces of the wing bones of pigeons.

Dancing.—The Önges dance in the open, men and women standing opposite each other bending their knees forward at the same time lifting their heels ; sexual thoughts are connected with such dances.

Conclusion.—The Önges undoubtedly belong to the *Eremtaga* or Jungle dwellers division in contrast to the *Aryoto* or Coast-dwellers. They do not possess the skill and dexterity shown by the coast tribes of Great Andaman in fishing and turtling. As a type von Eickstedt places them as being the " best representatives of the old type of Negrito, being the least affected of all the tribes by changes due to contact with the outside world ". Despite their lack of contact with the outside world the Önges like the Andamanese are undoubtedly a dying race. Estimated figures for the last thirty years are unfavourable.

Census 1901	Estimated	672
Census 1911	,,	631
Census 1921	,,	346
Census 1931	,,	250

A decrease of about 63 per cent. is hence shown in the last thirty years.

Experience has shown that the aborigine as a type is dying out whenever he comes in contact with civilization. In Little Andaman conditions are better than in Great Andaman owing to greater isolation from alien destructive influences, yet the numbers decrease year by year mainly from infections such as influenza introduced at times of contact with civilization. Some septs have almost completely disappeared during the last 30 years.

The Önges have not assimilated the vices of civilization in the same way as the Andamanese and every effort has been made by the local administration to keep them in their isolation.

Note by Census Commissioner for India.—The disappearance of aborigines is perhaps not an invariable concomitant of contact with a more advanced culture. Such contact probably leads in all cases to a serious decline at first, but provided the tribe in question can be saved from extermination for a period long enough to enable it to adapt itself to the change in its contacts and environment, the period of decline seems to give way again to one of increase. The Tasmanian is extinct but the Maori is at last reviving. In the case of the Andamanese the period required for adaptation is likely to be abnormally prolonged on account of the exceedingly long period during which these islanders have been isolated in a peculiar environment of their own to which they have become specially adapted. They appear incidentally unable to survive if without the shelter of the forest to which they have become accustomed (*vide* Portman, *History of our Relations with the Andamanese*, page 875).

J. H. H.

CHAPTER V (*d*).

Points of affinity between the Semangs and the Andamanese.

It has been mentioned at the beginning of this chapter that the Semangs of the Malay Peninsula are the nearest in type to the Andamanese. Sir R. Temple, in his Census Report of 1901, has laid down certain points of affinity between the Andamanese and the Semangs ; the publication recently of a book entitled *Among the Forest Dwarfs of Malaya* by Paul Schebesta has drawn the link still closer, as being the latest original research on the subject.

The " Orang-Utan ", or Forest men of Malaya, inhabit the dense forests in the Kedah, Patani, Perak, Kelantan, and Pahang districts of the Malay Peninsula. Like the Andamanese, they lead a typically nomadic life, ever in search of food and game, and may be classed as being relics of the so-called " Bamboo-age ". As a type the Semang seems to be more akin to the Önge-Jarawa group of Andamanese than to the Northern group. A comparison of illustrations in Schebesta's book with photographs taken of Önges exhibits a similarity of general physical features, stature, physiognomy, and expression, which lead one to believe that both groups are very closely related and undoubtedly identical in origin. A similarity is recorded in customs, habits and primitive cultural implements, which fully substantiates this premise.

Cultural Affinities.—Habitations. Huts are of the ordinary lean-to type as found among the northern groups of Andamanese, and are thatched with palm leaves fastened together by means of rattan strips. There is no habitation of any kind resembling the Önge-Jarawa communal hut ; but the Semangs erect raised cane-work beds such as are found among the Önges and not among the northern group of Andamanese. There appears to be among the Semang no such segregation of sexes as is common among the Andamanese.

Weapons.—The bow used by the Semangs is identical with that used by the Önges, with no special markings on it. Of recent years however, owing to alien influences, the bow is becoming obsolete among the Semangs, and has been superseded by the blowpipe borrowed from the Ple and Jahai tribes.

Burial Customs.—Nothing is known of Önge burial customs, but the Semangs, like the Andamanese of the northern group, bury their dead. Both races place food on the grave so that the spirit may be nourished, and make aggressive demonstrations to frighten away the evil spirits of the dead. Like the Andamanese, the Semangs immediately desert the spot, but return after a fixed period of mourning to celebrate a feast for the dead person. If there is any disinternment of bones later, as among the Andamanese, Schebesta makes no mention of it.

Beliefs.—The Semangs and the Andamanese possess certain similarities in their types of belief. In the Cosmos of both groups, there exists the same Tree on which the Heavens rest, and the same Bridge or ladder to Paradise (*jereg* of the Andamanese) whereby entrance is gained to the upper regions. In Kaeri, the Thunder God and Ta Pedu, the Creator of the Semangs, we have the Puluga or the Omniscient Creator of the Andamanese who unites both divinities in one person. As the disturbing of elements is supposed to denote signs of anger on the part of Kaeri the Thunder God, so it denotes similar feelings on the part of Puluga. Both races also believe in an after life, but there seems to be no practice among the Andamanese of blood atonement for sin, as among the Semangs.

Physical Peculiarities.—According to Sir R. Temple, the stature, pigment, colour and growth of hair, as well as colour and shape of eyes, are of the same type both in the Semang and the Önge-Jarawa groups.

N.B.—I am indebted to Mr. Man's book on the Andamanese for information as to their beliefs, and to Paul Schebesta's book for all information regarding the Semangs.

M. C. C. B.

COPY OF A MEMORANDUM NO. 3005, DATED 18TH MARCH 1932, FROM THE SENIOR MEDICAL OFFICER, PORT BLAIR, TO THE SUPERINTENDENT OF CENSUS OPERATIONS, PORT BLAIR.

Report on the blood grouping of the Andamanese.

The bloods of the Andamense and others tested here showed that they all fell in group I, indicating that standard sera with which the tests were carried out were probably inert. Therefore sera of the following Andamense were sent to Pasteur Institute, Rangoon, to have the tests carried out with the cells of known donors. The results are as follows :—

1. Kin. Great Andaman . . . . Group III of Jansky.
2. Dundey K. Gasay of Little Andaman . . . Group I of Jansky.
3. Female Bora. Great Andaman . . . . Group IV of Jansky.
4. Charaman of Great Andaman . . . . . Group I of Jansky.
5. Ukla. Little Andaman . . . . . . Group III of Jansky.
6. Ta Kie Keay Ganay. Little Andaman . . . Group III of Jansky.

Note by the Census Commissioner for India.—Colonel R. B. Lloyd, I.M.S., the Imperial Serologist, tells me that Jansky's group I corresponds to international group O. His II to international A, his III to international B, his IV to international AB. Group A is therefore not yet reported from the Andamans, but as group AB is present, it may be assumed to exist. Mydlarski working on Polish soldiers has correlated different groups with different head forms. Group A with meso- or sub-brachycephalic heads, group B with brachycephalic, group O with dolicho- and mesocephalic heads. Kossovitch interprets these groups as corresponding to Nordic, Mongolian and Mediterranean races, and points out that although the anthropoids may belong to any group, orangs and gibbons appear inclined to groups B and AB, and gorillas and chimpanzees to groups O and A (*Reveu anthropologique*, June 1931). The Andamanese according to Risley are all meso- or brachycephalic.

J. H. H.

CHAPTER V (e).

Distribution and Movement of the Aboriginal Population.

Of the aboriginal population only the friendly Great Andaman tribes were counted, while the Önges, Jarawas and Sentinelese were estimated.

The following table gives the figures for the various friendly Andamanese tribes of Great Andaman as they stood at the beginning of 1931 :—

	Men.	Women.	Boys.	Girls.
Yere	9	20	4	1
Half Bred	2	2	6	2
Kora	6	12	2	4
Kede	..	1	..	..
Half Bred	1	..	..	..
Chariar	4	4	..	..
Half Bred	..	..	..	1
Balawa	..	..	..	..
Half Bred	1	..	1	..
Bojigyab	1	..	..	..
Tabo	1	5	..	..
Total Pure Bred	21	42	6	5=74
Half Bred	4	2	7	3=16
	25	44	13	8=90

The total is only 90 against 209 in 1921 or a decrease of 57 per cent. During the preceding decade the decrease amounted to 54 per cent. The causes for the decrease have already been explained in the chapter on the Andaman Home. It is certain that very few pure blooded Andamanese of the friendly Great Andaman tribes will survive another decade. Most of these Andamanese have lost tribal cohesion but they nevertheless often cling to some extent to their territory. For instance the writer failed to persuade a solitary couple at Port Cornwallis to join the remaining friendly tribes at Havelock in order to be able to give them some medical attention while a few Chariars from Landfall island could only be persuaded to live at Havelock during the monsoon on the promise that they would be taken to Landfall after the monsoon. It was desirable to bring them away from Landfall as some suffered from diseases which required medical treatment.

Table showing the estimated population of Önges, Jarwas, and Sentinelese :—

	1921.	1931.
1. Önges	346	250
2. Jarawas	114	70
3. Sentinelese	117	50

The Önges.—The Önges were estimated in 1921 at 346 persons. In the present Census they were estimated at 250 persons only. There has been a considerable decrease in this population mainly from deaths due to influenza and malaria which caused several septs on the south and west coast almost to disappear while most of the children at Jackson creek were found to suffer from enlarged spleens so badly that they could only walk with difficulty. The present estimate may however be on the low side and it is hoped to verify it in the coming cold weather.

The Sentinelese.—Very little is known of the number of aborigines which inhabit Sentinel Islands. Like the Jarawas they are entirely hostile. The present estimate of 50 persons is made on conclusions arrived at from several visits during the last decade and after counting the number of huts found

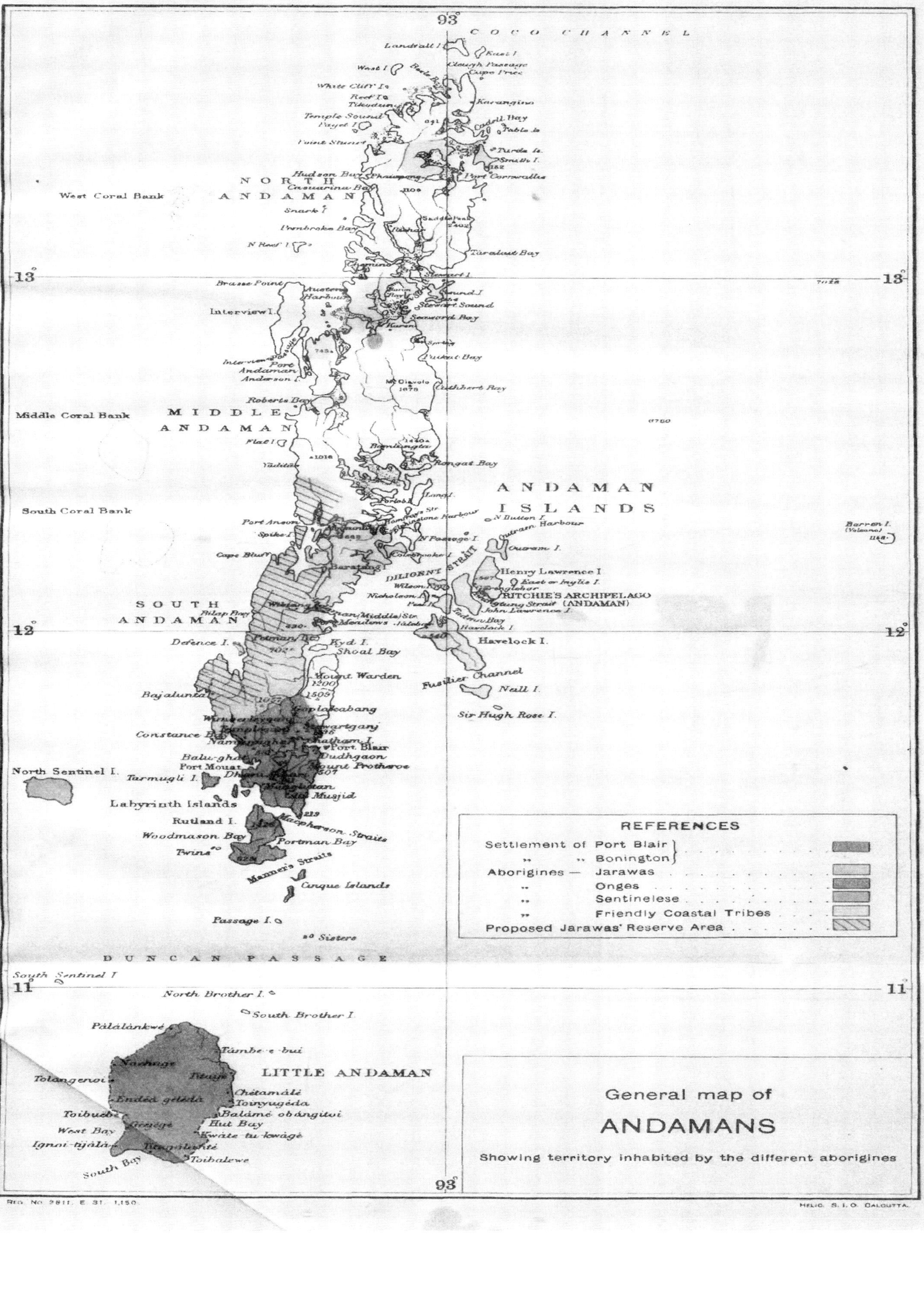
COCO CHANNEL
NORTH ANDAMAN
West Coral Bank
MIDDLE ANDAMAN
Middle Coral Bank
South Coral Bank
ANDAMAN ISLANDS
SOUTH ANDAMAN
RITCHIE'S ARCHIPELAGO (ANDAMAN)
Havelock I.
North Sentinel I.
Labyrinth Islands
Rutland I.
Port Blair
DUNCAN PASSAGE
LITTLE ANDAMAN
REFERENCES
Settlement of Port Blair
Bonington
Aborigines — Jarawas
Onges
Sentinelese
Friendly Coastal Tribes
Proposed Jarawas' Reserve Area
General map of
ANDAMANS
Showing territory inhabited by the different aborigines
HELIO. S. I. O. CALCUTTA.

and the sleeping places. Though the previous census showed 117 persons there has not necessarily been a decrease in the population, as even for that census no accurate data was available. It is believed that the population is stationary for the Sentinel islanders have been kept free from direct contact with civilization.

The Jarawas.—The Jarawas have been estimated at 70 persons only while the previous census showed 114. It is assumed that there has been some decrease in the Jarawas because quite a number of adults were killed or seriously wounded by Captain West's party in 1925. Apart from this the population like that of the North Sentinel is probably stationary. It does not necessarily follow that there has been a reduction in numbers of 44 persons during the decade, because the number estimated depends a great deal on individual opinion. The writer has often been through their territory and counted the huts and sleeping places and on this the present estimate is based.

Note by Census Commissioner for India.—The earliest estimate of the total Andamanese population on which any reliance can be placed is that of E. H. Man who estimated their number in 1883 after "the ascertained ravages of certain epidemics" at a maximum of 3,500 of which 2,000 were accounted for by the coastal tribes of Great Andaman and the remaining 1,500 (or possibly 1,000 only) by the Jarawa or Önge tribes of the interior of Great Andaman, of Little Andaman and of North Sentinel island. Portman writing at the end of the century after many years' intimate acquaintance with the Andamanese, put their total numbers in 1858 at the date of their first contact with the British at 8,000. This estimate was regarded by Sir Richard Temple as too high and in his census report on the Andamans in 1901 he estimated the total normal population of the islands up to 1858 at not more than 5,000 and the reasoned considerations on which he based that estimate will be found in chapter I of his 1901 Census Report. His estimate has been criticised by A. R. Brown, but as this writer had no experience of the Andamans remotely comparable with that of Portman, Man or Temple his criticisms in this respect carry little weight. Accepting therefore Sir R. Temple's conservative figure for the Andamanese population in 1858, we arrive at the following comparative numbers :—

Tribe.	*In 1858.*	*In 1883.*	*In 1901.*	*In 1911.*	*In 1921.*	*In 1931.*
Chariar	100		39	36	17	9
Kora	500		96	71	48	24
Tabo	200		48	62	18	6
Yere	700		218	180	101	46
Kede	500	2,000	59	34	6	2
Juwai	300		48	9	5	0
Kol	100		11	2	0	0
Bojigyab	300		50	36	9	1
Bea	500		37	10	1	0
Balawa	300		19	15	4	2
Önge	700	1,250	672	631	346	250
Jarawa	600		585	231	231	120
Total	4,800	3,250*	1,882	1,317	786	460†

* The intermediate figure between Man's maximum and his minimum.

† Of whom 16 Great Andamanese are half bred.

This devastating fall in the numbers of the Andamanese in less than 75 years of contact with administration paralyses comment, but it is impossible not to agree with von Eickstedt's view of the 'Andaman Home' policy. The relations with the Önges prove that the method was not without alternative.

J. H. H.

CHAPTER VI.

(*a*) The Penal Settlement.

The Penal Settlement was formed in 1858 after the Indian Mutiny as a solution to the difficulty of segregating the large number of mutineers, and also as a further attempt to establish a civilized population in the Andamans with the object of preventing the murder of mariners when sailing ships were wrecked, as they not infrequently were on the coasts inhabited by the aborigines, or put in to obtain water.

The system of treating prisoners was adopted from the original colony in the Straits Settlement, where convicts were divided into four classes and promoted from one class to another after definite periods of good behaviour or reduced to a lower class for any lapse of good conduct, the best behaved being selected as "sirdars" or "tindals" with a certain amount of authority over their fellow-convicts.

The penal system was revised from time to time according to the conclusions of the various committees appointed to investigate existing conditions. At one time conditions were too severe, perhaps unavoidably so, owing to the fact that a number of desperadoes of the mutiny had to be guarded extramurally without the prospect of ever returning to their homes. Later the policy was to ameliorate the conditions, and later again to make them more severe and deterrent because the Andamans became too attractive. The object, however, was always to reform the criminal by gradual relaxation of discipline over a decade, while holding out the prospect of a semi-free self-supporting existence during the latter half of his sentence.

Finally in 1921 the Jails Commission recommended the total abolition of the Andamans as a Penal Settlement. At that time the Settlement was administered by the Chief Commissioner assisted by 8 officers of the Andamans Commission and a subordinate overseer to every thousand convicts. No convict could be punished without a quasi-judicial inquiry held by an Assistant Commissioner, however trivial the offence might have been. The time of the overseers was fully taken up in posting convicts to various works supervising the issue and cooking of rations, preparing ration accounts, issuing clothing, inspecting convict stations and inquiring into complaints and offences. Consequently the enforcement of discipline rested to a great extent with the convict petty officers.

A convict on arrival was kept in the Cellular Jail for six months under strict discipline. During the day he had to complete a given task, such as pounding coir, or extracting coconut oil, at night he was kept in solitary confinement in a cell. After six months, provided he behaved well he was promoted to the 3rd class in which hard labour was still extracted from him but under less rigid discipline.

He was released from the Jail and posted to a gang working free from confinement except in a barrack at night. Under these conditions he had to pass four and a half years before being eligible for promotion as a petty officer or for domestic service. He still received convict rations and was not eligible for gratuity. He remained a further five years in 2nd class during which he received dry rations as well as a gratuity of 12 annas per mensem. Throughout these ten years he wore distinctive convict clothing according to the nature of his crime, an iron neck band and a wooden ticket indicating his number, the nature of his crime and the date of his conviction. Promotion to the first class made him eligible for a self-supporter's ticket, *i.e.*, he was allowed to earn his own living, to possess property, to send for his wife from India or contemplate the possibility of obtaining a woman to marry from the limited number of eligible women confined in the local female jail.

Fanatics and desperate criminals were kept in the Jail, habitual criminals and those convicted locally of serious offences were kept in separate gangs under different conditions and wearing distinctive clothing.

Female convicts were kept in a walled enclosure, slept in dormitories and were given suitable work. After five years they were allowed to enter domestic service and those who were eligible were paraded on fixed days when male convicts were permitted to interview them with a view to marriage. Having married a woman could be granted a remission up to five years so that her release might coincide with that of her husband. At one time the released convicts both husband and wife were forced to leave the Andamans. The average number of children of one of these convict marriages was very small.

The recommendation that the Penal Settlement should be abolished was, in effect, a proposal that the Andamans should be evacuated. For several reasons this was impracticable, the chief being (1) the existence of a free population of about 3,000 "local borns" (the descendents of convicts) who could not be repatriated to any particular province in India, (2) the commercial value of the forests, (3) the strategical importance of the islands and (4) the large amount of money spent on establishing the settlement.

It was eventually decided to discontinue transportation and to take only those convicts who volunteered to complete their sentences in the Andamans rather than in Indian jails and whose offences were such that they would not be unsuitable as settlers. On the offer of repatriation being made, the idea became prevalent that return to India would be a step further towards release, and but for the fact that the jail authorities in India expressed their inability to accommodate a large number of prisoners immediately, and the necessity for transportation of Mappilla rebels to the Andamans, the maintenance of a sufficient labour force to carry on essential public works during the transition period would have presented a serious problem. However, a beginning was made by the transfer of as many as possible of the convicts who had suffered in health or had proved incorrigible in conduct. Had the offer of more freedom and rights been made simultaneously with the offer to return to India, there is no doubt that a larger percentage would have elected to remain in the Andamans. This is borne out by the fact that many of the married Mappillas, who had experienced the benefits which the Government held out to them, have volunteered to remain here.

Efforts to introduce a free population from outside failed, chiefly on account of the sinister reputation of *Kala Pani* as nothing but a place of banishment, and efforts to induce convicts in Indian jails to volunteer for transfer to the Andamans met with little success.

Fortunately this set-back was only temporary and signs of progress can be traced to 1923 when the Government decided on the advice of the then Chief Commissioner, Lieutenant-Colonel Ferrar, to offer greater inducement to convicts to remain as free settlers after their release. Self-supporter tickets were granted more liberally and after a short term of confinement in the jail convicts' wages were increased. Wives and families were imported at Government expense and parties of convicts were sent to India to bring their families back with them, houses were built and rented at a nominal rent, restrictions on landing at Port Blair were removed; schools, hospitals and dispensaries were established in outlying villages, every encouragement was given to communities to build mosques, temples, etc., and to observe their religious festivities, and a boon to the convict cultivator was the liberal grant of *taqavi* and to the free tenant the conferment of occupancy rights over his holdings after five years tenure as a tenant at will.

These changes have had a marked effect on the outlook, bearing and conduct of the convict. Whereas formerly he was downcast, conspicuous and despised, with a reputation for malingering, now in the majority of cases it is impossible to distinguish him from the free person. He has his family, his land and his own house and cattle in the village; he may be a cooly earning daily wages, a contractor supplying large quantities of milk to local hospitals or timber to the Forest Department, or he may be employed on a fixed wage in any of the Government Departments. The wages of convicts with an allowance for wife and each child compare favourably with those paid in India for similar labour. In short, provided he behaves himself and observes the few rules framed for his welfare the convict has nothing to fear and is able to lead a normal life, especially if his family lives with him.

The most satisfactory result of the revised system is however the improved moral standard of the community. Many families from India and Burma have joined their respective husbands so that there are now 1,004 *married* convicts' wives with 1,447 children.

The most homogeneous communities in the Andamans are the Bhantus, Mappillas, Karens and Burmans. The Bhantus are a criminal tribe from the United Provinces. Most of the men are convicts with life sentences. They have been allowed to settle in the Andamans on the land with their families. Their children are being educated in their village school while as they grow up they find work in the local match factory, saw mills, etc. The total population of Bhantus in the Andaman is 285.

Male Adults	91
Female Adults	92
Boys	59
Girls	43

Had the families remained in India they would have been brought up to the hereditary criminal calling of their tribe. A note on the Bhantus is given in the Appendix.

The Mappillas were transported to the Andamans after the Malabar rebellion. A considerable number brought their families and settled on the land or set up as petty shopkeepers. Some of those have been released but have elected to remain in the Andamans because they find life easier than in their original home. As some point out, they have only to pay the Government tax whereas in India they had to pay their landlords two-thirds of their crops. Nevertheless it is reported that most of them will go as soon as all the Mappilla convicts are released. There are 1,885 Mappillas, of whom 714 are females, 365 of them being married. The Mappillas have separate villages with schools for their children.

The Karens form a separate free colony in the Middle Andaman near Stewart Sound. They migrated from Bassein in the year 1925 on the promise of a grant of land and employment in the Forest Department. All are Christians of the Baptist sect. At the time of the Census there were 133 males and 130 females. So long as the men can find forest employment in the Andamans they are likely to be permanent settlers.

Burmese.—During the last 5 years a considerable number of Burmans have brought their families to the Andamans and there are 400 Burmese females out of which 212 are married. Like the Bhantus, Mappillas and Karens they have separate schools for their children, and they have a Pongyi-chaung for religious worship.

As a result of the present policy it is therefore apparent that a free colony is in process of formation. The young generation will have their roots in the Andamans and as they grow up they will want to find work and thus replace the convict. Until then however some years must elapse during which the convicts must carry on the work of the Settlement. The Andamans seem to be ideal for the accidental type of prisoner who has committed a single capital offence in a brawl or owing to some dispute over his land in a fit of passion or perhaps owing to a vendetta forced on him by his tribal laws or as in the case of so many young Burmans has committed a single dacoity in a spirit of youthful exuberance. None of these men are real criminals, and it is just and fitting that such persons, instead of being compelled to spend their lives in intramural confinement surrounded by all types of habitual criminals, should be able to lead a normal life with their families, in exile it is true, but in not unpleasant surroundings where they have every chance of working out their own salvation and obliterating any stigma that may have marred their past career.

(b) Reclamation Works.

Swamp reclamation in the Andamans has an important bearing upon the health and permanency of the Port Blair Settlement. Owing to the hilly nature of the Andamans, and to the shortage of level ground it has been found necessary to use tidal swamps for the cultivation of paddy in addition to the limited area of the few alluvial valleys. Land elsewhere is undulating and unsuitable for wet cultivation. These swamps have been reclaimed by means of *bands* built up of adjacent soil and sludge along or near the half-tide level. At the outlets of the streams sluices were constructed with automatic wooden gates which were intended to let out the accumulated rain water at low tide and automatically close as the tide rises. These *bands*, which were many miles in length, required considerable labour for their upkeep as they were subject to erosion through continual wave action and undermining by crabs, and were among the preliminary works accomplished at the establishment of the settlement. In the past these have been maintained solely by convict labour, but long before the prospective closing of the settlement the problem of their continued maintenance had become serious. Owing to the scarcity of convict labour, and inability of the cultivators to maintain the *bands* and owing also to constant failure of gates, large areas of paddy and coconut plantations were destroyed and reverted to mangrove swamps. The danger of the situation was further increased as encroachments of the sea brought malarial infection further inland in their train and nearer to villages. Major Christopher, I.M.S., discovered the common malaria carrier in the Andamans to be *Anopheles Ludlowi* and that these mosquitoes only breed in brackish water as a rule, and were only found within half a mile of the breeding ground.

As an anti-malarial measure in the interests of the health of the future colony, as well in order to protect the fields, the Chief Commissioner, Colonel Ferrar, proposed the filling in of swamps by material taken from the sea-bed by means of cutter-suction dredgers. This scheme received the support of Sir Alexander Muddiman as well as the concurrence of the Financial Committee and the sanction of the Legislative Assembly. In 1927-28 seven lakhs of rupees were provided and a further sixteen lakhs in 1929-30 and 1930-31.

It is too early to forecast the actual results of the current year's work, but for the time being malaria has increased owing to the large number of men employed on reclamation in the swamps. The work however is certain to prove as beneficial as and the results to compare favourably with those of the year 1927-28 as well as former reclamation, which considerably reduced the sick and death rate as is evident from the accompanying medical records for the last 27 years. Perhaps the most successful reclamation of recent years has been that of some fifty acres from South Point to Atlanta Point, adjacent to the most populous area of the settlement. This was started by Sir Richard Temple some 25 years ago and took many years to complete owing to the extremely swampy character of the area and the fact that only manual labour was available.

Altogether by the end of 1931 some 900 acres will have been reclaimed. All the most important works have been completed, and the outlook of the local population is as bright now as it was gloomy when the closing of the convict settlement was first contemplated. The importance of these works both for the well-being and perhaps the very existence of the colony is brought out by the medical statistics and cannot be over-emphasized.

The medical statistics for the last 27 years show that most climatic diseases keep pace with malaria which undermines the constitution and lowers its powers of resistence against other diseases. The death rate within the last ten years has decreased from 43 to eleven per thousand.

It is also necessary to draw attention to the fact that Weil's disease was only diagnosed for the first time in 1927 and has been responsible for a large number of deaths. It is probable that this disease has existed for a considerable time in the Andamans, and owing to its comparatively recent discovery has been wrongly diagnosed in the past.

Admissions and death rate per 1,000 in various diseases.

Year.	Diseases for which treated.																	
	Dysentery.		Malaria.		Pulmonary Tuberculosis.		Pneumonia.		Respiratory diseases.		Diarrhœa.		Influenza.		Other Diseases.		Total.	
	Admissions.	Deaths.	Admissions.	Deaths.	Admissions.	Deaths.	Admissions.	Deaths.	Admissions.	Deaths.	Admissions.	Deaths.	Admissions.	Deaths.	Admissions.	Deaths.	Admissions.	Deaths.
1902	159	14	1,079	4·4	..	..	..	..	86	6	64	2	..	..	404	15	1,792	41·4
1903	133	7	1,091	2	13	·2	..	..	118	5·6	82·5	2	..	..	439	13·5	1,876·5	30·3
1904	162	7·9	1,176	4	..	..	..	..	80	4	66	1·5	..	..	422	14	1,906	31·4
1905	164	13	1,251	3·5	..	..	11·5	5	36	·4	55	·4	..	..	378	14	1,895·5	36·3
1906	94	4·9	1,454	3·2	6·9	5·5	17	5·5	33	..	36·5	·3	..	..	386·6	4·7	2,028	24·1
1907	109·8	3·1	1,320	2·2	..	..	14	4·3	33	..	31	·6	..	..	394	11·5	1,901·8	21·7
1908	111·1	3·2	854·1	2·2	..	..	10·2	4·1	23·5	·6	..	..	..	..	408	13·2	1,442·5	23·37
1909	149·6	·9	1,077·1	4·5	8·38	7	18·2	6	56·6	1·4	25·3	·6	..	..	405·9	10·5	1,741·08	39
1910	98·5	7·4	997·8	4·7	14·7	8·4	19·2	7·0	58·0	·7	25·1	·2	..	..	343	8·3	1,556·3	36·7
1911	94·0	3·7	681·6	1·9	5·8	4·9	15	4·4	67·8	·59	54·7	·7	..	..	333	4·8	1,251·9	20·99
1912	99·0	6·0	993·4	2·4	8·0	5·2	17·8	6·0	74·1	1·5	46·0	·44	..	..	383·3	7·4	1,621·6	28·94
1913	77·5	3·5	962·2	1·56	3·8	3·12	12·2	4·68	63·5	·78	29·4	·31	..	..	350·4	7·8	1,499·0	21·75
1914	85·7	3·2	839·4	1·7	4·8	2·4	13·3	4·8	53·1	1·6	19·6	·3	..	..	346·4	8·4	1,362·3	22·4
1915	50·1	3·8	1,341·7	3·2	5·3	3·8	23·2	10·1	52·3	3·8	43·7	1·1	..	..	358·0	14·9	1,874·3	40·7
1916	55·4	5·0	928·9	1·5	4·6	2·8	18·3	8·2	49·7	2·5	57·0	1·7	..	..	363·1	9·0	1,477·0	30·7
1917	67·3	5·05	1,018·8	1·7	4·1	2·8	18·0	7·3	62·5	2·4	44·7	1·2	..	..	330·2	18·4	1,545·6	38·85
1918	94·1	6·1	856·8	2·4	6·5	5·3	16·8	7·5	62·5	1·9	53·7	·7	192·6	10·7	375·7	18·3	1,658·7	52·9
1919	131·0	10·0	1,208·7	5·0	7·0	4·4	12·6	6·0	56·4	2·2	48·8	1·3	18·6	6·5	333·4	9·1	1,816·5	44·5
1920	67·3	4·3	870·6	2·9	5·6	4·8	12·0	6·0	63·0	·95	34·0	·7	72·1	7·7	384·0	9·9	1,508·6	37·25
1921	41·1	·9	502·4	1·35	4·1	2·7	8·1	2·7	57·5	·9	34·0	·45	23·9	·45	444·1	5·8	1,115·2	15·25
1922	37·0	1·2	272·6	2·6	5·7	1·2	8·4	3·6	43·2	·8	20·9	·09	·8	·09	361·0	7·0	749·6	16·58
1923	71·4	7·5	330·6	3·2	3·5	1·4	6·3	3·2	27·9	·8	25·7	..	13·5	..	324·7	10·7	803·6	26·8
1924	54·3	6·6	377·1	4·0	5·8	1·7	7·7	3·0	25·0	1·1	16·3	·2	·7	..	325·3	9·9	812·2	26·5
1925	51·3	5·1	279·5	1·6	4·2	1·7	8·1	3·1	28·8	·25	9·9	..	..	..	231·4	7·5	613·2	19·25
1926	22·1	1·9	208·2	2·25	3·1	2·25	7·1	2·7	32·4	·66	3·4	..	2·3	..	235·3	5·4	513·9	15·16
1927	10·1	1·1	123·5	1·38	3·5	1·38	8·1	2·1	33·3	·69	4·7	..	6·08	·42	231·2	4·8	420·48	11·87
1928	13·4	1·1	122·59	1·39	2·23	·62	5·58	2·01	35·59	·62	21·63	..	·97	..	277·9	6·4	479·89	12·14

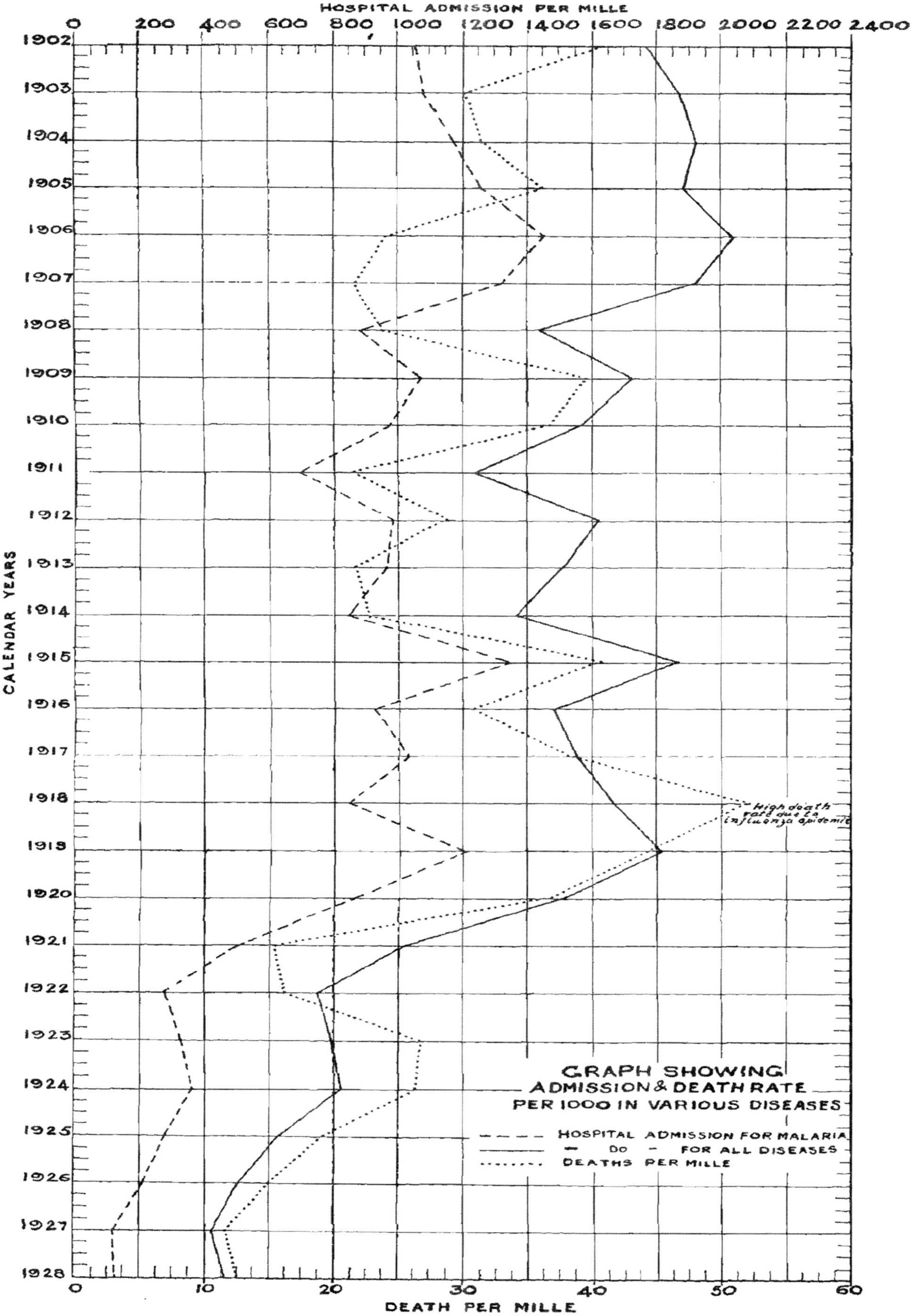
HOSPITAL ADMISSION PER MILLE
0 200 400 600 800 1000 1200 1400 1600 1800 2000 2200 2400
CALENDAR YEARS
1902 1903 1904 1905 1906 1907 1908 1909 1910 1911 1912 1913 1914 1915 1916 1917 1918 1919 1920 1921 1922 1923 1924 1925 1926 1927 1928
0 10 20 30 40 50 60
DEATH PER MILLE
GRAPH SHOWING
ADMISSION & DEATH RATE
PER 1000 IN VARIOUS DISEASES
HOSPITAL ADMISSION FOR MALARIA
DO FOR ALL DISEASES
DEATHS PER MILLE
High death rate due to influenza epidemic

CHAPTER VII.

The Local-Born Population.

The so-termed 'Local-Born' population is descended from Indian convict parents on both sides who settled in the Andamans; and this community is therefore of some interest.

Sir Richard Temple gave a fair criticism of their character in the Census report of 1901. While he points out their failings at that time, mainly in sex morality, he recognizes that they have shown themselves "to be upright, capable, hard-working, honest and self-respecting". At the time of Sir Richard Temple's report most of the local-born community were still in the first generation of convict descent, and if the morality of family life did not reach a high standard, it must be borne in mind that the proportion of males to females in the settlement was 12 to 1, and that convict marriage was more a marriage of convenience than anything else.

Since Sir Richard Temple's report the community has lived up to the favourable opinion then given, and local-borns hold many appointments in the higher grades of the subordinate services, where they have proved themselves trustworthy. As far as morality is concerned, a strong public opinion among them resenting immorality by individual members of their community has resulted in distinct improvement.

On the advice of Colonel Beadon, the local-borns have formed themselves into an association under the presidentship of a gazetted officer, and this association represents their interests to Government.

The community has laboured under many disadvantages in the past. For instance they have been looked down upon by Indian officials because they are descendents of convicts and because socially they do not strictly adhere to the orthodox customs of caste and religion, especially in matrimonial alliances. The latter is of course no fault of the community but due to the fact that races and creeds from all parts of India are represented in the Andamans and that there is therefore no homogeneous community of any caste. The social position of the community has however much improved since some of them have attained responsible posts, and many of the youths have received higher education and are thus qualified for posts for which men were recruited from India in the past. Moreover divergence from orthodox principles is more readily condoned by Indians generally than it was a generation ago.

Economically the community has had several set-backs which involved the loss of most of the savings of the more prominent members among them who had made extensive investments in land. Land had passed from hand to hand at rates varying from Rs. 100 to Rs. 200 per acre. This being contrary to the local laws of ownership of land the Chief Commissioner decreed that the law should be enforced, that non-cultivating ryots could not hold land and occupancy rights could not be admitted. All land which was owned by non-cultivators, therefore, reverted to Government without compensation, and savings representing Rs. 5,000 to Rs. 6,000 in the case of some individuals and perhaps several lakhs to the whole community were lost.

Fortunately for the local community Colonel Ferrar recommended later a change in the land tenure laws which received the assent of the Government of India, and occupancy rights were granted. This no doubt benefited some of the community but many of the original owners of land had lost their capital. Again when Aberdeen was declared a Municipal area, a standard pattern of building was prescribed by Government. Many of the householders belonged to the local-born community, and some of them had only built their houses a few years previously on plans approved by Government nevertheless they were forced to dismantle them, and had to borrow money at high rates of interest to build houses of the new pattern. These economic set-backs had an adverse effect on local development.

Government has however helped the community in other ways especially by giving them a long lease of the Rangachang coconut plantation at some

Rs. 50,000 lower than the best offer from outside the Andamans. Shares in this property can now be held only by members of the local-born community, and as it promises to provide a steady income it will benefit many of the members and their descendents.

Occupation.—There are 695 earners among the local-born community and of these 270 persons are in Government employ in various capacities, 278 persons earn their livelihood by agriculture and 125 follow various other callings as shown in the table below. The problem of the future is to find occupation for the increasing numbers of this community. The number of Government servants will diminish as the convict element becomes less in the Andamans. Suitable land for agriculture is limited, and it is very doubtful whether agricultural produce other than coconuts can ever be exported from the Andamans to compete in the Indian market. Land suitable for coconut cultivation is also limited. If the population of the Andamans is to be self-supporting it is essential that they should produce something for export to balance the cost of necessary imports. Any development of industry requires capital, and as has been shown above, the accumulation of capital has been seriously interfered with in the past. The only other important product of the Andamans is timber, the exploitation of which has always been more or less a Government monopoly. The Forest Department has recognized the needs of the local community and gives them a small share in the exploitation of timber for export. Further development in this direction will help the population to maintain themselves on an economic basis.

Occupations of Local-Born Population returned at the Census of 1931.

Occupation.	Persons.	Males.	Females.
Agricultural Field-men and agricultural Inspectors	4	4	..
Cultivating Owners	150	144	6
Cultivating Tenants	119	112	7
Cultivating Labourers	9	9	..
Clerks, Forest Department	33	33	..
Clerks, in other offices	67	67	..
Forest Department Labourers	57	57	..
Foresters	9	9	..
Forest Rangers	4	4	..
Gunners	4	4	..
Chaudhari	8	8	..
Motor Drivers	11	11	..
Motor Owner	1	1	—
Engine Drivers (secony, lascars, and other employees on boats)	44	44	..
Sweepers	3	3	..
Goldsmiths	4	4	..
Mason	1	1	..
Tailors	4	2	2
Blacksmith	1	1	..
Carpenter	1	1	..
Washerman	1	1	..
Fishermen	5	5	..
Graziers	2	2	..
Sawyers	10	10	—
Plantation clerk	1	1	—
Planters	5	5	—
Post and Telegraph service	5	5	—
Overseer	1	1	—
Timber Contractor	1	1	—

Occupation.	Persons.	Males.	Females.
Toddy sellers	2	2	..
Vegetable seller	1	1	..
Milkmen	3	2	1
Fowl seller	1	..	1
Shopkeepers	14	10	4
Sepoys	2	2	..
Havildar	1	1	..
Chaukidars	2	2	..
Firemen	6	6	..
Fitters	17	17	..
Patwari	3	3	..
Petition-writer	1	1	..
Sub-Assistant Surgeon	1	1	..
Compounders and Nurses	5	4	1
Veterinary surgeon	1	1	..
School Masters	18	16	2
Draftsman	1	1	..
Managers of Plantation	2	2	..
Pensioners	6	6	..
Domestic servants	11	7	4
Contractors unspecified	10	10	..
Cooly unspecified	22	22	..
Total	695	667	28

CHAPTER VIII.

Agriculture.

Prior to the establishment of the Penal Settlement in 1858 all the islands were covered by dense tropical forest, the aboriginal inhabitants living a nomadic life knowing no form of cultivation. During the early days of the settlement the Administration started clearing the jungle around Port Blair with convict labour in order to grow vegetables, fruit and other crops.

In 1870 Lord Mayo took up the question of making Port Blair self-supporting by the expansion of agriculture. Convicts were given tickets of leave, encouraged to marry convict women and settle on the land thus gradually bringing into being the free local-born population. These ticket-of-leave convicts and their descendents possessed no ownership in land but were tenants-at-will of the Government. This system, though a necessity for safeguarding the interest of the Government in a Penal Settlement, was a great handicap for agricultural development. The changing policies of the Government at times encouraged and at times set back progress from an agricultural point of view. Moreover with a mixed population, brought from all parts of India and Burma, from cities as well as rural areas it was impossible to get a homogeneous body of cultivating tenants who were really interested in agriculture. In spite of these adverse circumstances the past 73 years of occupation as a Penal Settlement has brought into existence a cleared area of 45,000 acres with an agricultural population of about 7,000 scattered in villages cultivating various crops on an area of about 12,000 acres.

The declaration of the Government of India of 1921 involving the gradual transformation of Port Blair from a convict settlement into a free colony has brought fresh plans for the development of local agriculture. A regulation was passed in 1926 dealing with land tenure which granted occupancy right to tenants who fulfil certain easy conditions and gave a secure tenure for 60 years to planters. Occupancy rights have been granted to 568 tenants under the new regulation.

The year 1927 saw the beginning of the Agricultural department with an Agricultural Officer and a staff of a clerk, a fieldman and a labour gang of 10 men. The department has slowly developed during the last four years and now a staff of 2 Inspectors, 2 fieldmen and a labour gang of 95 men are employed in carrying out its activities in the 2 agricultural stations, 1 coconut plantation, 1 coffee garden and 16 village demonstration plots. The work of the Department consists of experimenting at the agricultural stations with all crops of local importance and in demonstrating the proved results of these experiments on the cultivators' own plots selected in villages centrally situated. One of the objects is to improve the local method of paddy cultivation and the varieties cultivated. Seeds of some of the best varieties cultivated in India and Burma have been imported and grown in comparison with the best of the local varieties and the seeds which prove best in yield and quality are distributed to cultivators.

To show the advantages of careful cultivation and economic transplanting of seedlings, demonstration plots on the cultivator's own lands have been started. There the cultivators themselves do all the work under expert advice, and it is hoped that this arrangement will influence other cultivators in the neighbourhood. The department also devotes its attention to experiments with coconuts, sugarcane, cotton, *arhar, jowar, ragi* and tapioca as well as to the introduction of improved implements and manures and the organization of an annual agricultural exhibition and a ploughing competition.

Development of agriculture is essential for the food production of the islands but as has been found elsewhere the cultivator is conservative in his own methods and some years must elapse before the benefits of improved agriculture can be brought home to the ryot.

The total area under cultivation as furnished by the Revenue Assistant Commissioner is as follows :—

	Acres.
Paddy	4,123
Sugarcane	97
Turmeric	14
Maize	4
Pulses	118
Melons and Water Melons	21
Vegetables and other fruits	367
Coffee	95
Tea	163
Coconut	3,786
Rubber	276
Total	9,064
Grazing grounds	10,630
Total cleared area	19,694

Of the above, the rubber plantations have been closed since last year, because the cost of production of rubber exceeded the market value while the tea gardens have for the most part fallen into disuse for some years past. Further, land under cultivation is decreasing mainly because Mappilla convicts who had taken up agricultural tenures have returned to their provinces on release.

There was an over-production of paddy last year and many of the cultivators have been left with their surplus stock, owing to the fact that rice can be imported at a considerably lower rate from Burma than it can be produced locally. This position however is only a temporary one; it has arisen partly owing to the abnormal fall in the price of rice during last year and partly owing to the Andamans freight rate having been lowered by about 50 per cent. when the prices were exceptionally high in the preceding year, which rate still prevails. Under normal conditions the local harvest of paddy is still considerably below local requirements and there is therefore room for an expansion of the agricultural population by over 100 per cent. This estimate is based on the assumption that the average local paddy crop is about 14 maunds per acre or about 58,000 maunds at present, whereas at least 150,000 maunds of paddy are required to meet the full requirements of rice for the population.

A rice huller has recently been introduced into the Andamans. It has demonstrated that the local grown paddy is mostly of poor quality. To make the local population self-supporting as far as their staple food is concerned a good uniform high yielding variety of paddy is required. At present most of the surplus of the cultivators, who of course use their own rice for home consumption, is only considered fit for cattle by the remaining population of the islands who import their rice.

The following are the principal items of land revenue realized during 1929-30 :—

	Rs.	a.	p.
Land Rent	23,960	4	0
Coconut plantations	11,922	12	0
Coffee plantations	1,518	0	0
House Tax	3,451	0	0
Grazing Fees	7,604	0	0
Total	48,456	0	0

Cattle.

There are at present 10,278 cattle in the Andamans as under :—

Bullocks	1,771
Cows	2,092
Cow buffaloes	1,332
Bull buffaloes	868
Bull calves	1,222
Heifers	1,309
Bull buffalo calves	788
Buffalo heifers	896

The Commissariat Department have from time to time imported fresh stock to improve the breed in order to produce better animals for draught purposes and increase the production of milk. The present breeding stock consists mainly of Hissar and Sindhi cows and bulls and Murra buffaloes. The department also maintains a dairy farm for the supply of milk, cream and butter to residents and hospitals, the supply varying from 360 to 670 lbs. daily.

Of the 11,359 earners recorded in the Andamans 2,622 or 23 per cent. earn their livelihood by agriculture and pasture. It is however estimated that above 50 per cent. of the total population depend on agriculture for their means of livelihood since most agriculturists are married and their families comprise on an average five persons.

CHAPTER IX.

Distribution and Movement of the population of the Colony.

The total convict population in 1921 was 11,512 whereas the 1931 census shows 7,552. In order to illustrate the movement of the population and the effect on the formation of a free colony, the residents of the islands, excluding aborigines who are dealt with separately, may conveniently be classified under different heads as follows :—

	1921.	1931.	Increase.
1. Wives of Convicts	230	1,004	774
2. Forest Department labour	1,581	1,897	316
3. Match industry	..	103	103
4. Children aged 0—15	1,427	4,075	2,648
5. Females over 15 years excluding wives of convicts	1,086	1,842	756
6. Ships' crews	..	320	320
Total	4,324	9,241	4,917

The following is the explanation of the differences :—

1. Wives of Convicts. The increase is due to many convicts having brought their families from India during the last decade.

2 and 3. Increase accounted for by labour brought from India since last census.

4. Increase of 2,648 children under 15 years of age is due mainly to children born of free women imigrants, mostly wives of convicts, who have come to the Andamans during the 10 years.

5. Increase mainly due to females who have come from India since last census.

6. This only includes crew of vessels temporarily in the Andamans.

The total free population, excluding convicts and aborigines, was 5,473 in 1921 whereas it is now 11,211. The free population has therefore increased by 5,738. An increase of 4,917 has been accounted for above, and the remainder, that is 821 in number, may be accounted for by assuming that they are ex-convicts and free immigrant labourers. There has been a decrease of 231 in the garrison, which in 1921 was 978 against 747 in 1931, but other free immigrants have also replaced that loss making a total of 1,052 in addition to the increase of 4,917 accounted for under 1, 2, 3, 4, 5 and 6. These 1,052 may be assumed to have taken employment in the Andamans. Public Works Department works of construction which were formerly done by convict labour are now mainly carried out by free labour. Further about 2,000 acres of coconut plantations which were formerly worked by convict labour are now worked by free labour, while most of the men now employed by private individuals are free whereas formerly self-supporting convicts were employed.

The fertility tables of the local-born community, *i.e.*, those born of convict fathers and of convict mothers are given below :—

I.—*Sex of First Born.*

Natural Division.	Number of females first born.	Percentage of such families where female children predominate.	Number of males first born.	Percentage of such families where males predominate.	Number of females first born per 1,000 males first born.	Number of slips examined.
Andamans	246	40·8%	290	48%	848	603

II.—*Size of Families by Occupation of Husband.*

Occupation of Husband.	Number of families examined.	Total number of children born.	Average per family.	Number of children surviving.	Proportion of surviving to total 1,000 born.
Cultivators	211	982	4·65	782	796
Cooly and Labour	38	85	2·2	68	800
Shopkeepers and Merchants	71	197	2·8	132	670
Clerks, etc., serving in offices	58	192	3·3	143	745
Washermen	11	53	4·8	37	698
Carpenter, Tailor, Blacksmith, Fishermen, Sawyers, Barber, etc.	63	179	2·8	145	810
Orderlies, Village Chaukidars	45	127	2·8	102	803
Mechanical labourers	22	62	2·8	53	855
Other miscellaneous occupations unspecified	22	81	3·7	49	605

III.—*Size of Families by Religion.*

Caste or Religion.	Number of families examined.	Total number of children born.	Average per family.	Number of children surviving.	Proportion of surviving to 1,000 born.	Number of families with wife married at 13—14	15—19	20—30	30 and over.
Hindu	290	926	3·2	691	746	150	79	46	14
Muslim	254	754	2·97	576	764	120	96	35	4
Buddhist	52	138	2·65	111	804	14	18	18	2
Christian	22	64	2·9	49	766	9	8	4	1
Tribal	4	5	1·25	5	1,000	*Nil*	3	1	*Nil*
Unspecified	19	70	3·7	46	657	11	5	2	1

IV.—*Average size of Family correlated with age of wife at marriage.*

Age of wife at marriage.	Number of families.	Number of children born.	Average observed.	Number of children surviving.	Average observed.
13 years	234	705	3·0	593	2·53
14 years	68	193	2·8	154	2·27
15 years	62	205	3·3	154	2·5
16 years	43	123	2·8	87	2·0
17 years	40	85	2·1	71	1·75
18 years	43	113	2·6	92	2·1
19 years	22	51	2·3	43	2·0
20 years	26	76	2·9	52	2·0

These tables show that the average of surviving children is about 2·3 per family. It is highest among cultivators where the average number of surviving children is about 3·7. No figures are available of the natural increase of the local-born population as they were not enumerated separately. Figures of the natural increase of the population of the Nicobars, which do not migrate, however exist and fertility tables were also prepared for that population. It is therefore interesting to compare these figures for the Andamans and Kar Nikobar. On the latter island the indigenous population increased by 18 per cent. in a decade whereas the fertility tables showed an average survival rate of 2·5. Assuming that a survival rate of 2 would leave the population stationary and that a survival rate of 2·5 shows an increase of 18 per cent. on the same basis a survival rate of 2·3 would only give about 11 per cent. which is therefore probably near the normal increase of the local-born population in a decade.

CHAPTER X.

Birth-Place.

The statistics of birth-place by provinces are contained in Imperial Table VI. Statistics were also taken of birth-place by districts and these are given below. Out of 504 districts of India and Burma 347 are represented in the Andamans which of course is mainly due to the fact that convicts come to the Andamans from most provinces.

The following are the provinces of birth which are represented by over 150 individuals :—

	Persons.	Males.	Females.
Andamans	4,244	2,269	1,975
Burma	2,953	2,439	514
Madras	2,754	1,897	857
United Provinces	2,431	2,007	424
Punjab	1,983	1,598	385
Bengal	949	797	152
Bihar and Orissa	619	564	55
Bombay	495	435	60
Central India	426	366	60
Assam	152	134	18

The figures of the female immigrants are of considerable interest because the females, excepting 141 convicts, are voluntary immigrants, while 50 per cent. of the male population are convicts who cannot leave the Andamans at will. Of the females born outside the Andamans, Madras heads the list with 857. Of these 714 are Mappillas, 75 per cent. of whom will probably return to Malabar on the release of their husbands in the near future. Burma and the United Provinces, the Punjab and Bengal come next with 514, 424, 385 and 152 female residents. These figures give an indication of the proportion of the various races of which the future population will probably be composed. It is also apparent that the Burmese population is increasing to a considerable extent. Immigration of Burmese women is being encouraged for Burmans make the most suitable form of forest labour and forestry is the main industry of the islands. Judging by the influx of Burmese women in recent years it is probable that the Burmans will preponderate in the near future.

Table showing the number of persons born in districts of India and Burma and enumerated in the Andamans and Nicobars.

Birth Districts.	Persons.	Males.	Females.
Ajmer-Merwara	24	24	..
Assam.			
Balipara Frontier Tract	1	1	..
Cachar	1	1	..
Goalpara	7	7	..
Kamrup	7	7	..
Khasi States	1	1	..
Lakhimpur	31	26	5
Manipur State	35	30	5
Naga Hills	2	2	..
Nowgong	3	3	..
Sadiya Frontier Tract	1	1	..
Sibsagar	8	7	1
Sylhet	55	48	7
Baluchistan.			
Kalat State	1	1	..
Quetta-Pishin	2	2	..
Sibi	1	1	..
Unspecified	16	16	..
Bengal.			
Bakarganj	94	78	16
Bankura	6	6	..
Birbhum	9	2	7
Bogra	11	8	3
Burdwan	18	16	2
Chittagong	136	128	8
Dacca	82	54	28
Darjeeling	12	4	8
Dinajpur	6	6	..
Faridpur	47	36	11
Hooghly	18	16	2
Howrah	11	10	1
Jalpaiguri	5	3	2
Jessore	11	10	1
Khulna	27	20	7
Midnapore	31	27	4
Murshidabad	9	7	2
Mymensingh	30	28	2
Nadia	4	4	..
Noakhali	141	139	2

Birth Districts.	Persons.	Males.	Females.
***Bengal*—contd.**			
Pabna	15	11	4
Rajshahi	8	6	2
Rangpur	9	6	3
Tippera	15	14	1
Tripura State	9	9	..
24-Parganas	9	7	2
Unspecified	194	159	35
Bihar and Orissa.			
Angul	1	..	1
Balasore	10	7	3
Bhagalpur	6	5	1
Bonai	1	1	..
Champaran	5	5	..
Dharbanga	3	2	1
Dhenkanal State	7	5	2
Gangpur State	2	2	..
Gaya	23	20	3
Hazaribagh	11	9	2
Hindol State	1	1	..
Kalahandi State	1	1	..
Manbhum	7	6	1
Mayurbhanj State	4	4	..
Monghyr	4	3	1
Muzaffarpur	4	1	3
Nayagarh State	1	1	..
Palamau	11	11	..
Pal-Lahara State	2	2	..
Patna	22	18	4
Puri	10	9	1
Purnea	14	14	..
Ranchi	310	294	16
Ranpur State	18	17	1
Sambalpur	8	6	2
Saran	12	10	2
Shahabad	1	1	..
Singbhum	3	2	1
Talcher State	1	1	..
Unspecified	117	107	10
Bombay and Western India States Agency.			
Ahmedabad	23	19	4
Ahmednagar	5	4	1
Akalkot State	2	2	..
Belgaum	33	30	3
Bhavnagar State	1	1	..
Bijapur	16	15	1
Bombay Suburban	94	77	17
Broach	2	2	..
Cutch	11	11	..
Dharampur State	1	1	..
Dharwar	55	49	6
Dharangadhra State	2	1	1
Dhrol State	3	3	..
Gondal State	1	1	..
Hyderabad Sind	22	22	..
Kaira	8	6	2
Karachi	8	8	..
Khandesh	15	13	2
Kolhapur State	4	3	1
Larkhana	19	19	..
Nasik	20	18	2
Nawabshah State	6	5	1
Palitana State	1	1	..
Phalean State	1	1	..
Poona	19	15	4
Porbandar State	1	1	..
Rajkot State	3	3	..
Ratnagiri	41	38	3
Sangli State	2	2	..
Satara	27	21	6
Sholapur	13	12	1
Sukkur	15	14	1
Surat	6	5	1
Thana	22	19	3
Thar and Parkar	3	3	..
Unspecified	32	32	..

Birth Districts.	Persons.	Males.	Females.
Burma.			
Akyab	20	18	2
Amherst	6	4	2
Arakan Hill District	37	32	5
Bhamo	7	7	..
Bassein	157	111	46
Beik	3	3	..
Chin Hills	4	4	..
Dawe	10	7	3
Hanthawaddy	77	59	18
Henzada	113	85	28
Insein	87	69	18
Katha	5	5	..
Kyaik-Kami	1	1	..
Kyaukpyu	20	18	2
Kyaukse	14	14	..
Lower Chindwin	1	1	..
Magwe	60	49	11
Mandalay	107	89	18
Maubin	83	40	43
Meiktila	36	28	8
Mergui	27	25	2
Minbu	26	26	..
Monywa	17	14	3
Moulmein	141	119	22
Myaungmya	64	53	11
Myingyan	41	31	10
Myitkyina	10	10	..
Pakokku	55	47	8
Pathein	13	12	1
Pegu	132	118	14
Prome	74	57	17
Pyapon	102	89	13
Pyi	9	8	1
Rangoon	342	264	78
Sagaing	16	12	4
Salween	7	7	..
Sandoway	10	10	..
Shan Pyi	7	4	3
Shwebo	41	36	5
Sittwe	11	2	9
Tavoy	51	48	3
Thandwe	18	16	2
Tharrawaddy	189	134	55
Thaton	67	65	2
Thayetmyo	44	42	2
Taungu	78	74	4
Yamethin	59	40	19
Districts unspecified	454	432	22
Central Provinces and Berar.			
Akola	17	15	2
Amroati	19	19	..
Balaghat	16	11	5
Bastar State	1	1	..
Betul	5	4	1
Bhandara	6	4	2
Bilaspur	31	22	9
Buldana	6	5	1
Chanda	6	5	1
Chhindwara	8	6	2
Damoh	5	4	1
Drug	1	1	..
Hoshangabad	4	4	..
Jashpur State	1	1	..
Jubbulpore	32	24	8
Kanker State	1	1	..
Kawardha State	1	1	..
Khairagarh State	1	1	..
Mandla	8	7	1
Nagpur	45	36	9
Nimar	1	1	..
Raipur	31	20	11
Sarangarh State	1	1	..
Saugor	14	12	2
Seoni	9	7	2
Surguja State	8	5	3
Udaipur State	4	4	..
Wardha	6	6	..
Yeotmal	4	4	..
Unspecified	141	141	..

Birth Districts.	Persons.	Males.	Females.
Coorg.			
Coorg	7	7	..
Madras.			
Anantapur	18	16	2
Arcot	34	24	10
Bellary	21	19	2
Chingelput	16	10	6
Chittoor	12	9	3
Coimbatore	73	62	11
Cuddapah	24	15	9
Ganjam	41	36	5
Godavari	67	52	15
Guntur	11	6	5
Kanara, South	24	20	4
Kistna	13	11	2
Kurnool	24	22	2
Madras	299	172	127
Malabar	1,731	1,146	585
Madura	33	29	4
Nellore	12	8	4
The Nilgiris	5	4	1
Ramnad	18	18	..
Salem	23	21	2
Tanjore	41	33	8
Tinnevelly	61	52	9
Trichinopoly	25	16	9
Vizagapatam	65	50	15
Bangalore	24	17	7
Cochin State	15	9	6
Travancore State	12	8	4
North-West Frontier Province.			
Bannu	74	61	13
Dera Ismail Khan	19	16	3
Hazara	50	41	9
Kohat	27	21	6
Peshawar	190	163	27
Phulera	1	1	..
Unspecified	37	32	5
Punjab and Punjab States Agency.			
Ambala	88	73	15
Amritsar	200	161	39
Attock	82	63	19
Dera Gazi Khan	40	40	..
Faridkot	3	3	..
Ferozepore	151	114	37
Gujranwala	41	33	8
Gujrat	132	105	27
Gurdaspur	21	15	6
Gurgaon	14	13	1
Hissar	15	13	2
Hoshiarpur	91	80	11
Jhang	25	20	5
Jhelum	120	102	18
Jubbal State	1	1	..
Jullundur	28	22	6
Kangra	92	87	5
Kapurthala State	3	1	2
Karnal	9	8	1
Kuthar State	1	1	..
Lahore	161	130	31
Ludhiana	41	34	7
Lyallpur	37	33	4
Madhan State	4	4	..
Maler Kotla State	2	2	..
Mianwali	49	30	19
Montgomery	26	18	8
Multan	22	18	4
Muzaffargarh	8	8	..
Nabha State	4	2	2
Patiala State	42	34	8
Rawalpindi	200	165	35
Rohtak	30	23	7
Sangri State	1	1	..
Shahpur	76	58	18
Sheikhupura	27	21	6
Sialkot	58	46	12
Simla	6	4	2
Unspecified	30	10	20

Birth Districts.	Persons.	Males.	Females.
United Provinces of Agra and Oudh.			
Agra	81	64	17
Aligarh	87	69	18
Allahabad	49	38	11
Almora	7	5	2
Azamgarh	23	19	4
Bahraich	67	54	13
Ballia	20	17	3
Banda	16	12	4
Bara Banki	64	49	15
Bareilly	146	120	26
Basti	27	21	6
Benares	27	12	15
Bijnor	46	33	13
Budaun	58	43	15
Bulandshar	35	33	2
Cawnpore	95	71	24
Dehra Dun	4	2	2
Etah	113	74	39
Etawah	25	22	3
Farrukhabad	56	48	8
Fatehpur	29	25	4
Fyzabad	62	56	6
Garhwal	4	4	..
Ghazipur	20	12	8
Gonda	24	21	3
Gorakhpur	66	60	6
Hamirpur	1	1	..
Hardoi	61	51	10
Jalaun	9	9	..
Jaunpur	5	5	..
Jhansi	14	13	1
Kheri	75	52	23
Lucknow	53	46	7
Mainpuri	38	30	8
Meerut	82	63	19
Mirzapur	20	14	6
Moradabad	126	108	18
Muttra	20	19	1
Muzaffarnagar	24	17	7
Naini Tal	19	13	6
Partabgarh	18	16	2
Pilibhit	17	17	..
Rae Bareli	16	15	1
Rampur State	18	17	1
Saharanpur	5	3	2
Shahjahanpur	72	67	5
Sitapur	171	136	35
Sultanpur	15	13	2
Unao	37	34	3
Unspecified	267	267	..
Central India Agency.			
Ajaigarh State	1	1	..
Alipura "	4	4	..
Alirajpur "	3	3	..
Barwani "	5	5	..
Bhopal "	1	1	..
Dhar "	2	2	..
Indore "	19	12	7
Jaora "	1	..	1
Kilchipur "	1	1	..
Kurwai "	1	1	..
Narsinghgarh State	1	..	1
Orchha State	1	1	..
Rajgarh "	1	1	..
Rewa "	4	3	1
Sitamau "	1	1	..
Sohawal "	3	1	2
Nagod "	5	2	3
Rajputana Agency.			
Alwar State	1	1	..
Bharatpur "	13	12	1
Bikaner "	1	1	..
Bundi "	2	2	..
Dholpur "	11	10	1
Dungarpur "	1	1	..
Jaipur "	15	12	3
Jodhpur "	3	3	..
Karauli "	1	1	..
Kotah "	4	3	1
Lawa Estate	8	6	2
Marwar State	1	1	..

Birth Districts.	Persons.	Males.	Females.	Birth Districts.	Persons.	Males.	Females.
Rajputana Agency—contd.				*Delhi.*			
Mewar State	1	..	1	Delhi	8	6	2
Shahpura "	4	4	..	*Jammu and Kashmir State.*			
Sirohi "	1	1	..				
Baroda State.				Jammu	10	8	2
Baroda	9	9	..	Kashmir	4	3	1
Dwarka	6	5	1	*Hyderabad State.*			
Naosari	4	3	1				
Gwalior State.				Hyderabad (Deccan)	7	6	1
Garha	3	2	1	*Mysore State.*			
Gwalior	29	28	1				
Khanidhana	1	1	..				
Raghugarh	1	1	..	Mysore	5	5	..

Persons born in Andaman and Nicobar Islands and enumerated in other Provinces or States in India.

	Total.	Males.	Females.		Total.	Males.	Females
Assam	4	3	1	Gwalior State	*Nil*	*Nil*	*Nil*
Baluchistan	2	2	..	Hyderabad State	*Nil*	*Nil*	*Nil*
Baroda State	1	..	1	Jammu and Kashmir State	*Nil*	*Nil*	*Nil*
Bengal	17	13	4	Madras	Figures not available		
Bihar and Orissa	4	3	1	Mysore State	10	6	4
Bombay	81	66	15	N.-W. F. Province	2	..	2
W. I. States Agency	2	1	1	Punjab	105	69	36
Burma	82	43	39	Rajputana and Ajmer-Merwara	*Nil*	*Nil*	*Nil*
Central India Agency	4	3	1				
C. P. and Berar	96	73	23	Travancore State	2	2	..
Cochin State	*Nil*	*Nil*	*Nil*	United Provinces	140	29	111
				Total	552	313	239

CHAPTER XI.

Civil Condition and Social and Linguistic proportions.

(With map.)

Infant marriage is seldom resorted to by the "local-born" and by marriage condition here dealt with consumated marriage only is referred to. Re-marriage of widows is common owing to the shortage of women.

Statistics of the civil condition obtaining in the Andaman Settlement cannot be analysed on a scientific basis on account of the fact that the male element naturally predominates because convicts are sent to the Andamans and the proportion continually changes according to the policy adopted by Government from time to time; only practical conclusions are therefore attempted.

There have been considerable changes during the last decade. Of 7,404 convict males 1,004 have their wives in the Andamans or nearly one in seven convicts is married locally whereas only 230 convicts out of 10,960 or 1 in 47 convicts had a wife in the Andamans in 1921. This increased proportion of married convict families is one of the outstanding features of the new regimé and the improved moral tone among convicts is very noticeable, moreover since the convict husband or father is now usually of the accidental type, perhaps mentally unbalanced but otherwise not very criminal and the wives or mothers are free women, normally quite uncriminal, joining their husbands while both are young, they should raise large families of quite another type than that propagated by the old type of convict parents.

As regards the free population of 4,438 adult males only 1,450 have their wives in the Andamans, that is of about 3 adult free males 1 is married. The 1921 census showed 3,535 adult males and 773 married females, and of the latter 363 were convicts leaving only 410 married females to 3,534 adult males, so that only about one in nine free persons could have had a wife in the Andamans. The position has therefore also considerably improved as far as the free population is concerned and the Andamans do not now seem to be looked upon as being unfit for respectable families as was formerly the case. The percentage of free families, it is true, is not nearly normal but this is due to the large proportion that the Garrison and Military Police bear to the rest of the population as well as the large number of crews employed in vessels and immigrant labour of the Forest Department whose families do not come to the Andamans because they are settled on the land elsewhere.

The figures for adults are arrived at as follows :—

Children aged 0—15	4,075
Free wives of Convicts married locally	856
Free females over 15 years excluding wives of Convicts	1,842
Crews of vessels (Free)	320
Adult males over 15 years excluding crews (Free)	4,118
Convict males	7,404
Convict females	148
Aborigines	460
Total Population of Andamans	19,223

The following are the actual number of persons and percentages of various religions as represented by different colours in the map :—

(*i*) GREAT ANDAMAN—*Total Population*	*18,923*	
Andamanese	160	0·85%
Hindus	7,603	40·12%
Muslims	6,434	34·00%
Buddhists	2,902	15·34%
Christians	1,123	5·93%
Sikhs	649	3·53%
Others	52	0·27%

Under "Others" the following religions are included :—

Confucian	37
Tribal	14
Zoroastrian	1

(*ii*) SENTINEL ISLAND—*Total Population*	*50*	
Andamanese	50	100%
(*iii*) LITTLE ANDAMAN—*Total Population*	*250*	
Andamanese	250	100%

Although the colours have been shown against the whole of Great Andaman, 90 per cent. of the Indian population is confined to the Settlement of Port Blair, an area of about 473 square miles. Another map of the Andamans (page 22 above) gives the distribution of the various surviving Negrito tribes. Some 10 per cent. of the Indian population lives in camps and Forest settlements outside Port Blair.

The following are the principal mother-tongues of the population of the Andamans :—

Language.	Number of persons.	Percentage to the total population.
Hindustani	4,618	24·02
Burmese	2,745	14·27
Urdu	2,311	12·02
Punjabi	2,228	11·58
Malayalam	2,073	10·78
Bengali	1,171	6·09
Others	4,077	21·20

Under 'Others' most Indian, including the Andamanese tongues, and 7 Western languages are represented and these are shown in Imperial Table XV. The common vernacular used in the Andamans is however a colloquial form of Hindustani which every one acquires after a few months' stay in the islands.

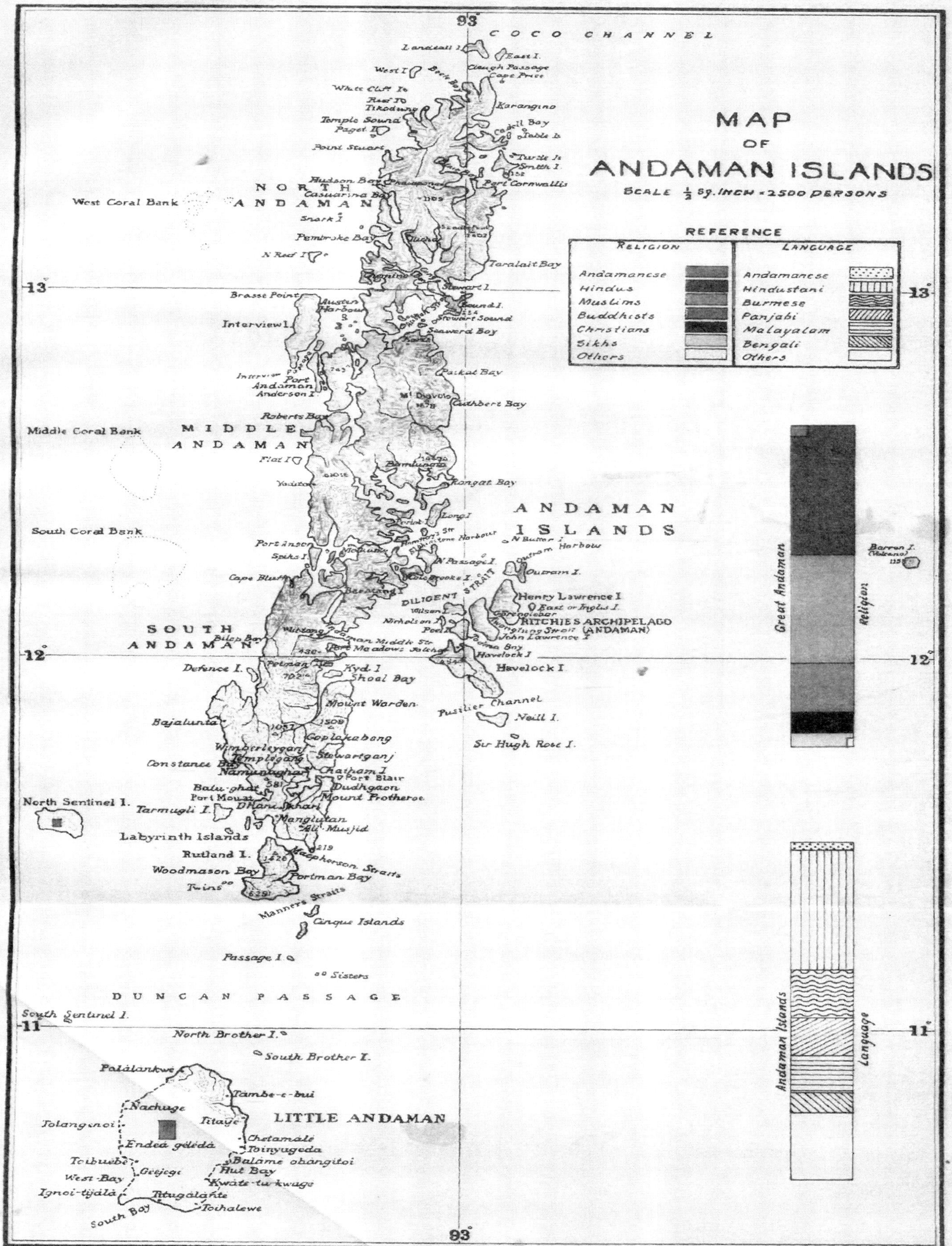

Reg. No. 2511. E. 31. 805.

HELIO. S. I. O. CALCUTTA.

APPENDIX I.

The Bhantus.

A criminal tribe of India.

The Bhantus are one of the many wandering gipsy tribes of India who subsist by organized robbery and dacoity and who are for this reason proscribed by the Indian Government as criminal tribes. They are found in North and Central India, branches of the tribe also existing in Eastern India where they are known as Karwal Nats. Their area of operations even extends as far as Burma, but they are not distinguishable there from the other Indians because they do not wander about in gangs. Being a proscribed criminal tribe, and probably the most dangerous of all such tribes, even in India the Bhantu invariably covers his identity by adopting an *alias* such as Kanjar, Sansia, Habura, Beria, Chaparband, Kuchband, etc., with which he has no connection whatsoever as a tribe.

For years the Government of the United Provinces has tried to confine them to settlements under the care of the Salvation Army, where they have been taught industries, but it is with great difficulty that they have been secured and confined within the limits of the settlement. A large gang of Bhantus in 1926 voluntarily came to the Andamans from Indian jails and from free Bhantu settlements. These were settled on the land under the care of Staff Captain Sheard of the Salvation Army, and their wives and children were allowed to accompany them. In the Andamans their conduct has been good and the colony comprises 285 individuals. Here they cultivate the land, the younger men and boys also being employed in the saw-mills and on coolie labour in various other industries.

Owing to their antecedents as a criminal tribe, there is very little information available about these people, except that found in Police records. Hollins in his "Criminal Tribes of the United Provinces" gives an account of their activities, but it is obviously difficult to obtain correct information, because they usually have a past of hitherto undetected history, or being good Bhantus, and there are few such, they do not wish to have their identity known, owing to the stigma attached to the name. In the Andamans no such concealment is necessary because their previous history is known, and they themselves are intimately known to the Salvation Army Officer in charge, who has been connected with them for many years. It is due to the latter's co-operation that I have been able to place on record some data on their tribal organization, habits and customs.

Adjutant Sheard supplied most of the information in reply to a questionnaire, which I set, and spent several months verifying it, his experience obtained by daily contact with them for many years being unique. The writer is extremely grateful to him for his care and willingness and for the thoroughness of his replies to the questionnaire.

Origin.—The Bhantus claim descent from the Chauhan Thakur clan of Chitorgarh, which they regard as their mother city. Ethnologically they are perhaps of Dravidian origin,[1] being a branch of a great nomadic race. According to tradition, most of the clan perished when the state was raided by Musalmans many years prior to the advent of the East India Company. Those who were fortunate enough to escape took to the jungles, becoming wanderers, and thus started their gipsy form of existence. Legend has it among them that the sacred threads of the Brahmins who were butchered in this particular Muslim raid weighed seventy-two maunds or 5,760 lbs.

As far as one can judge, the Bhantus probably have an ethnological connection with the Sansias, Haburas, Kanjars, Karwal Nats, and Jats; but the present day members of the tribes named differ considerably. Prior to their proscription it was usual for the Bhantus to meet every rainy season on the plain of the old ruined city of Nuh-Khera to the north of Jalesar in the Kheri district of the United Provinces for the settling of disputes and marriages. No definite information can be obtained as to the etymological meaning of the word Bhantu, but one villager suggested that it might have sprung from the practice of villagers and others, who on seeing strangers on their land, invariably yelled out, *Bhag-tu*—"Run away", obviously an aetiological derivation. Hollins is of the opinion that the term comes from "Bhante" in the sense of "broken" and that the name implies that the tribe is composed of various mixed elements, which is perhaps supported by its tradition of Rajput origin.

Gots.—The Bhantus are said to be divided into some thirty-six *gots* or clans but only the names of twenty-four have been ascertained. Almost every *got* differs in the observance of customs relating to worship, marriages, burial, etc., of a few of which differences mention will be made later. Information with regard to this must be taken with a certain amount of reserve as most of the Bhantus themselves had no idea there were so many *gots*. One man on being questioned gave the information that there were twelve and a half *gots*, explaining that eunuchs were given half a *got*, which is called the *Hijara Got*.

As far as has been ascertained the system, of marriage is exogamous with the exception of one *got* the Bhanswale. No particular explanation is offered as to why the names of the *gots* were chosen, many of them being selected from words in every day use. Several of the *gots* I have been able to identify with those mentioned by Inspector Baldeo Sahai's report on the origin, habits and customs of the wandering tribes, which he classes as Khanjars and Behrias inhabiting the Agra district in 1875. The Behrias usually marry Bhantu women and the difference from the Bhantu is therefore merely in that they follow a different profession while the Sansias, Haburas, Kanjars, and Karwal Nats may have a common origin with the Bhantus. The Mahe *got* is referred to as one of the three principal Kanjar *gots* and the Dhapo *got* has a

[1] W. Crooke's "*Tribes and Castes of the N.-W. Provinces*".

distinct affinity with the Dhapu mentioned by Baldeo Sahai, who refers to it as one of the 'Puckas' of the five *gots* which claim their descent from Bidhu, one of the three persons whom legend ascribes to have been born in the west at a place called Garwar.

The Kanjar is more of a hunter than a criminal, but Kanjars have been known to work with Bhantus as the local adherents of a raiding party. It is probable that owing to the continual adoption of aliases, confusion has arisen as to the identity of the *gots* as well as that of the various criminal tribes as a whole.

The names of the *gots* ascertained are as follows, a description following later in a tabulated form of the essential differences between the more important :—

1. Sade.
2. Dhapo.
3. Chareli.
4. Chanduwale.
5. Gadho.
6. Mahes.
7. Gehla.
8. Bhanswale.
9. Chhede.
10. Koran.
11. Timachi.
12. Marwarie.
13. Dhaneke.
14. Rorke.
15. Pophat.
16. Mataike.
17. Ghasive.
18. Dholive (High).
19. Dholive (Low).
20. Mire.
21. Range.
22. Gange.

General Appearance.—The Bhantus are experts in all kinds of dacoity and robbery, and are skilled in the use of fire-arms. They are of good physique and are reputed to be good runners. The women are strong and handsome and are gifted with exceptionally strong voices. They are clever and intelligent and are well able to take care of themselves and their families when the men of the clan are away on raiding expeditions.

Dress.—They wear the "*lenga*" or pleated skirt. This consists of some twenty to forty yards of material. The two ends are sewn up and a hole is made at one edge through which a cord is threaded. When the cord is drawn tight the skirt is "kilted". An edging of contrasted material is sewn on the bottom edge to make it hang properly. Women who are not suckling children wear coloured "armlets"; a shirt made similar to a man's and of any kind of cloth is worn loosely and hangs down over the *lenga*, a white or coloured cloth completing the dress. Girls wear clothes on the same lines. The men and boys have no distinctive dress. Jewellery is also freely worn by the women, and the men invariably wear some small gold ear-rings, and occasionally a small necklace of gold ear-rings. On the whole the women are far more distinctive as a type than the men, both in their dress and physical appearance ; they are completely different to other Indian women, a stout Bhantuni is not usually met with, while the men would pass easily for ordinary villagers. The women however are very "gipsy" in appearance and are dirty and untidy in their habits owing no doubt to the fact, that they lead a nomadic life, and are always on the move leaving their filth behind. They also tatoo each other with an ink of burnt *akaua* leaves in oil. The Bhantus possess no particular physical quality peculiar to themselves and the fact that they never oil their hair, a custom which is a direct contrast to that throughout India, is no doubt due to the fact that they are wanderers and unable to carry oil about or resort to the barber, but there is no special tabu on the use of hair oil except in case of children in certain circumstances (See paragraph on *Child birth*).

Internal Administration.—The Bhantus lead their nomadic life in gangs consisting of a dozen families, keeping as far as possible away from villages when they camp ; men from different gangs would however combine in the event of a raiding expedition. The system of internal administration of the clan is communal, all disputes being dealt with by the Panchayat or council of elders. In theory this may be composed of any five members of the tribe called together to settle any particular dispute, but in practice certain persons by reason of their knowledge of tribal laws, etc., come to be regarded as the Panchayat of any particular gang. Age has little to do in deciding who shall sit on the Panchayat. On a dispute arising, the parties concerned appear before the Panchayat, each party having its own advocate to state its case and wrangle for it. The whole however has the appearance of a debate more than anything else, for others (including women and children whatever the nature of the enquiry may be) attend, and most have something to say in the matter. Generally speaking the Panchayat aims at reconciling parties rather than punishing them. They have however considerable powers to inflict punishment, usually in the shape of pecuniary fines, some of the fines becoming the Panchayat's perquisite. Besides disputes, all manner of offences against tribal custom such as incest (marriage within a *got* is so regarded), divorce, adultery, etc., are dealt with by the Panchayat, not to speak of trials by ordeal, settlement of marriage-prices, and questions of general importance affecting tribal life ; for their services they may also charge from ten to fifteen rupees.

Crime.—As has already been said, the Bhantus prior to being confined to settlements lived entirely by crime. A few were ostensibly engaged in agriculture but this only covered up their real activities. Their nefarious practices found most scope in dacoity or robbery by violence but being a community organized for crime, nothing came amiss to them.

On deciding to commit a dacoity in any particular locality spies would be sent out to select a suitable victim, study the general habits of the villagers and the distance from any effective aid, and enumerate the number of men and firearms. Inspector Baldeo Sahai also asserts in his report "That they have been known to travel very great distances in disguise by rail for the purposes of committing thefts, robberies, and dacoities, never committing offences of any kind near their encampment". The raid usually took place at midnight. Acting on the information given by the spies, men would be posted at various points in the village, and by firing off their guns attract attention from the main gang which would attack the particular house or houses previously appointed. The gang would usually consist of some thirty to forty men and would not be over-scrupulous in their methods. If resistance was shown they were merciless, indeed, the particular gang sent to Port Blair had committed over fifty murders in one series of outrages. As they were working against time, cruel, and violent methods were often adopted to compel the victims to reveal the hiding place of their treasure, such as forcing women to sit on burning charcoal, etc. Rape was common. The traditional weapon of attack was a short hard stick, thrown with tremendous force, while the lathi was used for defence. In more recent years, however, guns have been adopted and khaki worn. Having secured their plunder, they buried it immediately in the vicinity to avoid any incriminating evidence and dispersed. In the event of a murder being committed, no serious action is taken, though it is regarded as *pap* or sin, and if a stranger has been murdered, the murderer distributes *gur* among the brotherhood. This costs Rs. 1-4-0. Should one of the tribe however be murdered the offender must give a feast costing Rs. 101. When the whole affair has blown over, the plunder is dug up and given to the women who dispose of it to the goldsmiths who act as receivers.

It is essential to emphasise the great part played by crime in the general life of the clan. A boy is initiated into crime as soon as he is able to walk and talk. No doubt the motive is practical to a great extent, in so far as it is always better to risk a child in petty theft, who, if he were caught would probably be cuffed, while an adult would immediately be arrested. An important part is also played by women, who although they do not participate in the actual raids have many heavy responsibilities. Besides disposing of most of the stolen property, they are also expert shop lifters thus participating in the material support of the tribe. They also arrange for the legal defence of arrested men, as well as supporting and visiting relations in jail.

A raiding party is composed of men who only operate at some distance from the district in which the rest of the gang containing old men and women and children have camped. Thus in the absence of the men on a raiding expedition, the women are responsible for the camp and the main body is in the charge of a woman and may be known by her name. It is no doubt this, which induces Hollins to remark that "A feature of the tribal organization is that many gangs are led by women". Mr. Sheard informs me that he has never heard of an active gang being under the leadership of a woman or women while actually engaged in dacoity or raiding. Quite recently a number of Karwal gangs wished to come to the Andamans, and in every case a woman's name was given as the leader of the gang; he was convinced however that this was merely for ease in reference to any particular gang and had no connection with leadership in crime. It is also apparently legitimate for a Bhantni to use her womanly wiles in the advancement of the tribe's criminal activities, but such aid cannot be termed prostitution.

W. Crooke in his "Tribes and Castes of the North-Western Provinces and Oudh" (pages 136—139) refers to the Bhantu as "one who lives by stealing and thieving cattle". With the exception of stealing goats for food, cattle thieving is not indulged in. The Bhantu is essentially a high way robber and dacoit, and the difficulties and risks incumbent in the disposal and transport of cattle would be too great; besides this, beef as an article of diet is forbidden.

Morality.—The Bhantus, have a tribal code of morality which is strictly enforced. The moral standard is high and any offence is severely dealt with by the Panchayat. Many writers have ascribed to this tribe a very low state of sex morality, due no doubt to the confusion regarding the identity of the tribe owing to the adoption of aliases, such as Behria, the morals and discipline of which tribe are notoriously lax.

Promiscuous intercourse before or after marriage is condemned. It is usual for Bhantus to marry Bhantus, but union with Behrias is common. A strict rule is maintained to prevent marriage with blood relations, that parties should not marry within the same *got*, there is however one exception, that of the Bhanswale *Got* who may marry within their own clan. Should it accidentally happen that two persons within the same *got* marry one another, they are brought before the Panchayat and fined Rs. 100. Where intercourse or adultery between two people of the same *got* is proved, the parties are guilty of incest, a serious offence, mention of which is made later.

Marriage.—The ceremony and arrangements for marriage differ greatly according to *gots*. Beneath follows a description of marriage according to the Sade *Got*, all essential differences between *gots* being mentioned in the tabulated form appended. A system is in force throughout the clans whereby it is incumbent upon certain clans to intermarry according to certain rules; for instance a boy of the Dhapo *Got* marries a girl from the Chireli *Got*. A Dhapo boy may not marry a girl of the Dhapo *Got* but may marry a girl of the Chireli *Got*, provided there is no blood relationship with the grandmother, *i.e.*, the marriage system is patrilineal and exogamous, and the female line is barred for two generations. He may however marry a girl of any other *got*.

Formerly the age of marriage for both a man and a woman was from 20-23, but latterly, prior to the Sarda Act, young children could be married at the age of ten with consummation on puberty. Much depended on circumstances and the ability to pay the money demanded. In the Sade *Got* the parents of the boy send male friends to the parents of a suitable girl. If the prospects are favourable the Panchayats and the father of the boy call on the girl's parents and in their presence two pigs are killed. The spilling of some liquor on the ground seals the engagement (*mangni*). These preliminary arrangements are called the *baithak*. Two or three days later the price to be paid is settled at the *bol* when one or two more pigs are given. The price generally accepted is according to *got* and this varies considerably. The terms are settled by the Panchayats and vary according to circumstances. For instance Behrias have paid as much as Rs. 1,500 for a Bhantu girl, whilst the lowest price is paid in the Timaichi *Got, viz.*, Rs. 280. This price may be lowered for any or all of the following reasons, (*viz.*): —

	Rs.
Lameness	140
Squint	140
Broken teeth	25
Unchastity	60

These items may cost more or less according to *got*. If the girl has not had small-pox and dies before giving birth to two children, the parents will refund the money paid for the girl. Should she die from small-pox after giving birth to two children nothing can be claimed from the parents. Questions are also asked as to whether the performance of any acts of worship have been promised in the name of the girl.

A few days later, the third and last of the preliminaries known as *mokhan* is settled. A pig is killed and prior to killing it, the following recited :—

" *Ai Maharaj Sri Thakur Ji, Karan kisi ka nam pahile tera nam. Hamare Pir Purke ke nam, jaise bap dadonki jat men hota aya hai ham waise hi karte. Tumhari larkiki ham shadi karte hain. Achchhi tarah se rakhna, Donon taraf achei tarah rakhna* ", " O Maharaja Sri Thakur Ji (or any other Deity named) no matter in whose name we do this, thy name is taken first. In the name of our ancestors and as our fore-fathers have done in our tribes before us, so do we. This is your girl. We are arranging her marriage. Be kind to her and to both parties in this contract ".

The pig is then killed by a pointed stake being inserted behind the shoulder piercing the heart. On the day of the Khatmi Shadi, the boy is dressed in clean clothes and is decked out in borrowed jewellery. The women paint round both his eyes with black and white, and when all is ready escort him to the house of the bride singing songs and abusing any relations of the bridegroom they may meet on the way. A coloured shawl or *Chadar* is held over the bridegroom's head by two women who lead the procession.

On arrival at the house of the bride, the boy enters but is stopped by two females who hold up a curtain and demand money before he can see his bride. When this has been given he is permitted to push under the bottom edge of the curtain a small bowl containing a mixture of water and *gur*. The girl touches this with her lips. Meanwhile the mother of the bride having smeared her right hand with *haldi* slaps the bridegroom on the back, leaving the impression of her hand on his clothes. She also stamps a grain of rice (steeped in *haldi*) on his forehead. Presents are given, the curtain is taken down and the bridegroom is free to take his bride home. The next morning, the near male relations of the bride meet at the bride's house and are given liquor. A basket or bowl is put under a *chadar* placed in the centre of the circle of squatting men and as the liquor is passed round a present of money or jewellery is placed in the bowl by the men and is afterwards given to the married couple. This is termed *piyale chelti*. The Panchayat also receive their fee at this gathering.

It is a custom for portion of a sum demanded for a bride to remain owing. This is called the *baqaya*. Should the girl be given trouble or be illtreated payment of the *baqaya* is demanded. Until this sum is paid, the parents of the girl have a right to interfere in the affairs of their daughter. " *Maje ne mal mol liya hai, tere ko kya ?* " " I have bought this property ; mind your own business", is the answer of a husband to any interference when the *baqaya* has been paid. Exchange weddings are very popular as the expense is much less. A brother and sister from one family will marry a brother and sister from another family. Should however one girl be illtreated by her husband, her brother, will promptly give his wife trouble although, otherwise, he may have no cause to do so. As a rule the eldest son in a family is married first, but should he be in jail or absconding when a suitable girl is available she may be married by proxy to another brother, who may with the elder brother's sanction take her to his house. On the return of the elder brother he may either take his wife or marry someone else. Should, however, the elder brother claim his wife, any children born while living with the younger brother remain with the younger.

Divorce.—Divorce is permitted by the clan, but not looked upon with favour. The Panchayat deals with the matter and decides how much of the original purchase price shall be refunded by the family of the girl. No particular ceremony is performed. A divorced woman may remarry, but a reduction is made in her original price of Rs. 60-8-0 according to *got*. If at the time of her husband's death a woman has a grown up family, she may please herself whether she remarries or not. She may live with the family of her brother-in-law, nearest in age to her husband, preferably the next brother in age below. In the event of a man's first wife failing to give him a son, he may, if he can afford it, take a second wife; this is however as a rule uncongenial to the rest of the tribe.

Child-birth.—In child-birth a woman is considered unclean for six days after the birth of the child and during this time is not permitted to touch any of the family cooking utensils, she also keeps apart from her husband for between two and three months. In the event of the mother dying within the unclean six days, she is considered to have died a " bad death " and is said to return and take possession of members of the family. This possession takes a form of mental affliction, for which the sole remedy is a good beating administered with a shoe by the *bhajat*. For persons of either sex to die in their teens unmarried is considered as a "bad" death and they are termed *Shaitan* because of the trouble they give their relations; convulsions of children are supposed to be due to their influence. A person secretly committing incest and subsequently dying is held to have died a " bad death ", his ancestors having caused the fatal sickness. In all bad deaths however, no difference is made in the treatment of the corpse, but the spirits of those who died are likely to cause troubles.

The ghost or *bhut*, that is the spirit of one who dies a " bad death " is confined to the district in which the person dies and can never enter a community. The *bhut* of a virgin is called *balai* while that of a woman who dies in child-birth is known as *churel*. This exclusion of the *balai* and *churel-bhuts* from the spiritual *biradari* or brother-hood, makes them most unhappy and particularly jealous of a child which appears to be well-fed and cared for. It is therefore dangerous for this child to enter their *hadd* as they are apt to cause it to be possessed. If ever this happens they can only be driven out by a *bhajat*. Should there be a suspected case of possession, or should a child be attacked with convulsions, all the children in the vicinity are given old cloths to wear and their hair is left unoiled and untidy, children remaining at home being immune. Sometimes, when driving out a *churel* the *bhajat* beats himself on the back with a *chamte*. This is an iron ring about three inches in diameter, from which are hung two chains on the ends of which are thirty-six pieces of sharpened iron *phale*. The whole weighs two and a half seers. More often than not the back of the *bhajat* is not cut. He also cuts his tongue and spitting the blood into some liquor, drinks the lot.

Incest.—Mention has been already made of the severity with which incest is treated by the Bhantus. The commission of incest involves *pap*. Should any member of a particular *got* be found guilty of incest in his own *got*, the whole *got* is debarred intercourse with the rest of the clan until the parties have been restored. In addition to a fine the culprits undergo a purification ceremony. Part of the fine is used in buying materials for a feast, which as a rule no adults but children alone attend. The culprits are kept apart from other members of the tribe in the charge of one of the Panchayat and must fast for twelve hours. The next morning the man and woman bathe and the Panch give them two pieces of khaddar. The man wears one as a *dhoti* and the woman the other in *sari* fashion. In front of the assembled tribe, the pair walk three times around a fire of *kundi*, two men (usually of the Mahes *Got*) throwing the same burning *kundis* at them. These however cause no serious damage. Wine and the blood of either a goat or a pig is also sprinkled over them. The hair of the woman and the moustache of the man together with the eyebrows are shaved off and hung up in the village as a warning to others.

Religion.—The Bhantu religion is a form of Animism inter-mixed with ancestor worship. In a sense they are Devi worshippers and many of them consider themselves low-caste Hindus, but they neither visit Hindu temples nor use Brahmins in any ceremony.

The Bhantus believe that after death the spirits of the departed meet again as Bhantu communities in the spirit world and that the spirit can only enter such communities after the prescribed number of feasts have been given to the tribe by the living members of the family. Until the whole of these feasts have been given, the spirit is said to be *bhandha* and is regarded as an outcast in the spirit world. Poor families often neglect to provide or else delay the provision of these feasts, so the spirit chafes at the delay and worries the family by causing some member to fall sick.

When any member of the tribe dies in peculiar circumstances such as in jail and the body is burnt by strangers, as soon as is possible an effigy is made of the deceased by his relations. This they proceed to bury or burn with all the ceremony usual in cases of death. In time of epidemics it is often impossible to deal with the dead according to custom, so it is permissible to get rid of the bodies as convenient and to perform the customary rites only when able to do so. The *putli* or effigy may be made of old or new cloth or even of an old quilt. It is merely roughly shaped by being partly rolled at both ends. One roll makes the arms and the head, the other the legs, while the middle portion is gathered together to make the trunk. Occasionally a shirt and pants are stuffed with straw and serve as the *putli*.

Ancestor worship plays a considerable part in tribal life. The spirits of the ancestors are supposed to be familiar with the doings of individual members of the tribe and in fact are regarded as a species of " guardian " spirit. Ancestors of three or four generations are known as *Purkha* or *Pir Purkha* while those of older generations are known as *Devta*.

Should there be a case of an individual committing an offence against tribal morality, such as adultery, the spirit community show their displeasure by outcasting the ancestors in that family. These vent their displeasure on the living members of the family by causing some member to fall sick. Whenever a Bhantu falls ill, the question arises as to the cause; certain members of the tribe are known as *bhajats* or mediums, who profess to receive communications from the spirits, and so the sick invariably seek their advice.

After squatting on the ground, the *bhajat* fills his huqqa and enquires as to the symptoms. When these have been described he sits smoking a while, then putting aside his huqqa, he commences the peculiar oscillations which appear necessary for him to get in communication with the spirits. The practice varies a little with individuals but it may generally be described as a rhythmical shaking of the head accompanied by forceful ejaculations of " Hu " " Hai " which gradually work up to a necessary frenzy. After a little while the sick one who sits in front of the *bhajat* with clasped hands will say to him " *Ai Maharaj, main ne kya kasur kiya ki mijh ko satata hai ?* " " Oh Maharaj, what is my fault that you are troubling me ? " The Bhantus are not very clear whom they address, although while using a term which to them indicates God, they address themselves to the spirit of the departed but first take the God's name. The *bhajat* then replies in somewhat the following manner. " *Main Devta hun tu ' ne hamare puja qabul kiye aur abhi tak tu' ne nahin kiya* " " I am a godling. You promised to perform a sacrifice for me, and you have not yet done so ", to which the sick one replies " *Main fulana din zarur kadunga* " " I will certainly perform it on such and such a date " and receives the assurance that " *Ab main tujhe chhor deta hun, meghe ainde men mat bhulna* ". When the message has been delivered, the *khel* stops abruptly and the *bhajat* takes to the huqqa. He does not take any payment for his services but when the *puja* is celebrated, he receives a goodly portion of the food and drink ! Many reasons are ascribed for a person taking ill, chief among them being the failure to perform the yearly *puja* to *Nagarkot Devi* or to do a *Puja* to *Parvati Devi* as thanks giving for the safe delivery of a child. The *bhajat* however is supposed always to be able to trace the cause of sickness.

Feasts of the Dead.—There are three feasts required for the dead, they are—

1. *Khuta*—given to those who attend the funeral.
2. *Teiya*—given to the tribe.
3. *Jagha*—a set quantity of provisions divided among those who attend the feast.

The *Teiya* Feast. When the party has assembled, the pig (which has been fastened up since the previous evening) is brought to the gathering. Taking up heavy sticks one of the male members of the party fractures the right hind leg of the pig with a heavy blow. The blood drawn as a result of the fracture of the skin, is smeared over the utensils used in the feast. If blood is not drawn the *puja* is abandoned and performed at some other time. The pig is next laid on the ground and following declaration is made :—

" *Ai Maharaj Sri Thakar Ji Tere nam ahile, jaise bap dadon men hota hai waise hi karte, Yih apna manzur kare. Mari ki roti ham karte hain ; hamare ghar par taklif na dena, bal bachhon par mehrban ho, ek roti rahgayi hai woh bhi ham karenga, aur isko jat biradari men jane do*". " Oh Maharaj, thy name shall ever be first. As our ancestors have done so do we. Accept this. We are giving the feast for the dead so do not give any trouble to our households. Be kind to our children. One feast remains that also will be given. Allow the departed one to enter his brotherhood ". The pig is then killed, and the four men who bore the deceased at the funeral, make a *chappati* and break it up in *karna* oil at the fire-place. Each then takes a little and puts it on the ground, the following declaration being made by the *tapnewale* : " *Ai Maharaj, is ke rote karte hain. Khandan par mehrban ho, aur jo Jagha rahgayi hai woh phir karenga. Ise chhor do. Jat biradari mea jane do* ". " Oh Maharaj, we are giving the death feast of the deceased. Be kind to our families. We shall also provide the feast that remains. Let him go. Allow him to join the brotherhood ". Four *pindi* or balls consisting of rice, wheat and gur are then given to the four men who partly eat it and throw the remainder into a hole which has been dug in the ground. The *tapnewale* gives *chappaties* to five women who dip them in gravy and throw them untouched into the hole. A large *nand* earthern pot is then filled with food. First a layer of rice is laid in the bottom of the *nand*, then follow successive layers of lentils, coconut, sugar, pork and sweetmeats. The process is repeated seven times. On the top of this the broken leg, the heart, kidneys and liver of the pig are placed. A small quantity of dried earth is sieved on to the ground and is covered over with a wooden bowl. The spirit is said to leave a mark on the dust under the bowl if the feast is acceptable to him. The food is distributed and when all has been consumed the earthen vessels are broken, thrown into the fireplace, and the whole party walk round the debris seven times. The broken leg, etc., are not eaten but are left in the empty *nand* for the dogs. The provisions for the feast consist of wheaten flour, ghee, sugar, and one pig, rice, etc.

The " Jagha " feast.—Chappaties are baked and then mixed with ghee and gur. The pig (*hink te*) is then killed, a similar declaration being made as in the " *Teiya* ". After the hair has been singed off the pig, a small portion of ground is cleared of grass and on this a small mound of earth is built. The right side of the carcass is then skinned, the head is cut off and after being wrapped in the skin is placed on the top of the mound together with a *pindi* of food. A small piece of skin is chopped up fine and scattered on the ground in front of the head and over it wine is poured. As this is done, the head of the family says " *Ai Maharaj, tumhare Jagha ham karte hain aur hamare upar kuch haqq nahin rahe, ab usko chhor do take* " " O Maharaj, we are providing the *Jagha* feast so there is now no further responsibility upon us. Let him go and enter the brotherhood. Be kind to our families ". One member of the party who has been fasting since the night before (the '*Nina*') is then given some wine, meat and other food, and when he has finished it the rest of the party eat the remainder of the food. The men only are given a portion of the skin which was wrapped round the pig's head. The mound is broken down and the head eaten by the men. Finally the whole party walk round the fireplace seven times and disperse.

Besides giving feasts to the dead, certain *pujas* are performed at various times of the year to various *Devtis*. The Bhantus say that the *gupta puja* has no reference in their case to human sacrifice but indicates that when a person ostensibly performs a *puja* to one Devti he really intends the puja for another.

In the case of an individual who has committed a secret *sin* for which he is being worried by his *Pir Purkhe* and which he is anxious that the rest of the tribe should not know about, he performs what is known as *gupti*, or *gupta* puja. The intention expressed is that relief should be obtained from the *Pir Purkhe* and at the same time the matter be kept from the knowledge of the rest of the tribe. Ostensibly a *puja* is performed to one Devti, but mentally it is offered to another.

In order that dark nights may accompany the commission of a particular dacoity, a *puja* is promised to the *Kalka Devi*. In performing this puja, the *bhajat* cuts off the head of the pig, and drinks a quantity of the blood mixed with liquor.

Superstition.—As a whole the Bhantus are superstitious and omens play a large part in their daily life, raiding expeditions, dreams, etc. Any enterprise or work is invariably put off should any of the following circumstances occur at the commencement of it :—

1. *A single sneeze*—More than one is regarded as a good omen.
2. *A corpse if met on the right hand*—If on the left it is a good sign.
3. A water pot if carried so that the inside can be seen. Whenever possible a raiding party will always include at least one *bhajat* or medium. As the spirits of the dead are believed to remain in the locality in which they die, it is customary for the *bhajat* to enquire from any ancestor of the tribe who may have died in the vicinity whether the intended raid has any prospects of success. Should a *bhajat* be not available a small *lota* of water is suspended by a string held by one of the members. If the *lota* swings in a circle, the omen is a bad one, but if it swings backward and forward the omen is good. The cry of a female jackal, the lowing of a cow, a snake crossing the path ahead or to the right of a raiding party is considered a bad omen. If however behind a party, the prospects are favourable.

No superstition is current with regard to any days of the week or month being particularly auspicious for raids, etc., nor is an individual credited with possessing supernatural or magical powers. Methods of divination, such as the consultation of grain current among the Haburas, are unknown, but the *bhajat* is often appealed to should property be stolen, cattle lost, etc. Dreams however have a peculiar significance. To dream of anything flying such as a bird, is very bad for women, who fear becoming barren and they invariably seek the aid of the *bhajat* to prevent this. A barren woman is always considered to have a bad influence and is supposed to possess the power of preventing conception. This power is exercised by tearing a piece of cloth belonging to another woman. Formerly it was not uncommon for a barren woman, to be "lost" in the jungles, and no questions to be asked. To dream of death, denotes death but not in the family of the dreamer, while to dream of marriage denotes death in the family. Dreaming of one's own death is a good omen. To dream of shallow water in a small stream is good, but a deep river means trouble. Eclipses are considered dangerous to the unborn, while earthquakes and comets note the death of a king. In the event of a man's going blind a *puja* of a simple nature is made to the sun (*Surya Narain Devta*) while it is rising.

Decision of cases by Ordeal.—In the event of the inability of the Panchayat to prove a charge of which they are doubtful it is usual to impose a "*qasam*" on the suspected person, who may depute a "Champion" to undergo the ordeal for him. This man receives Rs. 5 if he is successful, but only Rs. 2-8-0 if he fails. Those ordeals are of three kinds, the fire ordeal, the water ordeal, and another ordeal to pick out a "pice" from a *lota* of hot oil, but for obvious reasons this is seldom resorted to ; the fire test is the more popular.

Fire Test.—The suspected person or his champion is placed in charge of the Panchayat the night previous to the test. At day-break the man bathes and puts on a piece of *kaddar* and a piece of thread over his shoulder. A level piece of ground is chosen for the test, a *gudali, i.e.*, an iron hoe blade about a foot long and one and a half inches in diameter, is made red hot in a fire of *kundies*. From a point near the fire and with the back facing the sun, seven paces are measured off. The one taking the test stands on the starting line. Seven pipal leaves are then spread over his outstretched hands and fastened on with cotton thread. When all is ready and the iron is red hot, the head of the Panchayat with arm upraised, makes the following declaration. "*Sri Maharaj ham ne insaf kiye par thik nahin hua. Ab tere pas ate hain. Jhuth ko jhuth, sach ko sach*". He then takes the iron out of the fire, and balancing it on two sticks, lays it on the hands of the accused who carries it for the seven paces and throws it down. Should there be no burn he is considered innocent. The slightest blister is sufficient to leave him guilty, his hands being carefully examined by the Panchayat after the test. As the leaves are full of sap, there is little fear of the accused being burnt, provided he keeps his nerve. The Bhantus hold that should the person be guilty the fire will burn through the leaves at once, a miracle being worked to prove guilt and not innocence.

Water Test.—The water test is undertaken under similar circumstances. A pool or tank about 4 feet in depth is chosen. From the edge of this a course of 100 paces is measured, the test being taken as soon after day break as possible. A bamboo is stuck upright in the tank near the side, and the man to be tested stands in the water holding the pole with one hand. When all is ready the head of the Panchayat claps his hands three times and as the accused sits down on the bottom of the tank with his head under water, a man starts to run the course from the tank, to the spot 100 yards away where one of the Panchayat stands. After taking a small stick from him the man rushes back to the tank and, jumping into the water, lifts up the accused from the bottom of the tank. If the accused is able to remain under water until lifted out, he is proved innocent.

It is to be noticed that the pipal tree, the leaves of which are used in the fire test has a peculiar significance. It is regarded as a sacred tree and an oath sworn while touching it, is regarded as binding. An oath may be taken with reference to either past or future conduct. One is supposed to make a true statement when touching either pipal or the *akaua* tree. In cases of suspected theft the head of a cock is cut off and some of the blood, with salt and liquor are mixed in an empty coconut shell. A representative from each family dips his or her finger in the mixture and swears the following "*Agar main ya hamare khandan ke admion ne yih kam to jaise yih murga waise he hamare chandar*".

Should the leaves of the pipal not be large enough at the time of the fire test, *akaua* leaves are resorted to.

Disposal of the Dead.—As has been said, the Bhantus burn or bury their dead according to *got*. A description follows of both methods as used by the Dhapo and Dholiya *gots* respectively. *Dhapo Got-Cremation.*—If it is seen that a person is about to die a *kande* is lit and kept burning until the pyre is fired. The body is lifted from the bed and laid on an old blanket or rezai spread on the ground. Knives are stuck in the earth at the head and feet and removed later when the body is taken away. The following articles are then procured to clothe the body :—Two and a half yards of white cloth, cloth for a shirt and pagri and also a little thread. When the body has been clothed and while still on the ground a pice and a needle are placed on the mouth and a *pindi* of wheaten flour in the right hand. The right side of the bed is partly chopped through and is then broken by the relations with a blow from a heavy stick. The cot is immediately turned over and the broken side quickly repaired with rope. Having placed the body on the inverted bed four men carry it to the burial ghat. As this is neared, the *pindi* is taken from the hand of the corpse, is placed under a bush and is covered with a piece of cloth torn from the shroud. On arrival at the ghat the body is placed on a wooden pyre, which is lighted after the chief mourner has circled it three times with a small torch of burning grass lighted at the *khundi*. Some *gots* in the meanwhile break the skull. When the burning is finished the party walk round the spot seven times and then go to bathe in the nearest stream or pond. The chief woman stands in the water and makes the following declaration.

"*Ai Maharaj, jo kuch us ke upar bandha tha aur gubula thar agar wuh zinda rahta to ham puja dete, ab wuh margaya ishiye uske sang chale jao*". "Oh Maharaj, whatever puja or sacrifice has been promised in the name of the deceased would have been given if he had lived. Now he is dead, all these promises go with him". A little water is then thrown forward seven times. On the return of the party to the village, the relations and others gather in front of the house, and a small piece of unbaked chappati, wrapped in *akua* leaf is given to each. This is bitten and spat out on the ground. After partaking of food the party is sprinkled with water and disperses.

Dholiya Got Burial.—After death the body is laid on the ground. Knives are stuck in the ground at the head and the feet and the body is dressed in dhoti, shirt, and pagri. A pice is put in the mouth but the needle in this case is put in the cloth and not in the mouth, as in the Dhapo *got*. Nothing is put in the hand. The bed side is broken (this must be broken at one blow otherwise an extra pig will have to be sacrificed), the bed turned over, repaired and the body placed on it. On leaving the house an earthen pot full of water is dashed to the ground. Three times during the journey to the burial place, the bed is put on the ground and a pice and cowri are placed in a small hole in the ground and covered up. If the family are able to afford it, money is thrown in front of the party while the body is carried along. The grave is made after the arrival of the party and is usually about 5 feet deep, and when possible the sides and bottom are boarded. The body having been lowered into the grave (no women attend) the men take a little earth and throw it into the grave saying as they do so "*Aj tumhara nam gaya khuda ke pas,*" "To-day your name has gone to God". The grave is then filled and a lathi left lying along side it. All bathe and a similar declaration is made as in the Dhapo cremation. On arrival at the village they are sprinkled with water three times, the party lifting up their hands while this is being done. Assembling in front of the house, thin chappaties are cooked, wheat meal being boiled in water and served in different portions for men, women and children. A bottle of liquor is split on the ground while the head of the house says *Ai Maharaj, rish tadaran ne laya, isko mano am hamara pir purkhe milke pijawe* "Oh Maharaj, the relations have brought this, accept it and drink it with our ancestors". On the third day a young pig is purchased and swung round three times by one leg in the room where the death took place. After being killed, a portion of the right flank is cut off and finely chopped up and scattered on the ground while the following is repeated :—*Sri Thakur Maharaj tum lena, phir pir purkhe am hamare bap dada khale*—"Sri Thakur Maharaj, take this and eat it with our ancestors". The rest of the pig and other food is then consumed by the party.

Tabus.—Bhantus abstain from fish, beef, fox and duck but usually eat pig, goat, porcupine, *guil* and jungle cat. The Bhansware got however, which is regarded as the lowest *got*, and intermarry within their own clan, eat anything.

Dialect.—The Bhantus have a dialect which is peculiar to their tribe. *Tapi* is the term used for this dialect, which is not understood by the other criminal tribes such as Doms, Sansias, and Haburas, except when they come in contact with them in the settlements. There is an apparent relationship to Hindustani, which can be noticed from the list of words given below with the corresponding vernacular terms. Apart, however, from the actual changing of the words, they further mutilate their Hindustani by speaking somewhat in this way :—for *Kidhar ja rahe*? They will ask, *Kitar Jasi* or *Kidhar jahgre*. *Engra* and *Ágra* is apparently a suffix attached to many words and is apt to be confusing. It is not unlike a schoolboy's idea of producing a foreign language saying " Whera you arago gorogoing " for " where are you going ". The whole is species of thieves slang which however the settlers in Port Blair are rapidly losing, particularly the younger ones. Young women of the tribe often have a habit of speaking among themselves in this way. For example for *Kitna kam baqi hai*. They will say *Kamitha karam bavaqi hai*?

English.	Hindustani.	Dialect.
Bhantu	Bhantu	Chantu.
Woman	Aurat	Chintani.
Boy	Larka	Bohra.
Girl	Larki	Bohri.
Police officer	Daroga	Khagra.
Constable	Siphai	Chivra.
Stranger	Ajnabi	Kaja or Teha.
Mohr (Gold)	Mohr	Piskare.
Rupees	Rupiya	Kupaiya.
Cloth	Kapra	Richara.
Boots	Jute	Gonia.
Abuse	Gali	Rani.
Oil	Tel	Nel.
Ghee	Ghee	Rehuta.
Village	Gawn	Raun.
Dog	Kutta	Bhokara or Rutta.
Goat	Bakri	Beri.
Wheat	Gehun	Risu.
Water	Pani	Cheni.
Sweetmeats	Mithai	Kaddu.
Wine	Sharab	Kallu or Karu.
Run away	Bhag jao	Binti jao.
Have a smoke	Hukah pineko	Bukhta lo.
Earthenware pipe	Chillam	Nillam.
Arrested	Giriftar ho gaye	Chekra geya*.
Father	Bap	Dapap.
Mother	Ma	Maoti.
Sister	Bhain	Chaen.
Gun	Banduq	Tihari or Nanduq.
Revolver	Tamancha	Namancha.
Bed	Palang	Rahat.
Chair	Kursi	Rursi.
Grain	Anaj	Khanaj.
Sugar Cane	Ik	Rania.
Molasses	Gur	Rurcha.
To go to sleep	So jana.	Luni jana.
Drink	Pijao	Toge le.
Strike, Don't run	Maro, Bhago Mat	Lirpo Binto Mat.
Stop him and strike	Rokh ke maro	Koke se maro.
The enemy is upon us, run	Dushman a rahe, Bhago	Tiare aye binti jao.
Drink milk	Dudh Pio	Nud toge lo.

* ? for *Pakar giya*.

English.	Hindustani.	Dialect.
Hand	Hath	Khot.
Head	Sir	Nhir.
Eyes	Ankhen	Konke.
Ears	Kan	Ran.
Fingers	Ungli	Kongre.
Feet	Pair.	Gone.
Spear	Ballam	Kallam.
Fire	Goli chalao	Nahr.
Stop them	Unko rokho	Kirped.
They will run away	Wuhe bhag jaenge	We sab hinte jagre.
Severely wounded	Gehra gahow ho gaya	Rahra rahow ho gaya.
I have been caught, come	Pakra hua ajao	Mujh ko nurai lepo.
Take no heed	Fiqr mat karo	Rogan de.
Jewellery	Zewar	Newar.
Speak	Kahna	Kogna.
Shut up	Chup chap baitho	Thonke jao.

Note I—

Gots.—There are supposed to be some thirty-six *gots* but only the names of twenty-two have been ascertained.

1. Sade. Marry into other *gots*. Burn dead. Feast of either *Roti* or Sweetmeats. Second day after death collect bones and bury in earthen pot. Marriage Rs. 500.

2. Dhapo. Burn dead. Leave bones unburied until relative do a "Puja". If the bones are also consumed in the fire, the ashes and earth from the "Ghat" are buried. Marriage Rs. 500.

3. Chareli. Burn dead. At the funeral feast *Roti* is only part baked and is afterwards taken by the members, baked again and eaten. Marriage Rs. 500.

4. Chandu-wale. Bury dead. Clothe male corpse in shirt, a female in *Lenga*. Prepare boiled rice for the feast.

5. Gadho. Bury dead in Pyjamas and bind up the head. Feast as in Sadi *Got* except that when possible the body is kept overnight and a live pig is fastened near the house. In the morning the principal woman takes a heavy stick and stretching one of the pig's legs over a stone, recites the following :—"*Siri Thakur ji, tere nam ke sathki jai ja. Ae Maharaj iske ham kaj kiriye karte hain. Ae Maharaj, ise jatmen shamil karde, hamare bal bachche khaisala rakho.*"

The legs of the pig is then broken by a heavy blow of the stick, and the pig is immediately killed to be eaten at the feast. Marriage Rs. 500.

6. Mahes. Burn dead. When fines are inflicted by the Panchayat for any reason, any member of this *got* who may be present is asked to purify the money by touching it. When fire is thrown on offenders in a purification ceremony, the first to throw are members of this *got*. Marriage Rs. 500.

7. Gehla. Similar to Sade Got.

8. Bhanswale. Burn dead. Eat beef and jackal's flesh. Use rice in funeral feast. Can marry in own *got*. Marriage Rs. 600.

9 and 10. Chhede and Koran. Similar to Gadho.

Others. 11 Timaichi, 12. Marware, 13. Dhaneke, 14. Rorke, 15. Pophat, 16. Mataike, 17. Ghasive, 18. Dholive (high and low), 19. Mire, 20. Range, 21. Gange.

Note III—Bibliography—

1. Crooke.—*Tribes and Castes of the N. W. Provinces and Oudh.*

2. United Provinces Police Report, 1911.

3. Inspector Baldeo Sahai's Report on the origin, habits and customs of the wandering tribes known as Kanjars and Behrias inhabiting the Agra district. Agra 1875.

4. *Criminal Tribes of the United Provinces.*—S. T. Hollins.

5. *Report on the Ferrargunj colony for the year 1929.*—E. Sheard.

6. Mr. Sheard's reply to a questionnaire on the cultural anthropology and ethnology of the Bhantus.

C. J. B.

APPENDIX II.

The Fauna.

The mamalia of the Andamans and Nicobars has been examined by various scientists. Boden Kloss (In the Andamans and Nicobars) recorded 35 identified species, with 1 sub-species and 4 others whose status he describes as doubtful.

Mammalian Fauna of the Andaman and Nicobar Islands according to Boden Kloss :—

Name.	Where found.
Dugong dugon	Andamans.
Sus andamanensis	Andamans.
Sus nicobaricus	Nicobars.
Mus musculus	Andamans.
Mus palmarum.	Nicobars.
Mus bowersi	Andamans.
Mus stoicus	Andamans.
Mus taciturnus	Andamans.
Mus flebilis	Andamans.
Mus andamanensis	Andamans.
Mus pulliventer	Nicobars.
Mus atratus	Andamans.
Mus burrus	Andamans.
Mus burrulus	Nicobars.
Mus burrescens	Nicobars.
Mus alexandrinus	Nicobars.
Paradoxurus tytleri	Andamans.
Felis chaus	Andamans.
Tupaia nicobarica nicobarica	Nicobars.
Tupaia nicobarica surda	Nicobars.
Crocidura nicobarica	Nicobars.
Crocidura andamanensis	Andamans.
Scotophelus temminchii	Nicobars.
Tylonycteris pachypus	Andamans.
Pipistrellus tichelli	Andamans.
Pipistrellus tenuis.	Nicobars.
Pipistrellus camortae	Nicobars.
Miniopterus pusillus	Nicobars.
Rhinolophus andamanensis	Andamans.
Hipposideros nicobaricus	Nicobars.
Hipposideros nicobarulae	Nicobars.
Hipposideros murinus	Nicobars.
Pteropus nicobaricus	Andamans and Nicobars.
Pteropus faunulus	Nicobars.
Pteropus rampyrus	Andamans.
Cynopterus brachyotis	Nicobars.
Cynopterus brachysoma	Andamans.
Cynopterus scherzeri	Nicobars.
Macacus coininus (introduced)	Andamans.
Macacus umbrosus	Nicobars.

The larger mamalia is entirely absent in the Andamans so are monkeys.

Sambur, Barking Deer, Hog Deer and Spotted Deer have been introduced in the Andamans and the latter have increased to an alarming extent during the last 25 years.

The Birds of the Andamans and Nicobars have been collected by Hume Butler and Osmaston and the latter has kindly prepared a list of the birds. A list of butter-flies occurring in these islands has been kindly prepared by Brigadier W. H. Evans. At the request of the late Chief Commissioner Mr. Worsley the various lists are included in the Census Report so that they may remain on record.

Some authorities have disputed the presence of crocodiles in the Andamans. They are common in the Andamans and also in the Nicobars but they are not found everywhere. They breed in the Diglipoor stream of Port Cornwallis, where they are common, and in Jackson Creek of Little Andaman. To the Andamanese of North Andaman they are known as *thea* and to the Önges of Little Andaman as *tebichone*.

BIRDS OF THE ANDAMAN AND NICOBAR ISLANDS.

A. . . Corvus levaillanti andamanensis. The Andaman Jungle Crow.
A. . . Dendrocitta bayleyi. The Andaman Tree Pie.
A. N. . Elathea jocosa peguensis. The Burmese Red-whiskered Bulbul.
N. . . Iole nicobariensis. The Nicobar Bulbul.
A. . . Microtarsus atriceps fusciflavescens. The Andaman Blackheaded Bulbul.
A. . . Saxicola torquata indica. The Indian Bushchat.
A. . . Copsychus saularis andamanensis. The Andaman Magpie Robin.
A. . . Kittacincla malabarica albiventris. The Andaman Shama.
A. . . Geocichla citririna andamanensis. The Andaman Ground Thrush.
N. . . Geocichla citrina albogularis. The Nicobar Ground Thrush.
A. N. . Terpsiphone paradisi nicobarica. The Nicobar Paradise Flycatcher.
A. . . Hypothymis azurea tytleri. The Andaman Blacknaped Flycatcher.
N. . . Hypothymis azurea nicobarica. The Nicobar Blacknaped Flycatcher.
N. . . Hypothymis azurea idiochroa. The Car Nicobar Blacknaped Flycatcher.
A. N. . Lanius cristatus lucionensis. The Philippine Shrike.
A. . . Pericrocotus flammeus andamanensis. The Andaman scarlet Minivet.
A. . . Pericrocotus cinnamomeus vividus. The Burmese small Minivet.
N. . . Lalage nigra davisoni. The Pied Cuckoo-Shrike.
A. . . Graucalus macei siamensis. The Siamese Large Cuckoo Shrike.
A. . . Graucalus dobsoni. Dobson's Cuckoo-Shrike.
A. . . Artamus leucorhynchus humei. Humes White rumped Swallow-Shrike.
A. . . Dissemuroides andamanensis andamanensis. The Small Andaman Drongo.
A. . . Dissemurus paradiseus otiosus. The Andaman Racket-tailed Drongo.
N. . . Dissemuruds paradiseus nicobariensis. The Nicobar Racket-tailed Drongo.
A. . . Acanthopneuste borealis borealis. The Arctic Willow Warbler.
A. . . Muscitrea grisola grisola. The Grey Flycatcher Warbler.
A. . . Homochlamys pallidipes osmastoni. Osmaston's Bush Warbler.
A. . . Phragmaticola aëdon. The Thick-billed Warbler.
A. . . Phylloscopus fuscatus fuscatus. The Dusky Willow Warbler.
N. . . Oriolus chinensis macrourus. The Nicobar Black-naped Oriole.
A. . . Oriolus chinensis andamanensis. The Andaman black-naped Oriole.
A. N. . Gracula religiosa andamanensis. The Andaman Grackle.
A. N. . Lamprocorax panayensis tytleri. The Andaman Glossy Stare.
A. . . Pastor roseus. The Rosy Pastor.
A. . . Sturnia malabarica andamanensis. The Andaman White-headed Myna.
N. . . Sturnia malabarica erythropygia. The Nicobar White-headed Myna.
N. . . Sturnia malabarica Katchalensis. Richmond's White-headed Myna.
A. . . Acridotheres tristis tristis. The common Myna. (Introduced.)
A. . . Uroloncha striata fumigata. The Andaman White-backed Munia.
A. . . Munia malacca. The Black-headed Munia.
A.. . Passer domesticus indicus. The Indian House-sparrow. (Introduced.)
A. N. . Hirundo rustica rustica. The Common Swallow.
A. N. . Hirundo rustica gutturalis. The Eastern Swallow.
A. N. . Hirundo javanica javanica. The Javan Swallow.
A. N. . Motacilla cinerea caspica. The Eastern Grey Wagtail.
A. N. . Dendronanthus indicus. The Forest Wagtail.
A. N. . Zosterops palpebrosa nicobarica. The Nicobar White-eye.
N. . . Æthopyga siparaja nicobarica. The Nicobar Yellow-backed Sunbird.
N. . . Leptocoma pectoralis blanfordi. The Kondol Yellow-breasted Sunbird.
N. . . Leptocoma pectoralis procelia. The Car Nicobar Yellow-breasted Sunbird.
A. . . Leptocoma flammaxilaris andamanica. The Andaman Sunbird.
A. . . Dicœum virescens. The Andaman Flower-pecker.
N. . . Pitta cucullata abbotti. The Nicobar Green-breasted Pitta.
A. . . Dryobates analis andamanensis. The Andaman Pied Woodpecker.
A. . . Macropicus hodgei. The Andaman black Woodpecker.
A. N. . Cuculus canorus telephonus. The Asiatic Cuckoo.

A. N. . Cuculus micropterus micropterus. The Indian Cuckoo.
A. N. Chalcites xanthorhynchus. The Violet Cuckoo.
A. N. . Eudynamis scolopaceus malayana. The Malay Koël.
A. . . Centropus andamanensis. The Andaman Crow Pheasant.
A. . . Psittacula eupatria magnirostris. The Large Andaman Paroquet.
A. . . Psittacula alexandri fasciatus. The Indian Red-breasted Paroquet.
A. . . Psittacula nicobarica tytleri. The Andaman Red-cheeked Paroquet.
N. . . Psittacula nicobarica nicobarica. The Nicobar Red-cheeked Paroquet.
A. . . Coryllis vernalis vernalis. The Indian Lorikeet.
A. . . Eurystomus orientalis gigas. The Andaman Broad-billed Roller.
A. N. . Merops philippinus. The Blue-tailed Bee-eater.
A. N. . Melittophagus erythrocephalus erythrocephalus. The Chestnut-headed Bee-eater.
A. . . Alcedo atthis bengalensis. The Common Indian Kingfisher.
A. . . Alcedo meninting rufigastra. The Andaman Blue-eared Kingfisher.
A. N. . Ceyx tridactilus macrocercus. The Andaman Three-toed Kingfisher.
N. . . Ramphalcyon capensis intermedia. The Nicobar Stork-billed Kingfisher.
A. . . Ramphalcyon capensis burmanica. The Burmese Stork-billed Kingfisher.
A. N. . Halcyon smyrnensis saturatior. The Andaman White-breasted Kingfisher.
A. N. . Halcyon pileata. The Black-capped Kingfisher.
A. N. . Entomothera coromanda mizorhina. The Andaman Ruddy Kingfisher.
N. . . Sauropatis chloris occipitalis. The Nicobar White-collared Kingfisher.
A. . . Sauropatis chloris davisoni. The Andaman White-collared Kingfisher.
A. . . Rhytidoceros narcondami. The Narcondam Hornbill.
A. . . Hirundapus giganteus indicus. The Brown-throated Spinetail.
A. . . Collocalia innominata. Hume's Swiftlet.
A. N. . Collocalia francica inexpectata. The Andaman Grey-rumped Swiftlet.
A. N. . Collocalia linchi affinis. Beavan's Swiftlet.
A. . . Caprimulgus macrourus andamanicus. The Andaman Long-tailed Night jar.
A. . . Tyto alba deroepstorfi. The Andaman Barn Owl.
A. . . Otus balli. The Andaman Scops Owl.
A. . . Ninox scutulala affinis. The Andaman Brown Hawk Owl.
A. N. . Ninox obscura. Hume's Brown Hawk Owl.
A. . . Falco peregrinus calidus. The Eastern Peregrine Falcon.
A. . . Limnaétops cirrhatus andamanensis. The Andaman Hawk-eagle.
A. . . Haematornis cheela davisoni. The Pale Andaman Serpent Eagle.
A. N. . Haematornis elgini. The Dark Andaman Serpent Eagle.
N. . . Haematornis cheela minimus. The Nicobar Serpent Eagle.
N. . . Haematornis cheela klossi. The Great Nicobar Serpent Eagle.
A. . . Haliaetus leucogaster. The White-bellied Sea Eagle.
A. . . Circus æruginosus æruginosus. The March Harrier.
A. . . Circus pygargus. Montagu's Harrier.
N. . . Astur badius butleri. The Car Nicobar Shikra.
N. . . Astur badius obsoletus. The Katchal Shikra.
A. . . Accipiter gularis nisoides. The Indo-Chinese Sparrow Hawk.
A. N. . Dendrophasa pompadora chloroptera. The Andaman Green Pigeon.
N. . . Muscadivora ænea insularis. The Nicobar Imperial Green Pigeon.
A. . . Muscadivora ænea sylvatica. The Indian Imperial Green Pigeon.
A. N. . Myristicivora bicolor bicolor. The Pied Imperial Pigeon.
A. N. . Calænas nicobarica nicobarica. The Nicobar Pigeon.
A. N. . Chalcophaps indica indica. The Emerald Dove.
A. . . Streptopelia Senegalensis cambayensis. The Indian Little Brown Dove.
A. . . Ænopopelia tranquebarica humilis. The Burmese Red Turtle Dove.
A. N. . Macropygia rufipennis. The Andaman Cuckoo-Dove.
N. . . Excalfactoria chinensis trinkutensis. The Nicobar Blue-breasted Quail.
A. . . Francolinus pondicerianus pondicerianus. The Southern Grey Partridge. (Introduced.)
N. . . Megapodius nicobariensis nicobariensis. The Nicobar Megapode.
N. . . Megapodius nicobariensis abbotti. Oberholser's Nicobar Megapode.

A. N. . Turnix maculatus tanki. The Indian Button Quail.
A. N. . Hypotoenidia striata obscurior. The Andaman Blue-breasted Rail.
A. . . Rallina canningi. The Andaman Banded Crake.
A. . . Amaurornis phœnicurus in sularis. The Andaman White-breasted Waterhen.
A. . . Orthoramphus magnirostris magnirostris. The Australian Stone Plover.
A. . . Glareola maldivarum maldivarum. The Large Indian Pratincole.
A. . . Dromas ardeola. The Crab Plover.
A. . . Gelochelidon nilolica affinis. The Javan Gull-billed Tern (once only).
A. N. . Sterna dougalli korustes. The Eastern Roseate Tern.
A. N. . Sterna sumatrana sumatrana. The Black naped tern.
N. . . Anous stolidus pileatus. The Philippine Noddy.
A. . . Arenaria interpres interpres. The Turnstone.
A. . . Eupodella vereda. The Eastern Sand Plover.
A. . . Cirripedesmus mongolus atrifrons. The Pamirs Lesser Sand-Plover.
A. . . Numenius arquata arquata. The Curlew.
A. . . Numenius phæopus phæopus. The Whimbrel.
A. . . Tringa hypoleucos. The Common Sandpiper.
A. . . Erolia minula ruficollis. The Eastern Little Stint.
A. . . Erolia subminuta. The Long-toed Stint.
A. . . Calidris tenuirostris. The Eastern Knot.
A. . . Capella gallinago gallinago. The Fantail Snipe.
A. . . Capella stenura. The Pintail Snipe.
A. . . Lymnocryptes minima. The Jack Snipe.
A. . . Ardea purpurea manillensis. The Eastern Purple Heron.
A. . . Egretta garzetta garzetta. The Little Egret.
A. N. . Demi-egretta sacra sacra. The Eastern Reefheron.
A. N. . Ardeola grayi. The Indian Pond Heron.
A. . . Ardetta bacchus. The Chinese Pond Heron.
A. . . Butorides striatus spodiogaster. The Andaman Little Green Heron.
N. . . Gorsakius melanolophus minor. The Nicobar Bittern.
A. . . Ardetta sinensis. The Yellow Bittern.
A. . . Ixobrychus cinnamomeus. The Chestnut Bittern.
A. . . Nettapus coromandelianus. The Cotton Teal.
A. . . Dendrocycna javanica. The Lesser Whistling Teal.
A. N. . Nettion crecca crecca. The Common Teal.
A. . . Nettion albigulare.

The above list has been drawn up with the help of the Fauna of British India. (Revised Edition, 7 volumes.)

The list is probably fairly complete for the Andamans, which have been well worked by ornithologists.

The list for the Nicobars on the other hand is probably far from being complete.

Many of the birds marked "A" in the list will undoubtedly subsequently be found to occur also in the Nicobars when these islands are better known and more thoroughly explored.

B. B. OSMASTON.

5th August 1931.

List of butterflies recorded from the Andaman and Nicobar Islands.

By Brigadier W. H. Evans, C.S.I., C.I.E., D.S.O. (following his identification of Indian Butterflies, 2nd edition).

A.—Papilionidae.—

1. (*a*) *Troides helena heliconoides*, M. and male variety *aphnea*, Jordan. Andamans, common.
   (*b*) *Troides helena ferrari*, Tytler. S. Nicobars, not rare.
2. *Tros coon sambilanea*, Doh. S. Nicobars, very rare.
3. *Tros rhodifer*, But. Andamans, not rare.
4. *Tros hector*, L. Andamans, stragglers from India.

5. (*a*) *Tros aristolochiae goniopeltis*, Roth. Andamans, common.
   (*b*) *Tros aristolochiae sawi*, Evans. Kar Nikobar, common.
   (*c*) *Tros aristolochiae camorta*, M. Central Nicobars, common.
   (*d*) *Tros aristolochiae kondulana*, Evans. S. Nicobars, common.
6. *Chilasa clytia flavolimbatus*, Ob. Andamans, not rare.
7. *Papilio memnon agenor*, L. Stragglers on Andamans and Kar Nikobar : S. Nicobars, not rare.
8. *Paplio mayo*, Atk. Andamans, not rare.
9. *Papilio fuscus andamanicus*, Roth. Andamans, rare.
10. (*a*) *Papilio polytes stichioides*, Evans. Andamans, common.
    (*b*) *Papilio polytes nikobarus*, Fd. Nicobars, common.
11. *Pathysa antiphates epaminondas*, Ob. Andamans, not rare.
12. *Zetides eurypylus macronius*, Jord. Andamans, not rare.
13. (*a*) *Zetides agammemnon andamanica*, Lathy. Andamans, not rare.
    (*b*) *Zetides agammemnon decoratus*, Roth. Kar and Central Nicobars, not rare.
    (*c*) *Zetides agammemnon pulo*, Evans. S. Nicobars, rare.

B.—Pieridae—

14. (*a*) *Leptosia nina nina*, F. Andamans, not rare.
    (*b*) *Leptosia nina nicobarica*, Doh. S. Nicobars, not rare.
15. *Belenois mesentina mesentina*, Cr. Great Nicobar, stragglers.
16. *Huphina nerissa lichenosa*, M. Andamans, not rare.
17. *Huphina nadina andamana*, Swin. Andamans, not rare.
18. *Appias libythea olferna*, Swin. Kar Nikobar, stragglers.
19. (*a*) *Appias lyncida nicobarica*, M. Kar and Central Nicobars, not rare.
    (*b*) *Appias lyncida galbana*, Fruh. S. Nicobars, not rare.
20. *Appias albina darada*, Fd. Andamans, not rare.
21. *Appias paulina galathea*, Fd. (=*roepstorfii*, M.) Nicobars, not rare.
22. *Appias panda chrysea*, Fruh. S. Nicobars, not rare.
23. *Catopsilia crocale*, Cr. Andamans, stragglers.
24. *Catopsilia pomona*, F. Andamans and Nikobars, stragglers.
25. *Catopsilia pyranthe minna*, Herbst. Andamans, stragglers.
26. *Catopsilia florella gnoma*, F. Andamans, stragglers.
27. (*a*) *Gandaca harina andamana*, M. Andamans, not rare.
    (*b*) *Gandaca harina nicobarica*, Evans. Nicobars, rare.
28. (*a*) *Terias blanda silhetana*, Wall. Andamans, not rare.
    (*b*) *Terias blanda moorei*, But. Kar and Central Nicobars, not rare.
    (*c*) *Terias blanda grisea*, Evans. S. Nicobars, not rare.
29. (*a*) *Terias hecabe hecabe*, L. Andamans, common.
    (*b*) *Terias hecabe nikobariensis*, Fd. Nicobars, common.
30. *Terias andersoni andamana*, Swin. Andamans, not rare.
31. *Ixias pyrene andamana*, M. Andamans, common.
32. *Hebomoia glaucippe roepstorfii*, Wm. Andamans, common.
33. *Pareronia ceylanica naraca*, M. Andamans, common.

C.—Danaidae—

34. *Hestia lynceus cadelli*, Wm. and De N. Andamans, not rare.
35. *Danais aglea melanoleuca*, M. Andamans, common.
36. *Danais agleoides*, Fd. Nicobars, not rare.
37. *Danais melaneus plateniston*, Fruh. Kar Nikobar, stragglers.
38. *Danais similis nicobarica*, Wm. and De N. Nicobars, not rare.
39. *Danais limniace mutina*, Fruh. Kar and Central Nicobars, not rare : straggler on Great Coco Island.
40. *Danais melissa septentrionis*, But. Stragglers on Andamans and Nicobars.
41. *Danais gantama gantamoides*, Doh. Nicobars, not rare.
42. *Danais plexippus*, L. Andamans and Kar Nikobar, not rare.
43. (*a*) *Danais melanippus camorta*, Evans. Central Nicobars, not rare.
    (*b*) *Danais menanippus nesippus*, Fd. S. Nicobars, not rare.
44. *Danais affinis malayana*, Fruh. Central Nicobars (Kachal), rare.

45. *Danais chrysippus*, L. Andamans, Kar and Central Nicobars, rather rare.
46. *Euploea mulciber*, Gr. Andamans, stragglers.
47. (*a*) *Euploea climena scherzeri*, Fd. Kar Nikobar, common.
(*b*) *Euploea climena camorta*, M. Central Nicobars, common.
(*c*) *Euploea climena simultatrix*, Wm. and De N. S. Nicobars, common.
48. (*a*) *Euploea crameri esperi*, Fd. Kar and Central Nicobars, common (= *biseriata*, M.).
(*b*) *Euploea crameri frauenfeldii*, Fd. S. Nicobars, common.
49. (*a*) *Euploea andamanensis andamanensis*, Atk. Andamans, common.
(*b*) *Euploea andamanensis bumila*, Evans. Little Andaman and N. Sentinel, common.
50. *Euploea harrisi harrisi*, Fd. Andamans, stragglers.
51. *Euploea corus phoebus*, But. Nicobars, rare.
52. *Euploea leucostictos novarae*, Fd. Kar and Central Nicobars, not rare.
53. *Euploea roepstorfii*, M. Andamans, very rare.
54. *Euploea midamus brahma*, M. Central Nicobars, stragglers.

D.—Satyridae—

55. (*a*) *Mycalesis anaxias radza*, M. Andamans, rare.
(*b*) *Mycaleis anaxias manii*, Doh. S. Nicobars, rare.
56. *Mycalesis mineus nicobarica*, M. Nicobars, common.
57. *Mycalesis visala andamana*, M. Andamans, common.
58 (*a*) *Lethe europa nudgara*, Fruh. Andamans, not rare.
(*b*) *Lethe europa tamuna*, De N. S. Nicobars, very rare.
59 (*a*) *Orsotrioena medus medus*. F. Andamans, common.
(*b*) *Orsotrioena medus turbata*, Fruh. Nicobars, not rare.
60. *Melanitis leda ismene*, Gr. Andamans, common : Nicobars, rare.
61. *Melanitis zitenius andamanica*, Evans. Andamans, rare.
62. *Elymnias cottonis cottonis*, Hew. Andamans, not rare.
63. *Elymnias panthera mimus*, Wm. and De N. Nicobars, not rare.

E.—Amathusiidae—

64. *Amathusia phidippus andamanica*, Fruh. Andamans, rare.
65. *Discophora continentalis and andamanensis*, Stg. Andamans, rare.

F.—Nymphalidae—

66. *Charasces polyxena agna*, M. Andamans, stragglers.
67. *Eriboea schreiberi tisamenus*, Fruh. Andamans, very rare.
68. *Eriboea athamas andamanicus*, Fruh. Andamans, rare.
69. *Herona marathus andamana*, M. Andamans, rare.
70. *Euripus consimilis consimilis*, Wd. Andamans, straggler.
71. *Euthalia cibaritis*, Hew. Andamans, common. (=*vinaya*, Fruh.)
72. *Euthalia garuda acontius*, Hew. Andamans, rare.
73. *Euthalia teuta teutoides*, M. Andamans, rare.
74. (*a*) *Parthenos sylvia roepstorfii*, M. Andamans, not rare.
(*b*) *Parthenos sylvia nila*, Evans. S. Nicobars, rare.
75. *Limintis procris anarta*, M. Andamans, not rare.
76. *Pantoporia nefte rufula*, De N. Andamans, rare.
77. *Neptis columella kankena*, Evans. S. Nicobars, very rare.
78. (*a*) *Neptis jumbah amorosca*, Fruh. Andamans, not rare.
(*b*) *Neptis jumbah binghami*, Fruh. Nicobars, recorded only by Fruhstorfer.
79. (*a*) *Neptis hylas andamana*, M. Andamans, common.
(*b*) *Neptis hylas nicobarica*, M. Kar and Central Nicobars, common.
(*c*) *Neptis hylas sambilanga*, Evans. S. Nicobars, common.
80. *Neptis soma mananda*, M. Andamans, rare.
81. *Neptis nandina clinia*, M. Andamans, common.
82. *Neptis sankara* nar, De N. Andamans, very rare.
83. *Neptis ebusa ebusa*, Fd. S. Nicobars, only record some specimens in the British Museum.
84. *Neptis hordonia cnacalis*, Hew. Andamans, not rare.
85. *Cyrestis cocles formosa*, Fd. and var. *andamanica*, Wm. and De N. Andamans, rare.
86. *Cyrestis thyodamas andamanica*, Wm. and De N. Andamans, not rare.

87. *Cyrestis tabula*, De N. S. Nicobars, not rare.
88. *Hypolimnas misippus*, L. Andamans and Kar Nikobar, rare.
89. *Hypolimnas bolina*, L. Andamans and Nicobars, stragglers.
90. *Hypolimnas antilope anomala*, Wallace. Kar Nikobar, not rare.
91. *Yoma sabina vasuki*, Doh. Andamans, not rare.
92. *Doleschallia bisaltide andamana*, Fruh. Andamans, Kar and Central Nikobars, rare.
93. *Kallima allofasciata*. M. Andamans, rare.
94. *Precis hierta hierta*, F. Andamans, common.
95. *Precis orithyia ocyale*, Hub. Kar Nikobar, straggler.
96. (*a*) *Precis almana almana*, L. Andamans, common.
   (*b*) *Precis almana nicobariensis*, Fd. Kar Nikobar, common.
97. *Precis atlites*, L. Andamans, Central Nicobars, not rare.
98. *Vanessa cardui*, L. Andamans, stragglers.
99. *Cupha erymanthis andamanica*, M. Andamans, not rare.
100. *Cupha erymanthis nicobarica*, Fd. Nicobars, common.
101. *Atella phalanta*, Drury. Central Nicobars, straggler.
102. (*a*) *Atella alcippe andamanas*, Fruh. Andamans, not rare.
   (*b*) *Atella alcippe fraterana*, M. Central and S. Nicobars, rare.
103. *Cynthia erota pallida*, Stg. Andamans, not rare.
105. *Cirrochroa tyche anjira*, M. Andamans, common.
106. *Cirrochroa nicobarica*, Wm. and De N. S. Nicobars, common.
107 (*a*) *Cethosia biblis andamana*, Stich. Andamans, not rare.
   (*b*) *Cethosia biblis nicobarica*, Fd. Nicobars, not rare.
108. *Laringa horsfieldii andamanensis*, De N. Andamans, rare.

G.—Erycinidae—

109. *Abisara echerius bifasciata*, Wm. and De N. Andamans, not rare.

H.—Lycaenidae—

110. *Spalgis epius nubilus*, M. Andamans, Nicobars, rare.
111. *Castalius rosimon alarbus*, Fruh. Andamans, not rare : S. Nicobars, rare.
112. (*a*) *Castalius ethion ethion*, Db. and Hew. Andamans, not rare.
   (*b*) *Castalius ethion airavati*, Doh. S. Nicobars, not rare.
113. *Castalius elna nolitaeia*, Fruh. Andamans, not rare.
114. (*a*) *Castalius roxus roxus*, God. Andamans, not rare.
   (*b*) *Castalius roxus manluena*, Fd. S. Nicobars, rare.
115. *Neopithecops zalmora*, But. Andamans, not rare.
116. *Everes parrhasius pila*, Evans. Nicobars, not rare.
117. *Megisha malaya sikkima*, M. Andamans, not rare.
118. (*a*) *Lycaenopsis puspa telis*, Fruh. Andamans, not rare.
   (*b*) *Lycaenopsis puspa cyanescens*, De N. Nicobars, rare.
119. *Zizeeria lysimon*, Hub. Andamans, rare.
120. *Zizeeria gaika*, Trimen. Andamans, rare : Kar Nikobar, common.
121. *Zizeeria otis otis*, F. Andamans, Nicobars, common.
122. *Euchrysops cnejus*, F. Nicobars, not rare.
123. *Euchrysops pandava pandava*, Hors. Nicobars, common.
124. *Lycaenesthes ernolus andamanicus*, Fruh. Andamans, not rare.
125. *Lycaenesthes lycaenina lycambes*, Hew. Andamans, not rare.
126. *Catachrysops strabo*, F. Andamans and Nicobars, common.
127. *Catachrysops lithargysia*, M. Andamans and Nicobars, not rare.
128. *Lampides boeticus*, L. Andamans and Nicobars, rare.
129. (*a*) *Jamides bochus bochus*, Cr. Andamans, not rare.
   (*b*) *Jamides bochus nicobaricus*, Wm. and De N. Nicobars, common.
130. (*a*) *Jamides celeno blairana*, Evans. Andamans, common.
   (*b*) *Jamides celeno kinkunka*, Fd. Kar and Central Nicobars, common.
   (*c*) *Jamides celeno nicevillei*, Evans. S. Nicobars, common.
131. *Jamides ferrari*, Evans. Central and S. Nicobars, very rare.
132. (*a*) *Jamides alecto eurysaces*, Fruh. Andamans, not rare (=el Auct).
   (*b*) *Jamides alecto kondulana*, Fd. Central and S. Nicobars, rare.

133. (*a*) *Jamides kankena pseudelpis*, But. Andamans, not rare.
(*b*) *Jamides kankena kankena*, Fd. Kar Nikobar, rare.
(*c*) *Jamides kankena rogersi*, Bing. Central and S. Nicobars, rare.
134. (*a*) *Nacaduba pactolus andamanica*, Fruh. Andamans, not rare.
(*b*) *Nacaduba pactolus macropthalma*, Fd. Central and S. Nicobars, rare.
135. *Nacaduba hermus major*, Evans. S. Nicobars, rare.
136. *Nacaduba vajuva varia*, Evans. S. Nicobars, rare.
137. *Nacaduba pavana*, Hors. Andamans, not rare.
138. *Nacaduba ancyra aberrans*, Eleves. Tillanchong, Nicobars, recorded by Col. Ferrar.
139. (*a*) *Nacaduba helicon brunnea*, Evans. Andamans, not rare. (=*viola*, Auct.)
(*b*) *Nacaduba helicon kondulana*, Evans. S. Nicobars, rare.
140. (*a*) *Nacaduba kurava euplea*, Fruh. Andamans, Kar and Central Nicobars, not rare.
(*b*) *Nacaduba kurava nicobarica*, Toxopeus. S. Nicobars, rare.
141. *Nacaduba beroe gythion*, Fruh. Andamans, not rare.
142. *Nacaduba berenice nicobarica*, Wm. and De N. Nicobars, common.
143. *Nacaduba aluta coelestis*, De N. Andamans, not rare.
144. (*a*) *Nacaduba nora nora*, Fd. Andamans, common.
(*b*) *Nacaduba nora dilata*, Evans. Nicobars, not rare.
145. *Nacaduba dubiosa fulva*, Evans. Andamans, rare.
146. *Nacaduba dana*, De N. Andamans, not rare.
147. *Heliophorus epicles indicus*, Fruh. Middle Andaman, common.
148. (*a*) *Curetis saronis saronis*, M. Andamans, not rare.
(*b*) *Curetis saronis obscura*, Evans. Kar and Central Nicobars, not rare.
(*c*) *Curetis saronis nicobarica*, Swin. S. Nicobars, not rare.
149. *Iraota timoleon timoleon*, Stoll. Andamans, rare.
150. *Horsfieldia anita andamanica*, Riley. Andamans, not rare.
151. *Amblypodia alea constanceae*, De N. Andamans, very rare.
152. *Amblypodia centaurus coruscans*, Wm. and De N. Andamans, not rare.
153. *Amblypodia alesia*, Fd. Andamans, very rare.
154. *Amblypodia zeta*, M. Andamans, very rare. (=*roona*, M.)
155. *Amblypodia fulla andamanica*, Wm. and De N. Andamans, not rare. (=*subfasciata*, M.)
156. *Susendra quercetorum latimargo*, M. Andamans, not rare.
157. (*a*) *Loscura atymnus prabha*, M. Andamans, not rare.
(*b*) *Loscura atymnus nicobarica*, Evans. Nicobars, rare.
158. *Spindasis lohita zoilus*, M. Andamans, not rare.
159. *Pratapa deva lila*, M. Andamans, rare.
160. *Tajuria jangala andamanica*, Wm. and De N. Andamans, not rare.
161. *Tajuria cippus cippus*, F. Andamans, rare.
162. *Charana jalindra tarpina*, Hew. Andamans, rare.
163. *Charana mandarinus*, Hew. Andamans, very rare.
164. *Horaga onyx rana*, De N. Andamans, rare.
165. *Horaga albimacula*, Wm. and De N. Andamans, very rare.
166. *Chliaria othona*, Hew. Andamans, very rare.
167. *Hypolycaena thecloides nicobarica*, Evans. Central and S. Nicobars, rare.
168. *Hypolycaena erylus andamana*, M. Andamans, not rare.
169. *Artipe eryx*, L. Andamans, very rare.
170. *Deudoryx epijarbas amatius*, Fruh. Andamans, not rare : S. Nicobars, very rare.
171. *Virachola smilis maseas*, Fruh. Andamans, very rare. (=*nicevillei*, Tyt.)
172. *Rapala suffusa rubicunda*, Evans. Andamans, not rare.
173. *Rapala varuna orseis*, Hew. Andamans, not rare.
174. *Rapala schistacea*, M. Andamans, not rare.
175. *Rapala dieneces intermedia*, Stg. Andamans, not rare. (=*xenophon*, Auct.)
176. (*a*) *Bindahara phocides phocides*, F. Andamans, rare.
(*b*) *Bindahara phocides areca*, Fd. Nicobars, not rare. (=*kamorta*, Fd.)

I.—Hesperiidae—

177. *Hasora badra badra*, M. Andamans, rare.
178. *Hasora leucospila*, Mab. S. Nicobars, recorded.

179. *Hasora salanga*, M. S. Nicobars, recorded.
180. *Hasora vitta vitta*, But. Andamans, not rare.
181. (*a*) *Hasora taminatus malayana*, Fd. Andamans, not rare.
(*b*) *Hasora taminatus almea*, Swin. S. Nicobars, rare.
182. *Hasora alexis*, F. S. Nicobars, rare.
183. *Ismene jaina astigmata*, Evans. Andamans, rare.
184. (*a*) *Ismene harisa harisa*, M. Andamans, rare.
(*b*) *Ismene amara*, M. Andamans, very rare.
185. *Bibasis sena sena*, M. Andamans, rare.
186. *Badamia exclamationis*, F. Andamans and Nicobars, not rare.
187. *Celaenorrhinus leucocera leucocera*, Koll. Andamans, rare.
188. *Celaenorrhinus andamanica*, Wm. and De N. Andamans, rare.
189. *Tagiades obscurus alica*, M. Anadamans and Nicobars, common.
190. (*a*) *Tagiades atticus ravina*, Fruh. Andamans and Kar Nikobar, common.
(*b*) *Tagiades atticus helferi*, Fd. Central and S. Nicobars, not rare.
191. *Tagiades litigiosa andamanica*, Evans. Andamans, rare.
192. *Daimio bhagara andamanica*, Wm. and De N. Andamans.
193. *Sarangesa dasahara dasahara*, M. Middle Andaman, not rare.
194. *Astictopterus jama olivascens*, M. Andamans, very rare.
195. *Suastus rama aditus*, M. Andamans, not rare.
196. *Notocrypta paralysos paralysos*, Wm. and De N. Andamans, rare.
197. *Notocrypta curvifascia*, Fd. Andamans, not rare. (=*restricta*, M.)
198. *Gangora thyrsis yasodara*, Fruh. Andamans, rare.
199. *Erionota thrax aeroleuca*, M. Andamans and Nicobars, rare. (=*hiraca*, M. and *lara*, Swin.)
200. *Paduka lebadea adamanica*, Wm. and De N. Andamans, rare.
201. *Matapa aria*, M. Andamans, not rare.
202. *Matapa druna*, M. Andamans, not rare.
203. *Matapa shalgrama*, M. Andamans, rare.
204. *Hyarotis adrastus praba*, M. Andamans, rare.
205. *Zographetus ogygia andamana*, Evans. Andamans, rare.
206. *Halpe moorei moorei*, Watson. Andamans, not rare.
207. *Capitha purreea*, M. Andamans, not rare.
208. *Oriens gola gola*, M. Andamans, not rare.
209. *Padraona maesoides ottalina*, Evans. Andamans, rare.
210. *Padraona tropica nina*, Evans. Andamans, common.
211. *Padraona serina serina*, Plotz. Andamans, rare.
212. *Cephrenes palmarum nicobarica*, Evans. Nicobars, not rare.
213. *Baoris oceia scopulifera*, M. Andamans, not rare.
214. *Baoris oceia cahira*, M. Andamans, rare : Nicobars, recorded.
215. *Baoris conjuncta javana*, Mab. Andamans and Nicobars, rare.
216. *Baoris mathias mathias*, F. Andamans, not rare.
217. *Baoris zelleri cinnara*, Wallace. Andamans and Nicobars, common.

NICOBAR ISLANDS
DIAGRAM SHOWING THE VILLAGE NAMES

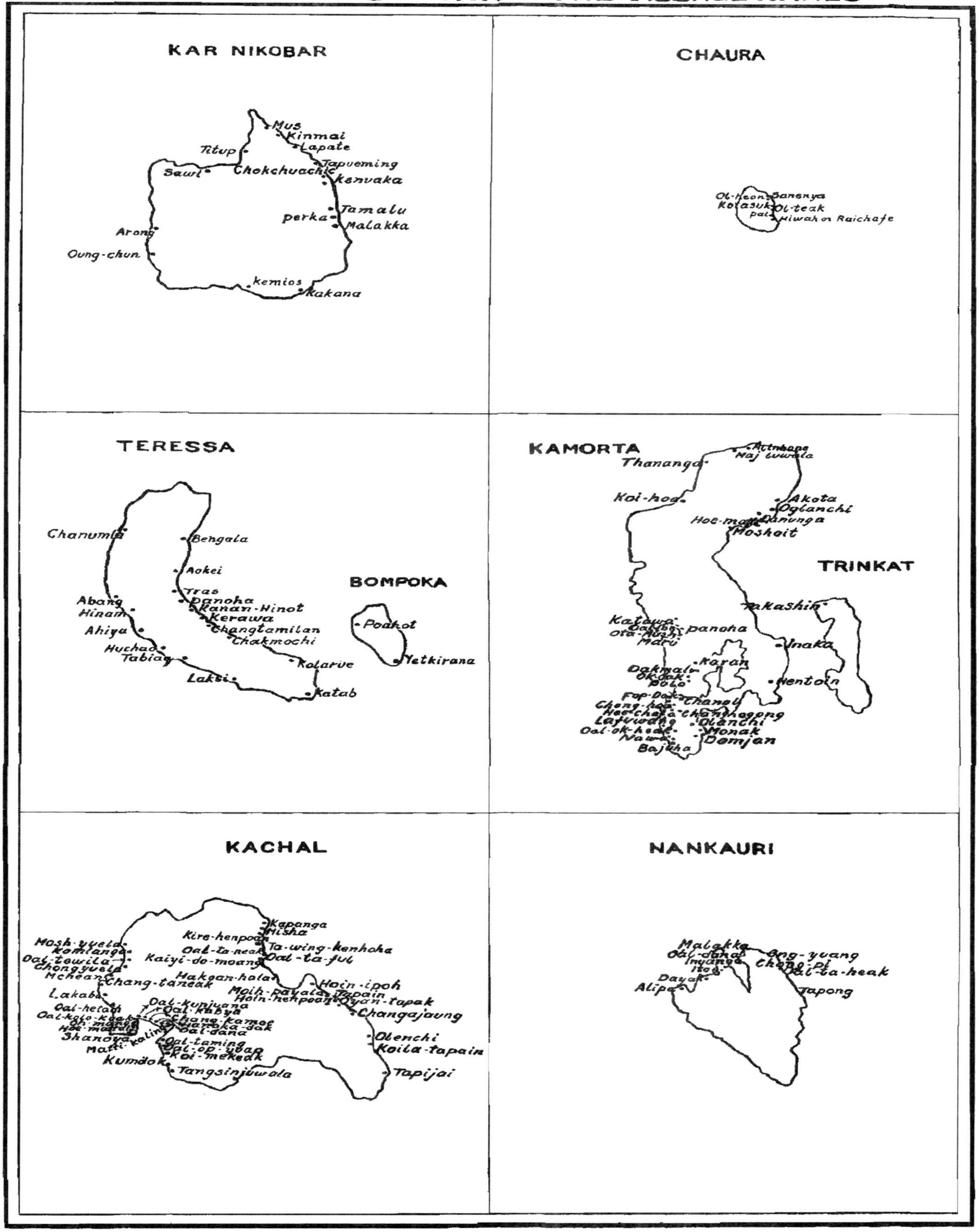

Part I-B.—REPORT ON THE NICOBARS.

CHAPTER I.

Geography.

The Nicobars comprising some 20 islands, large and small, are situated in South East portion of the Bay of Bengal between the 6th and 10th degrees of latitude North and between the 92nd and 94th degrees of longitude East. Kar Nikobar, the most northerly island of the group, is 143 miles from Port Blair and the "Ten Degree Channel", about 75 miles, separates it from Little Andaman. The islands of Nankauri, Kamorta, Trinkat, Kachal, Teressa, Bompoka, Chaura, and Tilangchong are known as the Central group. Sombrero Channel, some 35 miles wide, separates the Central and Southern group, which consist of Little Nikobar with Pulo Milo and the outlying islands Meroe, Trak, Treis and Menchal, and Great Nikobar with Kondul and Kabra; the extreme southern point of Great Nikobar is some 91 geographical miles from Pulo Brasse off Achin Head in Sumatra.

The extreme length of the sea-space occupied by the Nicobars is 163 miles and the extreme width is 36 miles, having an aggregate area of 635 square miles.

Names of the Islands.

Geographical Name.	Native name.	Area in sq. mile.
Kar Nikobar	Pu	49·02
*Batti Malv	Et	0·80
Chaura	Tatat	2·80
*Tilangchong	Laok	6·50
Teressa	Taihlong	34·00
Bompoka	Poahat	3·80
Kamorta	Nankauri	57·91
Trinkat	Laful	6·40
Nankauri	Nankauri	19·32
Kachal	Tehnyu	61·70
*Meroe	Miroe	0·20
*Trak	Fuya	0·10
*Treis	Taan	0·10
*Menchal	Menchal	0·50
Little Nikobar	Ong	57·50
Pulo Milo	Miloh	0·40
Great Nikobar	Loong	333·20
Kondul	Lamongshe	0·50
*Kabra	Konwana	0·20

The southern group of islands are known to the Malays as Sambilong or the Nine Islands.

The accompanying plan of the inhabited islands in the northern and central groups shows the sites of existing villages in three groups, no other map of which is known to be available.

*Uninhabited islands.

CHAPTER II.

A.—Configuration of the ground and underlying rock and soil.

The islands were explored by the writer of this report some years ago to examine the possibilities of colonization and since the results have some bearing on the future of the population they are recorded here.

The outer fringe of all the islands consists of a belt of sand and coral thrown up by the sea, only a few feet above high water, with a width varying from a few yards to a mile or even more. It is most in evidence at the low-lying island of Kar Nikobar. In other respects the physical characteristics of the various islands vary considerably.

1. *Great and Little Nikobar* are much intersected by steep sided ridges with very narrow valleys, rendering their exploration a difficult process. These irregular features are, no doubt, due to the action of the atmosphere and heavy rainfall which easily disintegrate the soft micaceous sandstone which is the principal formation of these islands. This formation is similar to that of the west coast of Middle Andaman. Numerous stream beds have cut up the surface in all directions, and the soil is washed down into depressions where it forms alluvial beds, sometimes of considerable extent. These flats are, however, occasionally below the outer fringe of coralline alluvium and are inundated in the rains. In such cases they are often a heavy clay and have the appearance of having been at one time below the sea.

2. *Nankauri, Kamorta, Teressa, Bompoka.*—Beds of polycistine clay predominate, the slopes of the hill are easier, but owing to the slow disintegration of the clay there is no more than a thin layer of soil on the surface, only capable of supporting grass. Other parts of the islands contain sandstone formations which are covered with forest.

3. The formation of *Trinkat* is similar to that of Kamorta and Nankauri, but the island is low, considerable areas are swampy, and there is a good deal of coralline diluvium which supports fairly extensive coconut plantations.

4. *Kar Nikobar.*—Is surrounded by large areas of flat ground consisting of coralline diluvium. The coral extends in places to the higher ground as on Kachal and appears to have been raised considerably above sea-level.

5. *Kachal.*—The island possesses flat and sometimes swampy ground of coralline diluvium over the whole of its north western portions and sandy alluvia similar to that of the southern group in parts near the north and south coast. A layer of limestone (coral) overlies a considerable portion of the south west coast and the hill above Oyantapa, and here the soil is a dark brown fertile loam. It may be mentioned here that a cave on this hill contains some 5,000 c. ft. of bat guano. The greater part of the island is suitable for cultivation and the island is the most suitable of all the groups for extension of coconut and other cultivation and would be the most suitable for a further overflow of the increasing population of other islands which is certain to follow if more attention is paid to medical treatment. Yaws for instance which now takes a heavy toll of the inhabitants of the central group could soon be eradicated.

B.—Forests.

(*i*) Great Nikobar, Little Nikobar, and Kachal are entirely covered with forests, while the larger part of the principal remaining islands, excepting perhaps Chaura, Tilangchong and Kar Nikobar, are covered to a large extent with *lalang* grass.

(*ii*) The littoral fringe of Kar Nikobar as well as that of the Central group is occupied by coconut trees. At Great Nikobar they occur in groves all along the shore, signs of past Nicobarese settlement, but since their abandonment their fruit never reaches maturity, as the monkeys destroy almost the entire crop. The areca palm tree is also fairly plentiful and the nuts are a commercial asset. The abandoned coconut groves in Great Nikobar indicate a larger population's having existed in this island in the past.

(*iii*) The forests do not compare favourably with those of the Andamans as far as timber producing trees are concerned. The most valuable Andaman timber trees, *i.e.*, Padauk, Pyinma and Gurjan are absent. Terminalias, *i.e.*, white and black Chuglam and White Bombwe, are not uncommon and the latter, in some of the alluvial valleys of the West coast of Great Nikobar and on Kachal, sometimes attains a girth of 12 ft. Toungpeing, Lakuch, Lalchini and various other soft wood species are also present; but the limited quantities will never make the timber exploitation of these islands a financial success apart from other conditions such as the want of good anchorages, indigenous labour, and adverse climatic conditions.

(*iv*) *Great Nikobar.*—Quantitites of red and white cane are collected by Shompens, and exported to the Strait Settlements by Chinese traders.

(*v*) The grass lands of the central group are excellent for grazing cattle; on Kamorta Island buffaloes were left by the Danes and cattle were left when the Penal Settlement was abandoned in 1888. Both have done so well that there are now considerable herds. These islands are suitable for cattle ranching and would supply the Port Blair settlement with slaughter cattle which are now imported from India.

(*vi*) The fauna and flora of the Nicobars differ considerably from that of the Andamans. This change is gradual as one goes from north to south and is most noticeable in Great Nikobar where the luxuriant tree-ferns on the banks of streams indicate the moist climate of the equatorial belt which with the chatter of monkeys and continual screeching of the megapod bring home to the casual visitor from the Andamans the great difference of the forests.

C.—Economic Zoology.

The economic zoology of the Nicobars is very similar to that of the Andamans. Trochus and turbo shells, trepang, and edible birds' nests are found in both groups of islands. There is a possibility of increased revenue if the right to collect this produce were let out as it is in the Andamans.

CHAPTER III.

Climate.

(*i*) *The climate.*—The atmosphere is damp and warm all the year round though when the sun is southing the nights may be chilly, while the temperature varies from 65 to 98 degrees in the shade. The rainfall is anything between 90 and 170 inches annually, and is considerably more on Great Nikobar; most rain falls during the south west monsoon, but hardly a month passes without it. The monsoon sets in at the end of May or beginning of June and strong south-westerly winds with heavy squalls are current till September. Easterly winds prevail from November till April, usually beginning from the south-east and veering round to the north-east. During October and from February to April it is usually calm. Cyclones have been recorded in May 1885 and March 1892, but as a rule the cyclones which traverse the Bay of Bengal orginate north of the Nicobars and do not affect these islands.

(*ii*) *Climatic diseases.*—Malaria fevers and elephantiasis are prevalent all over the group. Yaws, a disease which has often been confused with syphilis, is very common, and where it occurs frequently, as on Teressa, the fertility is very low. The appointment of a sub-assistant surgeon would be of great benefit to the people of the central group. Yaws could be eradicated and no doubt the population would increase in the central and southern groups.

CHAPTER IV.

History.

Sir R. Temple in his Census Report 1901 deals with the history of the Nicobars in detail. A short account, however, is here appended together with fresh information as a result of recent investigation of the Hindu occupation of the Nicobars in the XIth century A. D.

Owing to their situation in the middle of the Bay of Bengal, the Nicobars were along the ancient trade route to the East. The earliest mention of them is that made by the famous Chinese traveller and Buddhist monk I'Tsing in 672 A. D. who refers to them as the land of the 'Naked people' (Lo-Jen-Kuo) and this seems to have been the recognized name for them in China. Yule however identifies with the Nicobars the islands referred to by the Buddhist monk as 'Nalo-kio-chen' (*i.e., Narikel-dwipa* or coconut islands), where the men are 3 feet high and had beaks like birds, no cultivation, and lived on coconuts. The beaks might be taken as an allusion to the protruding mouths developed by the betel-chewing habits of the Nicobarese. In A. D. 607, the Empress of China, Yang-ti, sent an envoy to Siam who reached the Nicobars, spoken of as the country of Rakshasas—meaning demons. He reported that the inhabitants were very ugly, having red hair, black bodies, teeth like beasts and claws like hawks. Sometimes they visited Linyih (Champa) but traded at night; by day they covered their faces.

The Nicobarese have also been identified with the "Lankhabulus" "Langa balus" or Najabalus (Sanskrit *nagna nanja*-naked) of the "Arab Relations" 851 A. D. In Pinkerton's Voyages and Travels, Vol. 7, page 183, appears "an account of the travels of two Mahomeddans through India and China in the ninth century" translated by the Abbe Renaudot from the Arabic. The Nicobars are here referred to as "Najabulus which are pretty well peopled; both the men and the women there go naked, except the women conceal their private parts with the leaves of trees". Mention is also made that ambergris and coconuts are bartered by the inhabitants for iron. Gerini has fixed on "Maniola" for Kar Nikobar and "Agathodaimonos" for Great Nikobar among the *Satyrorum insulœ* of the 1490 edition of Ptolemy. Apparently Ptolemy however regarded "Agathodaimonos" and the "Maniolae" as an entirely different group. He mentions ten islands as called "*Maniolae*". As to the *Satyrorum insulœ* he mentions that the inhabitants are said to have tails like those with which Satyrs are depicted. The Nicobar Islands also appear in the Great Tanjore Inscription of 1050 as "Nakavaram" or land of the Naked*.

S. Krishnaswamy Iyengar, Ph.D., in his contribution to the Journal of Indian History describes the overseas expedition of Rajendra Chola II and includes among his conquests the Nicobars, Kar Nikobar appearing as Kardipa, Great Nikobar as Nagadipa, the whole being the islands of Naccavaram. This invasion has been fixed at the beginning of the 11th century. The name appears as Nocuveran, and Nicoveran in Marco Polo (1292) and Friar Odoric (1322) respectively. In the 15th and 16th century the islands are referred to as Nacabar and Nicubar by the Portuguese pioneers who attempted to try and evangelize them by means of missionaries, who had their headquarters in the neighbouring Mergui Archipelago. This is without doubt the cause of the vague monotheistic belief which exists in the Nicobars and identifies the Chaura word *Reussi* and the Teressa and Nankauri words

* *Note by Census Commissioner for India.*—The Nicobars have always been identified with *Lankhabalus* of the Arabs, *Nakavaram* of the Hindus and Marco Polo's *Necuveram*. The name no doubt survives in Nankauri. One is tempted to identify them with Ptolemy's *Nagadipa* (as the island of the Naked, *Nanga*, not of Snakes) east of Ceylon, but the traditional identification is with the *Satyrorum Insulae Tres* 'the inhabitants of which are said to have tails, as the Satyrs are depicted,' a reference perhaps to the tailed girdles worn by the men. Even the comparatively recent Swedish navigator Koeping reported the Nicobarese to be gifted by nature with anatomical tails (1647). An alternative identification is with Ptolemy's five Barussæ islands (inhabited, of course, by *anthropophagi*), which may be taken to correspond well enough to Teressa and the other islands of the Central Group [*vide supra*, page 5.]

J. H. H.

Reus, which signify a species of superior being who lives in the sky, with the Portuguese word *Deos* or Latin *Deus* meaning God.

European Occupation.—The history of the Nicobars since the 17th century is a long record of unsuccessful attempts at colonization and evangelization. As early as 1688 Dampier mentions the attempts of "two fryers to convert the Indians" followed by the French Jesuits Fauré and Taillandier in 1711.* In 1756 the Danish East India Company made one of the series of attempts to colonize and convert the Nicobarese. Dutch pirates appear to have occupied the island prior to the coming of the French Jesuits. The islands were made over to the Moravian (Herrnhunter) Mission, which effort lasted till 1768. During the Napoleonic wars the islands were in the hands of the British to be ceded back by treaty in 1814 to the Danes. In 1835 the Jesuits again fruitlessly attempted to convert the natives of Kar Nikobar, Chaura and Teressa, and after the failure of Pastor Rosen in 1837, the Danes officially gave up rights to the place.

In 1845 the Danes made an attempt to re-open the settlement and in 1846 the "Galathea" expedition arrived with a new settlement scheme. The results were as disastrous as all former attempts and in 1848 the Danes formally renounced all sovereignty and removed all remains of their settlement. During the years 1848-69 the islands were left to themselves despite the attempt of Franz Mauer, an officer who in 1867, tried to interest the Prussian Government in the islands, nine years before the Austrian scientific "Novara" expedition had arrived with a scheme for colonization which came to naught.

1869.—In spite of the occupation of the islands by Europeans the Nicobarese were developing a name throughout the Indian ocean of being little better than pirates. They came to the direct notice of the British Government because of the islanders having committed repeated murders on the crews of 26 vessels under the British Flag. With a view to putting an immediate stop to this, the British Government took formal possession of the islands, and established in Nankauri harbour, a Penal Settlement, attached to the Andamans.

British Penal Settlement.—While thus the primary cause for the foundation of the Settlement was the suppression of the piratical tendencies of the inhabitants and desire to afford protection to trading vessels visiting the islands, there was also a subsidiary reason in so far as the British Government wished to avoid the establishment of a rival foreign naval station in close proximity to the British settlements of the Indian seas.

The settlement was maintained at Nankauri till it was closed down in 1888. The total number of residents were 400 of which a mean average of 235 were convicts. The cause of the closing of the Settlement was the fact that the British Government had attained the object for which it was established. "Owing to the exceptional circumstances and conditions of the colony in incurring continued expenditure and no adequate return, even prospective, there remained neither inducement nor justification for maintaining an establishment in such a remote and malarious locality".†

In 1884 an attempt was made to colonize the islands with Chinese settlers. The attempt failed owing to the lack of capital and perseverance. In withdrawing the Settlement the British Government had no intention of renouncing annexation of the islands. For purposes of general administration two Government agents were left at Nankauri and Kar Nikobar respectively. Their duties were to assist the Chiefs in keeping law and order, to collect fees for license to trade in the islands, to give Port clearances, to report all occurrences, to prevent the smuggling of liquor and guns, and to settle petty disputes.

Recent administration.—Since 1888 the Nicobars have been in contact with the administration by the means of the two local government agents. Mr. Man in his report on the Penal Settlement at Nankauri, suggested the formation of a mission at Kar Nikobar to educate young intelligent Nicobarese.

* See "Letters Edifiantes," Paris, 1711.

† Extract from E. H. Man's Report on the Penal Settlement in Nankauri harbour.

This suggestion has since been carried out and an account of the action taken will be found in the Chapter on Education in the Report.

Owing to the remarkable increase in the population and the formation of a flourishing mission, Kar Nikobar has become the most important island in the group; it is the seat of an Assistant Commissioner, and possesses a Sub-Assistant Surgeon with a local hospital for the treatment of the Nicobarese.

CHAPTER V.

Anthropology, Philology and Ethnology.

Owing to territorial distinctions the Nicobarese are divided by customs, manners, physical and linguistic characteristics into groups. These groups are :—

I.	Kar Nikobar	Northern group.
II.	(*a*) Chaura	Central group.
III.	(*b*) Teressa	
	(*c*) Bompoka	
IV.	(*d*) Nankauri	
	(*e*) Kamorta	
	(*f*) Trinkat	
	(*g*) Kachal	
V.	(*a*) Little Nikobar	Southern group.
	(*b*) Pulo Milo	
	(*c*) Great Nikobar (coastal tribes)	
	(*d*) Kondul.	
VI.	The Shompen of the Interior of Great Nikobar.	

Anthropologically and ethnologically the Nikobarese have many points of affinity with the Indo-Chinese Race as distinguished from the Tibeto-Burese and Malay tribes, and their manners and customs point to an eastern rather than an Indian origin.

S. H. Roberts in his Population Problems of the Pacific mentions waves of migration which took place towards the Pacific, in the fifth and thirteenth centuries from Indonesia. Undoubtedly, there were even earlier migrations from the main land to the islands and it is not improbable that such migrations took place from the Penang Peninsula in the fine weather of the north-east monsoon for which the Nikobars would be a natural destination. All the Nikobarese are excellent sailors and build large sea-worthy outrigger canoes comparable with Hawaiian, Tahitian, Fiji and Maori types in which Cook in 1777 found Tahitians as far as 200 leagues from home.

There can be no doubt that the Nicobarese of the different islands have various mixtures of foreign blood which has been introduced at a date considerably later than the migration. In the people of Chaura, possibly, the purest type is represented, on account of their exclusiveness and isolation. In them the highest form of Nicobarese culture is found as well as a tribal and economic organization superior to that of the other islands. This exclusiveness is due to their refusal to allow any foreigners to remain on their islands and even within the last 40 years they are known to have killed two large canoe crews of Nicobarese who had come for pots and could not leave owing to a change in the monsoon. Although this had never come to the notice of the administration, it is admitted by the Chaura people and substantiated by John Richardson, the Nicobarese Honorary Tahsildar of Kar Nikobar, whose father was one of the massacred crew.

Owing to their position the Northern group as exemplified in Kar Nikobar appears to have assimilated a certain amount of Burmese blood while in the south the influence of the Malay is very noticeable. Père Barbe in his monograph on the Nicobar Islands in 1846 states that the natives of Kar Nikobar have a tradition that they are Burmese, who owing to rebellion were forced to fly from Tenasserim and seek safety in the Nicobars. This theory has very many supports both anthropological and philological to bear it out.

The Kar Nicobarese hold themselves to be descended from a man and a bitch, who got afloat on a raft. Dr. Hutton, has recorded a similar belief in the Naga Hills, where such an origin is ascribed to Europeans, pointing out that in Purchas' *Pilgrimage* (vol. V, Ch. V), "The Peguans ascribe ....their origin to a dog and a China woman, which escaped shipwreck". The stories are of the same nature and are probably of the same source, and were no doubt taken by a branch of the Mon race to the Nicobars together with the Mon language which is still spoken. Young Kar Nicobarese women when dressed in Burmese costume can hardly be distinguished from Burmese or Talaings. The Talaings speak a Mon language and are not identical with the Burmese by race, though now much mixed up with them, but there is evidence of later migration by the Burmese race, proper for in Kar Nikobar, there is a village *Oung Chun*, Burmese for coconut island, the inhabitants of which are said to have arrived about 100 years ago ; the Kar Nikobarese indeed assert that they killed several of them as they were cruel and obnoxious generally.

The "dog's ear" head band of the Kar Nicobarese is supposed to represent the canine ancestress' ears and the long end of the loin cloth her tail. Dr. Hutton mentions a resemblance between some forms of Konyak Naga head-gear and that of the Nicobarese. The Chaura people assert that the reason for the Kar Nicobarese being averse to dog's flesh is their presumed descent from a man and a bitch. In contrast the Chaura people themselves eat dogs' flesh which suggests that they and the Kar Nicobarese claim a different origin.

The strongest link which binds the chain of Nicobarese affinities to the Indo-Chinese group is that formed by the philology of the Nicobarese language. Various grammars and vocabularies have been prepared in the past by missionaries, officials, and others of the Nankauri dialect of the Central group. So far the Rev. G. Whitehead is the only person who has collected that of Kar Nikobar.

Among the many differences which exist between the islands the chief one is linguistic. Some six distinct dialects are in existence, though four of these, those spoken in Chaura, Teressa and the Central and Southern groups might be regarded as one, though there are distinct differences, due no doubt to the operation of "tabu" on words which here, as in various other regions where scattered communities exist speaking an unwritten language, and having infrequent means of intercourse and communication, has effected constant changes in the language.

The best attempt to reproduce the dialect is E. H. Man's dictionary of the Central Nicobarese language 1889. This has been identified by the great philologist Pater Schmidt and by Sir G. A. Grierson, as having "affinities with the Indo-Chinese language as represented now-a-days by the Mon or Talaing languages of Tenasserim and Malay Peninsular and Khmer languages of Cambodia amongst civilized peoples, and by a number of uncivilized tribes in the Malay Peninsula. Philologically the language is invaluable, as owing to isolation and inconsiderable miscegenation, it is the "true probable basis for the philology of the languages of the Indo-Chinese family". Lieutenant-Colonel P. T. Gurdon in the "Khasis" (1914) quotes Pater Schmidt that "Khasi possesses many words in common with Mon or Talaing, Khmer etc.,...................and to a lesser degree with those of Malacca and the Nancowry language of the Nicobar Islands."

The Central Groups.

Traces of miscegenation in the Central group are most noticed at Teressa and Nankauri. In Teressa, South Indian influence is predominent, the features and general physiognomy of some of the people pointing to a strong South Indian mixture at some period. The top tuft of hair, the "tiki" of the Hindu, is usually worn by males from childhood. They powder their head with a red powder and apply a concoction of turmeric to their body for medicinal purposes. It is possible that this has originated from Hindu customs, besides the general cast of feature and colour of the skin of some of the youths is such that they would not be distinguished from others on the streets of Madras. Further mention of this is made in the chapter on History, yet there are undoubtedly traces of old Hindu colonization in the Nicobars which is stated to have existed 900 years ago when King Rajendra Chola II invaded Sumatra and the Nicobars, *vide* S. Krishnaswamy Aiyangar Ph. D. "Journal of Indian History" *Rajendra, the Gangaikonda Chola.*

At Nankauri harbour anthropometrical measurements were taken which induced Dr. Naidu to believe that a mixture of nordic blood was present. According to history, the Nicobars were at various times during the last 300 years visited by European vessels, Dampier in particular, giving a long and interesting discription of his visit there in 1688. It is possible that the nordic shape of head noted in Nankauri may be accounted for by the former presence of a Danish garrison. A legend is current among the people of Teressa that the people of Nankauri are descendants of Malays who visited the islands on a fishing excursion and lost their boats.

The Southern Group.

The diverse differences between the inhabitants of the Northern, Central and Southern groups have given rise to a number of theories as to whether the Nicobars are inhabited by two different peoples, or the original inhabitants and an invading race or whether they are one people who have changed owing to successive influences of foreign blood. Boden Kloss advances the theory in his "Andamans and Nicobars" "that the islands were originally peopled by a race of Malays who were gradually driven south by the immigration from the coast of Burma of the Indo-chinese settlers, but that, in the process, there was a certain fusion of races which would account for the Malay element in the Niccbarese of to-day". The Shompen* or inland tribe of Great Nicobar are the last element of the Malay race, who were enabled to hold off the invaders, and maintain a separate existence in the dense forests of the interior of that island. Kloss also mentions a possible mixture by immigration in remote times from Southern India, to account for the dark skin, and curly or wavy hair met with among the Shompen. He further substantiated this by pointing out that the skull is brachycephalic with marked prognathism ; the type of people, approaches very nearly, to that described by Herr Baelz as typical of the Japanese of the lower Malay type, *i.e.*, Pithecoid.

This is supported by E. H. Man who notes that the differences are both racial and linguistic between the coastal and Pen tribes though the Shom-Pen are fairer than Malays. He holds that the Shom-Pen were the original inhabitants of Great Nikobar and that at a later date they were driven into the interior by aliens more powerful than themselves, who were wrecked on their coasts.† Sir R. Temple in his 1901 report, page 200 contradicts this, stating that there is no radical difference between a Shom-Pen and other Nicobarese. The differences are merely such as exist between islands and as are to be expected among people living an almost isolated existence.

During the visit of the Census party to Great Nikobar, a Shom-Pen village on the Alexandra river was visited and anthropometric measurements taken of a dozen individuals. As a type they appeared to be totally different to other Nicobarese and the men possessed distinct features. Some resembled the Papuan while the women had Mongoloid features and often the epicanthic fold. Several male children on the other hand showed features very suggestive of South Indian blood.

While the coastal tribes of Great Nikobar exhibit all the characteristics of a mongrel Malay race, the Shom Pen with their more primitive culture and nomadic habits are distinct and differ from the remaining groups and are really not part of the social economic group either. They alone of all the groups do not use Chaura cooking pots, while the "hentas and hentakois" and other signs of spirit propitiation and devil scarers common in the houses of the coast dwellers are absent in the crude huts of the Shom-Pen.

---

* *Vide* Appendix A. The Shom-Pens.

† *Vide* Appendix A.

With the exception of Chaura there is a considerable mixture of Malay, Chinese, Pre-Dravidian and even Indo-European blood in the Central and southern groups. At the present day Chinese influence is most apparent in the south and in parts of the Central group, where possessing most of the trade, the Chinese have families of hybrid stock.

The different ossuary practices prevailing on the islands of Kar Nikobar, Chaura, Teressa with Bompoka and Nankauri with the Southern group, indicate however the possible presence of different original stocks. Further details are given in the chapter on Ossuary Practices. Dr. Hutton has suggested that the practice of ancestor-worship and of preserving the bones of the family in little coffins in the dwelling houses, as prevails in Teressa and Bompoka, has Melanesian associations. Anthropological researches in the Pacific and Melanesia, *e.g.*, *Argonauts of the Western Pacific* by Malinowski, etc., reveal an environment and culture presenting many similarities to those found in the Nicobars, and point to a possible former connection.

During the Census some 200 anthropological measurements were taken, which were sent to the Calcutta Museum, and have been analysed by Dr. Guha as follows :—

"Though the Nicobarese are generally known to belong to the Mongolian stock, accurate information regarding their somatic characters was lacking due to the absence of definite metric data. The measurements of 121 males and 50 females on which the present analysis is based will go a great deal in removing this want.

"The mean stature of 121 males is 1589·25 which places the Nicobarese among the short-statured people, though not quite so short as the Andamanese. The proportion of the breadth of the head to the length is 76·76 and the auricular height is 127·14. The above figures show that the Nicobarese are not brachycephalic as is commonly supposed, but mesocephalic with a relatively high head. The nose verges on platyrhiny, as the mean basal index of 83·87 indicates, with a sunken bridge (mean orbito-nasal index 111·81). The face is low but broad, the mean total and upper facial indices being 82·08 and 48·05 respectively. The maximum bizygomatic diameter is as high as 138·31 and the bigonial breadth 102·26, showing that the face is of the square shape."

CHAPTER VI.

1. Internal Government and Social Organization.

The Nicobarese are divided in their various islands into a series of communities or clans which find expression as a unit in the village. To borrow a phrase from Sir R. Temple " Government is in fact simple democracy bound by customs ".* Though there is this detribalization, which finds expression in the complete independence of the individual, yet there are customs and uses which form unwritten tradition, to which the individual must bow. Throughout the islands, with perhaps the exception of Chaura, the government of the village lies essentially in the hands of the elders of the village rather than a head-man. The headman is usually an individual who owing to his superior wealth, symbolised in the number of his pigs and the size of his plantations, has reached a position of influence within the community. This position of influence is almost invariably hereditary. He is in most cases nothing more than *primus inter pares* who acts as the mouthpiece of the elders of the village. As an individual, his personality and wealth alone will increase or decrease the practical value of his position.

Within the clan or village a patriarchal family system holds sway. Owing to the procedure of inheritance, a number of individuals are economically

* Census Report, 1901, page 214.

dependant on the owner of the land and plantations; thus a whole village consists of a number of households, each head of a household having a large number of dependents both male and female. In return for their sustenance, these individuals are at the beck and call of the head of the house, performing all domestic duties for him, such as feeding his pigs, cultivating his plantations, building his huts, preparing his canoes, etc. The whole is remarkably akin to the feudal system except that the sustenance of the individual replaces the land tenure.

The prestige and influence of the headman has always been encouraged by the Administration, which presents him with a flag (Union Jack), a letter of appointment and a book in which all vessels and visitors can record their visits.

Each head of a family has a recognized position within the community as an elder, and it is before a council of these elders that all questions of weight and importance are decided which concern the general welfare of the community at large. The elders can also hear disputes and possess certain primitive powers mention of which is made under "Tribal Law and Justice". In Kar Nikobar, and to a lesser degree in the other islands excepting Chaura, tribal administration in the general run of community life, has lost its former power whereby the interests of the clan were safeguarded. Contact with the trader and civilization seems to be eliminating those economic and social qualities which are such an essential factor in the existence of a primitive race in its fight against the forces of civilization symbolised in a superior culture.

Owing to its position and size, which involve no commercial possibilities, Chaura has never really come in direct contact with the administration, or under its influence. The people being the purest of the race, have an intensely rigid and complicated tribal organization, in which the authority and dependance of the Chief or Captain of the village stand out. All points and decisions are referred to him by the community, and he settles all disputes deciding what the punishment of the individual should be.

2. Tribal Law and Justice.

The appointment of an Assistant Commissioner at Kar Nikobar has of late years induced the Kar Nicobarese to refer disputes and general offences to the local court. In other islands offences against tribal morality, custom and tradition are still referred to the elders of the clan who resort to punitive powers in the shape of fining an individual so many pigs, or physical correction in the shape of a good beating. On Chaura the individual is brought to the Captain who in conjunction with the elders inflicts a fine on him of at least one pig. This is immediately seized and the rest of the community participates in a feast at the culprit's expense.

Should the accused be a depêndent, the elders approach the head of his family and obtain the pig from him.

In the cases of disputes on Chaura, both parties, in the presence of the Captain, select a man each to assist them, thus with two men a side they proceed to fight with quarter-staves. The party which is adjudged to have been worsted, no real serious injury ensuing, loses the dispute and at the same time makes over a fee in the shape of a pig which is consumed by both parties.

Sir R. Temple in his Census Report mentions the settlement of quarrels by parties attacking each other at night, armed with quarter-staves, wearing coconut husk helmets and smearing their faces with blood. No serious harm ensued, and the idea expressed appears to be the moral retaliation for any offence suffered. This custom appears to have died out in the Northern group, but is no doubt still current in the South and Central groups.

Devil Murders.—Until recent years "Devil murders" were current in Kar Nikobar, Chaura and Teressa. The idea involved seems to have been the desirability of ridding a community of individuals who were dangerous to the general welfare of the village and in many respects is a primitive exposition of the modern lynch-law of the United States. Many cases appeared before the Administration, records of which will be found in Appendix D Census Report, 1901, which deals with this matter in detail. The murders appear to have been committed solely for the public benefit after a more or less open consultation of the elders of the village. The general cause appears to have been that the victim was possessed of an evil spirit and hence was both harmful and dangerous.

The causes of the murders proved to be—

(1) Possession by an evil spirit.

(2) Witchcraft to the public harm.

(3) Danger to the community.

(4) Homicidal proclivity.

(5) Threat on the part of the victim to kill.

(6) Failure to cure (by a "doctor", *menluana*).

(7) Theft.

In recent years owing to the powerful influence of the Administration and realization on the part of the Nicobarese that severe retaliatory measures would be taken, these murders have entirely ceased and are no longer a cause for anxiety and constant 'surveillance'. The orthodox method of killing a victim is very cruel. The legs and arms are broken or dislocated to prevent the individual's fighting. He is then strangled and thrown into the sea with a heavy stone around his legs.

(*a*) Marriage.

Among the Nicobarese boys attain puberty at about 14 and girls at about 13. They attain full growth at about 22 and 21. At an early age they are initiated into sexual life, no doubt as a result of the practice of a man's living with all his dependents in a communal hut. This feature of "free love" is however the rule rather than the exception among primitive peoples, and in no way offends their sense of morality. Among the young people games of hide and seek are played in the evening which are little more than opportunities for sexual intercourse.

The usual age for marriage is sixteen in the case of a girl and twenty-two in the case of a man. Girls are always free to choose their own husbands. Marriage is usually the outcome of some long-standing affection for a particular youth. The consent of the parents or head of the family is however necessary. In Chaura, before couples are able to marry, either the boy or the girl must possess at least three pigs which are given by their parents or the head of the house. To obtain a bride, the suitor must always give a present which differs with the clan status of the bride's father. In the case of a wealthy parent it would be ten pigs, 20 fathoms of cloth, 20 rupees, 2 large silver spoons, and 1 bundle of silver wire. Should this indemnity be too much for the suitor or should he be a poor man, he can enter the house of his father-in-law and work as his dependent, and should he possess a small coconut plantation this becomes the property of his father-in-law and stays for ever within the latter's family.

Although there is no ceremony or rite associated with marriage, a large feast is invariably held to which the whole community is invited. They are expected to bring presents for the newly married couple so that at some time they may set up in a new home. Pig and toddy form the chief attraction in the feast wherein the partakers invariably leave thoroughly intoxicated. It is usual for the woman to come and live in the man's house and though the opposite sometimes takes place it is rare.

The status of women socially is every whit on a par with that of men. Far from being inferior they exercise considerable influence in the councils of the men and are at complete liberty. On them also the majority of the work, both domestic and otherwise, devolves.

(*b*) Divorce.

As a rule after a couple have married infidelity is rare. Marriage however is by no means binding on either party in the Nicobars. Should a husband and wife fail to get on well they just leave one another to look elsewhere for a mate, no malice being borne on either side. Adultery is rare, but is good cause for divorce. It is treated as an offence against the community, and the delinquents are both fined three pigs each. On Kar Nikobar and other islands it is not unusual to beat severely both the man and the woman. Should there be any children they are divided between the couple. As an actual moral offence adultery is not regarded in a serious light, but the husband and sometimes the injured family get pecuniary compensation for the alienation of his wife's affections. A case happened a few years ago where the co-respondent had to indemnify the brother of the woman with whom he had committed adultery ; the brother in anger over his sister's conduct had destroyed his own racing canoe. The co-respondent was unable to pay for it and had to hand over a part of his coconut plantation as compensation.

3. Property and Land Tenure.

Ownership of land.—Throughout the Nicobars recognised proprietary rights exist in land. R. F. Lowis in Appendix G of his Census report gives an able and clear exposition of the rules as to ownership of land in Kar Nikobar.

Kar Nikobar.—Tradition and usage has vested the ownership of land in Kar Nikobar in the person of the village chief or headman as his personal property. Hence all land, jungle or otherwise in Kar Nikobar is the property of some village headman. In the course of time the headman has made grants of land to all families of his village. This land has either been cultivated or sown with coconuts, and is now the scene of thriving vegetable and yam gardens as well as fine coconut plantations. The headman would naturally keep the major part of the land for his own family to enable them to acquire greater prestige by the number and size of their plantations, and the number of their pigs, for it is by wealth alone that a family can show its importance.

All land therefore on Kar Nikobar is either unplanted, in which case it belongs to the headman, who owns the timber growing on it, or has been allotted by him to various families. The usufruct of this allotted land belongs to such a family, and remains with them as a family rather than as individuals, but not the soil itself. Thus in the Nicobars it will be found that a plantation has descended in a family for generations never changing hands. This considerably enhances the unity of the family which in turn strengthens the village and community, the tribal unit.

The headman has also powers to sell land to members of neighbouring villages, and sometimes even to make them free grants, but to such alienation the consent of the elders of the village is always necessary. It also often happens that plantation land in one village is exchanged for garden land in another, and in most cases of this nature there is usually trouble over the land alienated to other villagers and many of these cases are brought into the local court every year.

Throughout the Northern and Central groups of the Nicobars, the jungle is interspersed with large open spaces of *lalang* grass. This grass is used to form the thatching of the beehive huts and is the common property of all individuals, every villager having the right to cut and use it. The boundaries which divide the lands of one village from that of another one are recognized by certain marks ; a young coconut stuck on top of a stick is one such and constitutes a prohibition for the picking of coconuts.

Tribal custom allocates the land and the forest growing on it to certain villages and when the inhabitants of other islands wish to cut down trees for canoes they have to pay royalty to the owner. In Great Nikobar before attempting to cut down a tree in the jungle for canoe-building permission is always obtained from the Shom Pen who expect certain presents in return. Judging on inferences, it is concluded that the land in Great Nikobar is divided up by boundaries into the hunting grounds of the various groups or tribes, who would naturally retaliate at any attempt to encroach on their land.

Chaura.—The whole island is split up into numerous holdings, consisting of jungle and cultivated land. Contrary to the custom at Kar Nikobar, this land is the property of the owner of the trees upon it. A chief, of whom there are but five, has no rights over the land belonging to the members of his village. Comparably to the old English village land system, an individual owns strips of land all over the island, cultivated and otherwise, which have come into his family by inheritance or marriage. Even the conspicuous hill on Chaura, (which is supposed to be the resort of maleficent evil spirits, and is shunned by the inhabitants, and can only be climbed with one's person devoid of ornaments and wearing a white loin cloth for fear a snake should bite or the spirits seize one) is split up into a series of holdings from which individuals at certain times of the year cut fuel. All wells are the property of certain villages.

Inheritance.

With the exception of Chaura, the only property that goes by inheritance in the Nicobars, are coconut trees, canoes and sometimes huts. Whoever has planted a tree is the owner of it and his heirs after him. The land, as has been shown is not claimed, only the trees.

According to the primitive laws of inheritance current in the Nicobars, all real property, coconut and areca trees and gardens, will descend to the surviving members of the family who lives in the village. It remains with them as a family rather than as individuals as has been explained. Each village community is divided into a series of families, each family consisting of a number of individuals who have a right to be sustained from the plantations which are in reality their common property, though the head of the family assumes a despotic position. All persons both male and female have equal rights to the property. Should a son marry in Kar Nikobar he can either bring his wife to live in his own village, or he may go and live in her village with her relations. By doing this latter he renounces all claims to his own family inheritance, and thus virtually becomes a member of another family group. The same is the case with a daughter who leaves her family. For inheritance is communal to the family. Each individual has an unspecified but effective right to part of the produce of the plantation. It supports each member of the group it belongs to, and they can supply themselves at will. Should a family completely die out the plantation will of necessity go back to the chief who owns the land. He can either keep it for himself or allot the same to some other member of the community.

In Great Nikobar and in the Central Group where communities are smaller, the possession of coconut palms, that is of the source of all wealth, is usually vested in the headman and the eldest son succeeds to the inheritance, or the daughter if there is no son. Occasionally a man or woman will hold property in several villages, in contrast to the usage in Kar Nikobar.

The disintegration of the lands of a village would result in the breakdown of the community. Thus the land is never alienated to traders.

For inheritance of Property, other than trees and land see Chapter VI, Section 5 (*b*) Ossuary practices.

4. Economics of the Social Group.

Organization of labour.—In the organization of labour, the family, clan, village community, and ultimately the whole island are the groups which co-ordinate for the accomplishment of their various tasks throughout the

Nicobars. The duties which a dependent owes his family, and which the family owes the village community, are united to undertake the task. The building of huts, canoes, and plantation are economic factors which are undertaken by the various family groups. In these any member of the village may take part and as a reward or recompense will join in the large feast given by the owner who organizes the task. At the great ossuary feast which takes place at Chaura every three monsoons or eighteen months, the whole island community resort to the *al panam* or village near the shore. This contains 32 specially built large communal huts which house the whole population, and are vacant at other times of the year. All the pig in the island are driven into specially cleared areas surrounded by fences and are then killed and eaten at the feast which lasts a month. Some 1,280 pigs are eaten at the feast as 40 jaw bones of pigs stained red are hung in orderly rows in each hut. These are cleared just before the next feast takes place. This naturally exhausts the complete stock of pork on the island, so a new era of work and trading commences to replenish the stock before the next 18 months.

Pottery.—The importance of the pot to Chaura has been stated. In it are displayed the industrial qualities of the women. The clay is procured from Alheun village at the northern end of Teressa where it is obtained in the hill side. Clay was at one time procurable on Chaura but the Chaura people say it is of poor quality and very brittle. Each man is only allowed to take the equivalent of 2 cubic feet of clay every season from Teressa, much to the annoyance of the Chaura people who make it a subject of complaint. Thus Teressa controls the output of Chaura pots.

Prior to making pots the Chaura women sprinkle themselves with pig's or chicken's blood, in order, they say, to prevent the pots cracking, and wear collars of young banana leaves. The pots are handmade. The process adopted is that of coiling. Starting from the base, long pencils of clay some 9″ in length are coiled one on top of the other until the size required is made. This is then smoothed into the shape of the pot with a spatula of wood. Before it is fired it is left to harden in the shade under the hut for a day or so, so that any blemish or crack may be easily discerned. After firing, black stripes 2″ in width are painted on it. The paint consists of resin extracted from the husk of the coconut boiled over a fire.

A woman on Chaura is supposed to be able to make 2 large pots in one day. Each pot can be identified, as its maker leaves her special mark on the outside just below the rim.

Economic Wealth.—Dependents and children in the Nicobars are an economic asset, as from the age of ten till they reach manhood they do most of the domestic work around the house such as fetching fuel, drawing water, feeding the pigs, climbing coconut trees, etc. Owing to their extreme usefulness in this way an orphan is never without some support to fall back on, as any family are willing to adopt him or her as a dependent and as a mainstay in their old age when all of the hard work falls on the younger people.

On Great Nikobar several Shom-Pen children were found with the coast Nicobarese who said they had bought them for 1 *dah* and 2 fathoms of cloth from their parents. These children are in the same position as the remaining dependents of the community and are quite happy in their new surroundings.

In a rich man's household often as many as three hundred coconuts are consumed in one day. Some two hundred of these are used in feeding the family's many pigs in the jungle. One by one the pigs are brought to a large wooden trough filled with the contents of fresh coconuts. Each pig being given an allowance in accordance to its size.

Inter-Island Trading.—The trading season of the Nicobars opens with the fair weather but usually not before February. This is marked on Chaura by the many short journeys to Teressa to fetch clay, and under every hut women and children are seated the whole day preparing pots. The men gather round their large canoes, up to 70 feet in length, which have been drawn up during the s. w. monsoon and covered with coconut palms to prevent cracking. They prepare for the ceremony of burning the canoe, wearing necklets of young banana leaves, their bodies covered with pig's blood. The canoe is charred all over and then shaped and chipped with adzes and axes to make it lighter in the water. New rattan lashings hold new outriggers in place, and new pennants are fixed on the canoe, the whole accompanied by singing, toddy drinking, and general feasting by the men engaged. After all village canoes are ready, canoe racing takes place in the evenings to watch which the whole of the community line the shore criticizing the merits of the various canoes. At night feasting, dancing, and singing of canoe songs take place. Canoe songs usually have sex as a theme, and are either composed on the island or have been imported from Kar Nikobar. With the coming of the full moon the canoes set out for Kar Nikobar, Teressa, Bompoka, Nankauri and Kachal laden with pots. In return all islanders come to Chaura where they stay for a few days with their friends to trade and feast. As many as ten Kar Nikobar canoes will arrive in the fine weather to purchase pots and canoes, and put up in the empty huts of the *al panam* being fed by the Chaura community.

Culture.—All canoes in the Nicobars, are made either in the islands of the Central or of the Southern group, manufacture being completely "tabued" on Kar Nikobar, Chaura, Teressa and Bompoka. Besides there not being a large number of trees available for the purpose, there is a legend current in Chaura, that a chief once attempted to make a canoe from the wood obtained from the tabued hill, immediately his plantations were destroyed by pigs, his hut burnt down, and misfortune followed him in whatever he undertook.

All canoes made in the Central group are either cut out by parties sent from the various northern islands or are bought direct from the inhabitants. If bought direct the equivalent in pork, lime and general trade goods of 1,000 pair of nuts is given per fathom of canoe, otherwise if personally cut by the Chaura people for instance, a royalty is charged on the tree by the island owners. All Kar Nikobarese must either purchase their canoes through Chaura, or failing to do so must give the equivalent of the price they paid at Nankauri to any Chaura man. Most of the Kar Nicobarese have a friend or agent on Chaura to whom they pay this money, and will stay with him in the event of their visiting the island. Unless this price has been paid a canoe may never visit Chaura and as a pilgrimage to Chaura is as important as the *haj* to Mecca the necessity for it can be realized. The journey of a youth from Kar Nicobar to Chaura by canoe, is the first step in initiation to manhood. The price usually paid for a large racing canoe, if bought on Chaura by the Kar Nicobarese, is roughly Rs. 100, 20 fathoms of cloth, 20 pigs, 100 spoons, 10 large spoons, 3 or 4 empty tin boxes, silver wire, *dahs*, and betel boxes.

Navigation.—Primitive charts and drawings are not existent in the Nicobars. To go north from Nankauri to Chaura, or from Chaura to Kar Nikobar, the North Star or Plough is followed. To go south the Southern Cross is used as a guide. The Nicobarese have names for some of the more prominent stars.

Southern Group.—A few canoes find their way north from the Southern group, but the outturn is not as great as in the Central Group. Most southern canoes are brought from either Kondul or Pulo Milo. To make a canoe in Great Nikobar, permission must be obtained from some friendly tribe of Shom-Pen. These will assist in cutting down the trees and hollowing out the log, and in return will receive a *dah* or two, some cloth and other trade articles. Besides coconuts the chief export of Great Nikobar is cane or rattan. The coast villages of Great Nikobar trade for this with the Shom-Pen, and although the major part falls into the hands of the Chinese traders, a considerable amount goes north to be exchanged for Chaura pots, for Bompoka and Teressa tobacco and for general trade goods and to be used as canoe lashings and in hut building. For one tin of rice two large bundles of cane are obtained, while on Chaura, two large pots are exchanged for one bundle.

Tobacco.—Both Bompoka and Teressa grow excellent tobacco which is valued by the leaf in Chaura, Kar Nikobar and the Central Group. 600 leaves were obtained by the Census party in return for a bag of rice, while on Chaura it is sold at the rate of 40 leaves for one medium sized pot.

Lime.—Throughout the Nicobars the natives are much addicted to the chewing of betel nut from the areca palm mixed with lime, which is responsible for the hideous deformation of the lips and blackened appearance of the teeth. One of the steps of initiation to manhood is the permission given to chew betel nut. Both men and women are very fond of it. Lime is obtained by the burning of *tridacna* and other shells. On Chaura and Teressa this is "tabued", so that the Chaura people resort to Nankauri for their supply of lime while the Teressa people obtain it from the neighbouring island of Bompoka. Owing to the weather of the s. w. monsoon which prevents travel, it is necessary for the Chaura people to lay in a good supply of lime to last over the s. w. monsoon. For this purpose a whole canoe load of men go to Nankauri and will be charged at the rate of one pot per man if they wish to burn lime. While there, they are fed by the local community and in return are expected to help in the general duties of domestic life.

It can be seen how great a part the inter-island trade system plays in the daily life of the Nicobarese. It has an important place in their tribal economic activities which necessitates much work, and considerably engages the minds of the people. Its destruction would create a void in their lives, leaving them without interest or occupation.

5. Religion and Magic.

As the religion, magic, ossuary practices, etc., of Kar Nikobar have been fully described in Appendix A by the Rev. George Stevenson, the contents of this chapter deal purely with the Central and Southern groups which have similarities with the general customs of Kar Nikobar in fundamentals but differ considerably in details.

(*a*) Animism.

The religion of the Nicobars is animistic and consists in the propitiation or compulsion of evil* spirits, which are credited with possessing power to cause sickness, damage property, and generally harm individuals. To discover and frighten away these *iwi* (evil spirits), the Nicobarese erect "scare-devils" which differ considerably in form and number in the Northern, Central and Southern Groups. In the north, they are marked by either simplicity and adherence to two patterns only, while in the Central and Southern groups, they are noticeable by their numbers, elaborateness and general talent shown in their execution.

On Chaura, only two types of scare-devil are found, the first consisting of a man-headed post, with a slightly forked top, hung round with lalang grass and young banana leaves, found in every village clearing, the second an elaborately carved model canoe which is hung up inside the huts. Besides this on building a new hut or clearing a new plantation area, young coconuts are hung up on sticks to propitiate the good spirits or *iwi ka*.

The medium through which the Nicobarese communicate with the spirits is the *menluana* or witch-doctor, who is credited with powers of smelling out evil spirits and driving them away. These people are supposed to possess considerable powers, even to the extent of causing a person to become ill and die. This can however be countered by using the services of some other witch-doctor to counteract the former's evil influences. On all occasions of sickness the witch-doctor is immediately sent for, he smells out the offending evil spirit and drives it away, at the same time making a new scare-devil for the benefit of the patient, this being their peculiar privilege on Chaura.

* *Note by Census Commissioner for India*.—The conclusion is, I think, unavoidable that these spirits are not vague malicious Earth spirits but definitely ancestral spirits in a bad temper. The Chaura "scare-devil" posts to which Mr. Bonington refers seemed to me to take indubitably the form of the soul figure of a defunct ancestor, as the slightly forked top of the head suggested at once a vestigial survival of such a device as the prongs of a Naga soul-post intended to hold the skull in place during the downward transition of the soul into the wooden figure prepared for it [*vide* M. A. S. B. XI (1929), p. 19 and pl. 3]. This view is confirmed by photographs taken by Colonel Sewell of a so-called "scare-devil" on Teressa showing the headgear developed in just such curved hornlike prongs, and by Mr. Bonington's subsequent discovery on Teressa and Bompoka of the figure itself actually bearing the skull (see *Man.*, 1932, 133). Clearly the purpose of the man-headed post is to provide a local lodging for the fretful soul of a troublesome ancestor, while the miniature canoe hung up in the house is probably to provide for his return to the ancestral land overseas.

J. H. H.

At the annual feast of spirits, mention of which is made in the Economic Chapter, the fundamental idea underlying the whole festival is the propitiation of the spirits with pork, toddy, coconuts etc., so that the island may have good trade for the next two years, that their pots may not break, that the plantations may thrive and that general prosperity may come to the community.

Every canoe is supposed to be guarded by *iwi ka*, who are always propitiated when the canoe has been racing or has undertaken a long journey by large pieces of pork, young coconuts and fruit being placed inside it. The pennants which are always found on the bow and the stem of the canoe, besides being there for purposes of ornamentation are supposed to frighten away the evil spirits by their constant flapping in the wind, thus ensuring a successful voyage.

Central and Southern Groups.—The scare-devils of the Central and Southern groups are marked by their variety, and their aggressive theory symbolised in the forms they take. At Nankauri three types are found :—

(1) *Henta.*

(2) *Henta Koi.*

(3) Automatic bull roarers and bamboos with bushes of grass erected in the sea in front of the village.

(*i*) *Henta* are paintings worked on areca spathe screens or boards with considerable skill and a fineness amounting almost to art. On each screen some four to eight pictures are found depicting a man (probably representing an anthropomorphic conception of God, perhaps acquired from missionaries), the sun and the moon, domestic scenes, fishes, etc.

(*ii*) *Henta Koi* are carved wooden figures, animals, birds, crocodiles, fish and human beings, often monstrous and showing considerable skill and talent in creation, found both in the Central and Southern group. These are always aggressive in character so that the evil spirits may be readily scared.

(*iii*) *Automatic bull-roarers.*—These are found in the Central group on the sea front, being attached to trees and poles often 40 to 60 feet in height, and are thus described by Dr. Hutton :—"They are formed of a narrow plank to which a slight screw effect has been given by twisting and cutting so that they revolve in the wind about a central pin. At each end of the plank and facing in opposite directions is a node of bamboo the open end of which is partly blocked with rubber or wax. The result is that the revolving wood produces a very deep and loud booming noise identical with that produced by a bull-roarer" (*Tour notes in the Nicobars*).

When there is illness in the house, the *henta koi* are decorated with young nuts, leaves, lights burning in *tridacna* shells, and these together with young coconuts adorn the interior ; strips of pork and fowls are placed about to propitiate the spirits, their subsequent disappearance being ascribed by the people to consumption by the spirits. In Great Nikobar, *henta koi,* which are on wheels, are trollied about the gardens. Should these be of no avail, the *henta koi* are thrown away and new ones are made.

(*b*) Ancestor Worship and Ossuary Practices.

Burial customs vary greatly throughout the Nicobars. Dr. Hutton, Census Commissioner for India, in his tour notes of August 1930 has propounded a theory as a result of his enquiry. He came to the conclusion that the three forms of burial customs current indicate that the Nicobars are inhabited by two different peoples (*a*) the original inhabitants who buried their dead in or near their houses and dug them up again to fête the skull as is done by the Yimsungr of the Naga Hills ; (*b*) those who came later, to Chaura in the first instance, and brought with them the practice of exposing the dead in canoe coffins, presumably in order that their souls might return by sea to the land of origin further east. In Kar Nikobar there is a compromise between the two customs, the dead being first buried (on the sea shore and not to landward as in Nankauri) after which their bones are thrown into the jungle at the edge of the sea.

Since the Census Commissioner for India's tour, a visit to Teressa and Bompoka, where he did not touch, revealed that on these islands ancestor worship is current, the skull of a revered personage being preserved and placed on a life size wooden body in a sitting posture. The body is hollow and fitted with a door, the remaining bones of the deceased being inside the figure. Not only are the bones of important people kept but all the bones of the deceased family were found kept in little hollowed logs about 1 foot in diameter and 3 ft. long, as many as ten being found in one hut besides the wooden figure of a woman with a skull fixed into the head, who was said to be the mother of the present headman. Ram Kishen the headman of Malakka in Nankauri harbour also keeps the skull of his father in his house but it was ascertained that this custom had been brought from Teressa where Ram Kishen was born.

After death, a man on Teressa is buried with his head to the west and his feet to the East, near the village. "A soul figure in the form of a post"* is then placed over the grave which post is covered with cloths, and general belongings of the deceased such as spears, ornaments, silver wire, spoons, in fact all his personal property as well as the head dress of his wife worn on festive occasions and the skulls of pigs which he had killed and which were hung up in his life time as ornaments within the hut. It is customary for all relatives and friends to attend the funeral and bring pieces of cloth in which to swathe the dead. The body is then buried at sun-down so that no shadows (*i.e.*, spirits) of the attendants shall fall into the grave. This method of interment is common throughout the Central and Southern groups. Bodies of unimportant poor people or orphans are placed in canoes as on Chaura. At Nankauri and in the Southern group it is usual that a great feast should be given in honour of the deceased and that before burial certain expenses should be undertaken to procure silver wire and cloth to wrap around the dead man before interment. Should the children not possess the wherewithal with which to provide these, it is customary for a friend or relative to undergo the expense and in return seize all the landed property and plantations of the children, which circumstances may have prevented their turning into ready money for the funeral. The children then become the dependents of the new owner but completely lose their inheritance.

Beyond the real estate of the individual nothing is left by him after death, as all his portable property is destroyed by being left to rot; on the island of Kar Nikobar the huts too are burnt should the man not die in the *al panam*. One exception there is however to this general rule which makes the Chaura people unique in the Nicobars. They do not destroy any of the personal wealth of an individual but rather preserve it, avoiding the condition found in the rest of the Nicobars, where wealth only stays in the family during the life time of the deceased. By their preservation of all the property of the dead man, they accumulate wealth. On Teressa and Bompoka, after the bones of the relatives have been disinterred, cleaned, preserved, sometimes after many years, which has allowed the people to collect many pigs, a large feast, is held to which the whole community is invited, particularly those individuals who gave presents of cloth for the wrapping up of the corpse, all bones are then thrown into a common ossuary near the sea shore.

Chaura.—On the death of an individual on Chaura, the whole community ceases work for several days, the length of time varying with the importance of the man. Singing, fishing, dancing or any type of communal labour is forbidden. The body is then taken and washed and prepared for burial near the village. In the case of a man, he is buried with the top of his head pointing west and he lies on his back with his legs towards the east. This signifies that he has been on a long journey through life and like the sun constantly crossing the sky reaches the West after much travel; a woman

* Dr. J. H. Hutton.

Dwelling-house on Teressa Island with wooden coffins containing remains of deceased members of the household. Most houses on Teressa and Bompoka Islands contain such coffins.

Life-size wooden figure containing skull and bones of a venerated member of the household.

Canoe burial on Teressa for such as are not members of any household on the island (canoe burial is customary for all on Chaura Island).

OSSUARY PRACTICES ON TERESSA AND BOMPOKA.

From photographs by the author, with acknowledgments to *Man* by the kind permission of which journal they are here republished.

(*N.B.*—They appeared in the *Man* in May 1932—Volume XXXII, 133; the dwelling-house in fig. I was erroneously there described as an ossuary house.)

is always buried in the opposite direction*. As a sign of respect to the deceased it is customary for the whole village to shave their heads, which operation is performed with a sharp *dāh* by the women.

After the corpse has been in the ground for three days, it is disinterred; when this takes place the community may again resume the domestic routine and duties of tribal life. The corpse (*canopa*) is then put into one of the deceased's canoes which has previously been sawn in two, and placed in the ossuary (*laich*) in the jungle near the sea shore on a pair of forked wooden Y shaped posts, from four to six feet from the ground. The body is then left to rot, and in time owing to the breaking up of the canoe, falls to the ground, which is covered with the skulls and bones of many generations and there it stays, the bones being partly consumed by the village pigs. After disinternment a feast is given by the relatives to the whole village community and one of the trees of his coconut plantations, which lapse to his heirs, is ceremonially cut and burnt as a sign of his death. A cut is also made either in the floor or in one of the posts of his hut to mark his death, many huts being found covered with such marks.†

On the death of an individual it is customary to "tabu" his name to the whole community, while in the Central and Southern groups certain forms of food and drink are "tabued" for a time as a sign of respect to the deceased.‡

CHAPTER VII.

General adaptation and effects of contact with civilization.

The comparative isolation of the Nicobars has so far rendered the islanders immune to alien influences. The islands with two exceptions are in a thriving condition. The appointment in recent years of an officer at Kar Nikobar with magisterial powers is tending to break up the tribal system of Government, as it causes the Nicobarese to bring all complaints of a petty nature to the local court, instead of adjusting them within the tribe. The former policy of the Administration, in maintaining a Government Agent without magisterial powers, was to pursue an indirect form of Government through chiefs and elders, and only interfere in cases of violence, and it seems not unlikely that such a policy is sounder than that which involves direct action through British courts.

Education.—For many years past, a Mission has been established in Kar Nikobar, to educate and Christianise young Nicobarese, who are either orphans or who have been placed in the Mission by their parents. This is in a flourishing condition and is a source of much good, especially through a hospital which is kept up with the assistance of Government. The outlook of those who have been brought up in the mission from infancy is however changing and there is danger of this becoming inimical to the welfare of the race, for instance the younger generation thus brought up is inclined to treat tabus as superstitious customs. These tabus are however an important factor in the life of the people. The inter-tribal trade, indeed the whole social and economic life of the Nicobarese, is built up on them.

---

* *Note by Census Commissioner for India.*—This difference in the treatment of male and female corpses seems to me to go some way to confirm my theory of the immigrant nature of the Chaura burial customs. If male navigators from the east landed on Chaura and introduced the canoe and pottery cults, which Chaura controls, and Kar Nikobar tradition (*vide* Census Report of 1921, p. 49) very definitely ascribes the introduction and use of pots to Chaura, what more natural than that the men should be buried so as to face east and the women, who may be supposed to have belonged exclusively to the indigenous inhabitants, laid to face the other way. Similarly one may suppose that disinterment was originally followed by the preservation of the skull and bones in a wooden soul-post, for which treatment canoe exposure was substituted as a result of the immigrant culture. J. H. H.

† "P. Hamilton (1801) reports this to be a vicarious sacrifice of one of the widow's finger joints, inferring a survival of the actual sacrifice of the finger joint". (R. C. Temple.)

‡ There is no tabu to the forms of address adopted by an individual to any of his relatives, maternal, paternal or "in law". An individual is always addressed by name, be she wife, daughter, sister, mother, etc., a father or mother are always addressed by name by their children.

In this connection, it may be noted that experience in the Oceanic Islands of the Pacific where conditions of environment and culture bear a great resemblance to that of the Nicobars, depopulation has been rapid mainly owing to similar causes. "Destruction of tabu and its consequent interests, destroys the sociology of primitive tribes, and their minds are left a perfect blank."*

As the same writer proves in his book, destruction of the interests of the natives of Tahiti caused them to relieve themselves in endless dissipation ending in decimation of the population.

In order not to leave those who are the products of the Mission stranded between two worlds it is therefore of some importance to link up any form of education to their tribal environment and thus inculcate the necessity of keeping up tribal customs, tabus and economics. It is also desirable for their welfare to confine lessons in the missions to part of the day only, allowing the afternoon to be spent by the children at their ordinary occupations at home under the care of their parents or the elders, thus making them fit for their future place in Nicobarese society. The necessary ground and support will then be found against the blighting effect of a superior culture and alien influence which will never meet an inferior culture half-way, but completely destroys it.

Trade.—Although the trader may be classed as a necessary evil, it is possible that he favourably affects the adaptability of the race through a slow process of miscegenation. Prior to the annexation of the islands, the Nicobarese protected himself against the influences of the trader by murdering the crew and plundering the vessel in cases of dispute. It was mainly to put a stop to this that the British Government assumed possession of the Islands at the same time affording the trader complete protection. Left without their natural means of protecting themselves, the Nicobarese, in the course of years, steadily came under the influence of the trader, until it was found in 1915 that the natives were in debt to the extent of 29 millions of nuts, a sum representing the total output of 4 years crops. In several cases, the debtor was found to be without plantations, and was consequently reduced to a state of serfdom, as he worked without remuneration of any nature. To solve the problem Government decided that the traders should be allowed five years grace to collect debts, and at the end of the period closing March 31st 1920 the total debts outstanding were to be written off. At the same time traders were forbidden under the terms of their license to grant further credit to the Nicobarese.

Owing to the peculiar economic position of the Nicobarese whereby his total wealth is vested in the land, and can only be gradually drawn on, it was found necessary that the Assistant Commissioner should allow credit to certain individuals in certain circumstances. The death of the member of a family necessitates the realization of this wealth. Lack of tangible assets necessitates obtaining credit to procure cloth and silver wire for the deceased as well as giving feasts to all comers. In the Central group, should the heirs be unable to provide the necessary provision for the deceased it is usual for some wealthy relative or friend to provide it, but at the same time, all the plantations of the deceased fall to this benefactor, leaving the heirs without support and causing them to assume the position of dependents in his household.

Owing to lack of control in the Southern groups, it is difficult to gauge whether the rule regarding debts is adhered to. The Census party received the impression that the Nicobarese were heavily in debt as no goods were seen in the shops of the trader, but piles of nuts were collecting daily in his yards, giving the impression that the score of past debts had not yet been paid off.

Medical Treatment.—With the exception of the hospital at Kar Nikobar and a compounder at Nankauri, the islands are without medical supervision. Distances prevent cases being brought by canoe to these two stations. Mention has already been made of the presence of yaws on Teressa and Bompoka,

* S. H. Roberts *Population Problems of the Pacific.*

and of syphilis throughout the Southern group. It would be highly beneficial to the people if the services of a sub-Assistant surgeon were procured to visit the islands regularly and keep down the ravages of these diseases which are a danger to the fertility of the race. A small oil-driven schooner costing about Rs. 35,000 would possibly solve the question of inter-island communication, and at the same time enable the Assistant Commissioner and Sub-Assistant Surgeon to visit the islands, and allow of a judicious supervision of the Central and Southern groups which are at the moment in a state of isolation except for the very occasional visits of the Station Steamer.

CHAPTER VIII.

Trade—Exports—Revenue—Expenditure—Possibilities of economic development.

Trade.—1. The Islands are visited annually by a number of sailing vessels coming from Burma, and even from as far as the Gulf of Cutch, the Maldive Islands, and Penang. The average number of nuts exported per year for the last ten years was about eight millions including copra and khalis, of which two and a half millions come from the Central and Southern groups, the remaining five and a half millions from Kar Nikobar. The exports also include betel-nuts, trepang, shell, rattan, cane and occasionally tortoise-shell. A 10 per cent. export tax is levied by Government, the valuation of nuts being 64 to the rupee on the basis that the trader in most cases arranges to collect the nuts himself.

2. *Trepang,* or *bêche de mer*, a sea slug collected, boiled, dried and exported to China where it is a delicacy, varies greatly in the amount exported, and leaves room for increased revenue. The amount exported has varied between 3,000 and 54,000 per annum.

3. *Betel-nut.*—The average number of bags exported yearly is 130, but the annual output varies from sixteen to 240 bags.

4. *Tortoise-shell* is only mentioned in two years, once with 63 pieces, and another time 24 pieces. Undoubtedly tortoise-shell is exported which is not declared.

5. *Edible Birds' Nests.*—No returns are shown of Revenue from edible-birds' nests. They are undoubtedly collected by the Chinese.

6. *Shell.*—Trochus and Turbo shells are only shown to have been exported in two years out of ten, the returns being 100,000 one year and 36,000 another. The royalty on 100,000 shells, at the Port Blair rate of duty of Rs. 60 per ton, would alone yield Rs. 3,000. The shell is regularly collected, as whenever one meets a Chinese sampan, one sees in it trepang and shell.

7. *Rattan* is exported from Great Nikobar to Penang and Burma. The export averages 1,754 bundles per year, varying from *nil* to 4,700 bundles per annum. The value of this in Penang is about Rs. 2 per bundle, and the cost of collection is very small.

8. *Cattle.*—There is scope for cattle-ranching on Nankauri and Trinkat, which abound with wild cattle, if small stockades were erected and the cattle driven into them. In the event of this being started, no doubt lessors would soon be found who would export cattle to the Andamans and elsewhere on a royalty basis.

In the Central and Southern groups trade lies in the hands of the Chinese, a firm in Penang virtually owning the monopoly, keeping shops on all islands. They exercise a good deal of influence, as some of the agents marry influential Nicobarese women for the period of their residence in the Islands.

9. *Revenue.*—The revenue for the last ten years has averaged Rs. 21,000 per annum. There is scope for improvement but at present the movements of the Tahsildar at Nankauri are hampered and he cannot exercise sufficient control on the activities of traders and ships owing to the size of the launch at his disposal. A larger sea-going vessel is necessary. The upkeep and

depreciation of such a vessel would be fully compensated for by an increased revenue. Moreover, the station steamer with its heavy expenditure items of coal and charter would need to call less at the Nicobars, as the vessel would be of a size and cruising radius sufficient to reach Port Blair. Further with such a vessel an Assistant Surgeon could visit the outlying islands and the consequences on the welfare, outlook, and general administration of the people would be untold.

10. *Wrecks.*—During the last decade a cyclone visited the island in 1922, eleven vessels being lost, causing a temporary retardation of trade. The R. I. M. S. "Elphinstone" a comparatively new vessel was lost in Castle Bay, Tilangchong, in 1926.

Distribution and Movement.—The table given below shows the density of population in the various islands :—

Islands.	Area in sq. miles.	Population.	Density per sq. mile.
Kar Nikobar	49	7,492	153
Chaura	3	615	205
Teressa	34	437	13
Bompoka	4	105	26
Kamorta	58	548	9·5
Nankauri	19	201	10·6
Trinkat	6	65	11
Kachal	62	317	5
Great Nikobar	333	300*	0·90
Little Nikobar	58	57	0·98
Kondul	0·5	45	90
Pulo-Milo	0·5	43	86

The density of the population is governed by several factors, the principal one being the proportion of flat coralline soil to the total area of each island. The former alone is suitable for the cultivation of the coconut which forms the staple diet of the people ; with it they feed their domestic animals such as pigs and fowls and the surplus they barter for rice, cloth, silver wire and other luxury articles including among others, spoons, forks and soup ladles which are merely used for decorative purposes and as a visible sign of prosperity.

There are other factors which govern the density to a smaller extent and will be referred to presently. On Kar Nikobar the density is 153 souls to the square mile and there is still a surplus of 5½ million nuts annually for export. It is difficult to estimate the total population which the island is capable of supporting but the first sign of over population will probably be a reduction in the export of coconuts. Chaura which has probably a similar proportion of land suitable for cultivation has no surplus of coconuts for export with a population of 205 souls to the square mile. There is however room for a larger population on most of the islands especially on Kachal Island and on Great Nikobar. At the latter island the abandoned coconut plantations all along the coast are the remaining signs of a larger population in the past. Strife with the Shompen, and probably to a larger extent disease such as yaws, is responsible for the reduction in the population of the coast but this can only be surmised as no data are available earlier than 1911 since when there has been little change. It is however on record that the inhabitants of Laful village had to vacate it owing to repeated attacks by Shompens. The inhabitants of Laful took refuge on the island of Kondul.

* Represents 200 estimated Shompens, 98 enumerated Nicobarese and 2 Chinamen.

DIAGRAM SHOWING MOVEMENT OF POPULATION OF KAR NIKOBAR 1901—1931

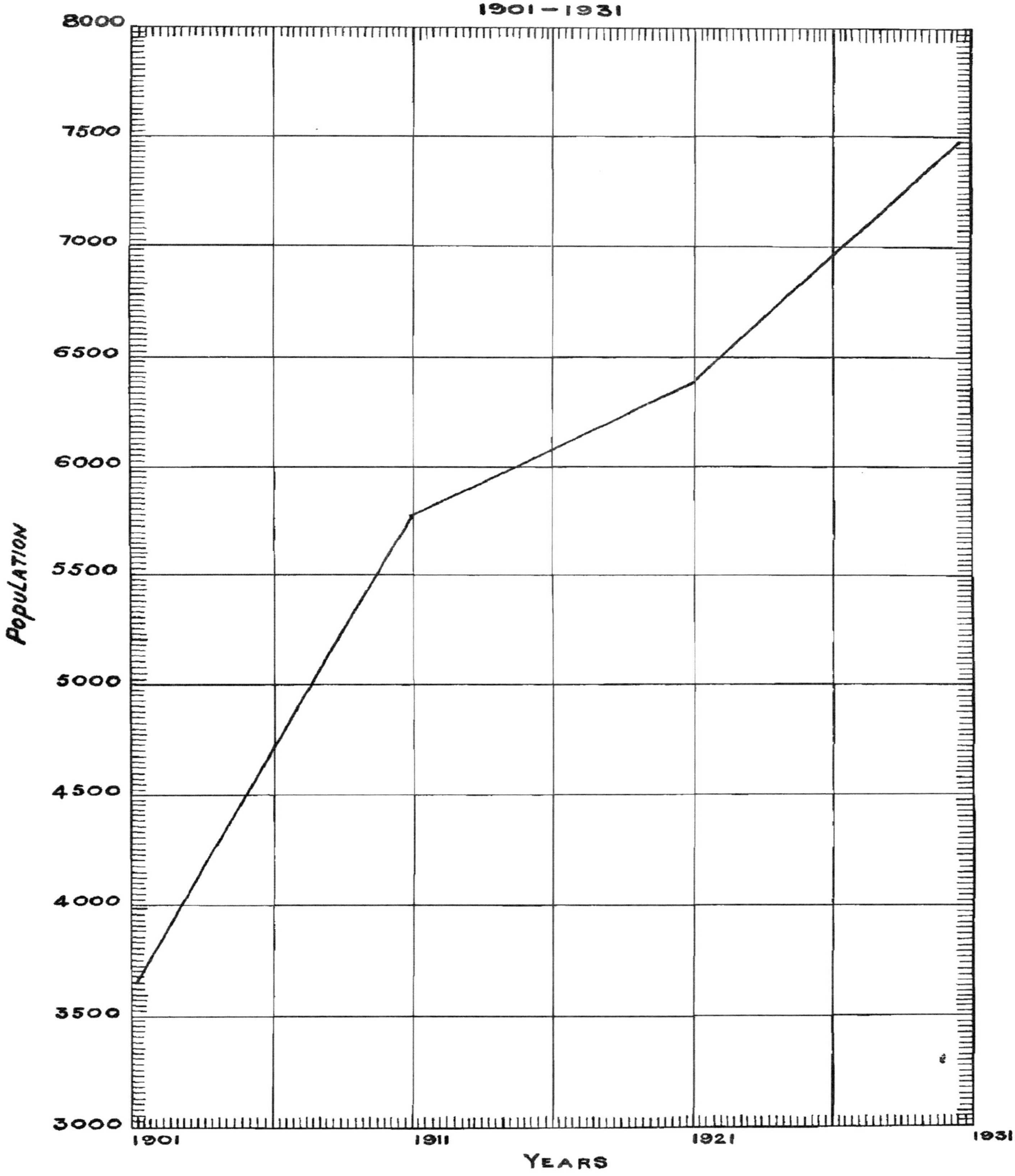

The Census of the Nicobars was taken non-synchronously. The following table shows the distribution and movement of the population on the various islands from 1901 to 1931.

Islands.	Year.	Number of Houses.	Nicobarese. M.	Nicobarese. F.	Nicobarese. Total.	Traders and officials. M.	Traders and officials. F.	Traders and officials. Total.	Grand Total.
Kar Nikobar	1901	748	1,830	1,621	3,451	201	..	201	3,652
	1911	768	2,892	2,658	5,550	237	7	244	5,794
	1921	1,098	3,268	2,819	6,087	250	15	265	6,352
	1931	1,134	3,708	3,474	7,182	242	68	310	7,492
Chaura	1901	130	272	250	522	..	..	..	522
	1911	92	196	152	348	..	..	..	348
	1921	82	141	93	234	..	..	..	234
	1931	142	344	271	615	..	..	..	615
Teressa and Bompoka	1901	130	382	320	702	..	..	..	702
	1911	139	357	299	656	36	..	36	692
	1921	147	332	308	640	39	..	39	679
	1931	131	263	243	506	31	5	36	542
Central Group	1901	235	561	534	1,095	..	..	..	1,095
	1911	225	613	552	1,165	63	3	66	1,231
	1921	220	591	480	1,071	85	..	85	1,156
	1931	301	540	501	1,041	85	5	90	1,131
Shompen (estimated)	1901	..	192	156	348	..	..	..	348
	1911	..	190	185	375	..	..	..	375
	1921	..	190	185	375	..	..	..	375
	1931	..	100	100	200	..	..	..	200
Crews of Vessels enumerated.	1911	6	..	..	..	95	..	95	95
	1921	11	..	..	..	243	..	243	243
	1931	1	..	..	..	15	..	15	15

During the southwest monsoon the indigenous population remain at the place of their permanent residence ; they only start going about to different islands during the fine weather months. As the canoeing season had not started at the time when the Census was taken the above table may be accepted as representing the stationary indigenous population of the various islands while it represents also the number of traders who reside normally on the different islands for trade purposes. It does not represent the number of ships crews correctly because mainly through coincidence, the sailing vessels which frequent these islands were absent at the time on voyages from island to island.

Kar Nikobar.—The indigenous population has increased from 6,087 to 7,182 during the last decade or by over one-sixth whereas it has more than doubled during the last 30 years. It is possible that the first Census was not as correct as the present one which has been taken by educated Nicobarese youths of the Mission under the supervision of the resident Assistant Commissioner. Nevertheless there has been a steady increase during the preceding decades. This increase may be due to the fact that a Sub-Assistant Surgeon has been resident in the island for some years.

The fertility of under 6 per cent. of Nicobarese families following the tribal religion and of over 50 per cent. Nicobarese Christian families was recorded and the following tables show the result.

Proportion of Fertile and Sterile Marriages.

Duration of Marriage Years.

Age of wife at marriage.	0—4 Fertile.	0—4 Sterile.	5—9 Fertile.	5—9 Sterile.	10—14 Fertile.	10—14 Sterile.	15 and over. Fertile.	15 and over. Sterile.
Kar Nikobar.								
14 and under	5	1	..	..	..	..	..	..
14 to 20	47	10	15	1	..	..	1	..
21 to 25	30	2	1	..	..	..	..	..
26 to 30	9	3	..	..	..	..	..	..
31 to 35	4	2	..	..	..	..	..	..
Central Group.								
14 and under	11	1	2	..	1	..	..	..
15 to 20	42	2	6	2	2	5	..	12
21 to 25	30	3	10	1	..	2	..	3
26 to 30	13	13	5	3	1	4	..	..
31 to 35	1	..	..	..	..	..	..	..

Sex of First Born.

Natural Divisions.	Number of females first born.	Percentage of such families where female children predominate.	Number of males first born.	Percentage of such families where male children predominate.	Number of females first born per 1,000 males first born.	Number of slips examined.
Kar Nikobar . .	49	45·4	65	50	754	130
Central Group . .	69	39·6	61	35·56	1,131	174

Size of Families by Religion.

Caste or Religion.	Number of Families.	Total number of children.	Average per family.	Number of children surviving.	Proportion of surviving to thousand born.	Number of families with wife married. 13-14	15-19	20-30	30 and over.
				Kar Nikobar.					
Tribal . . .	92	302	3·2	237	785	3	39	44	6
Church of England .	38	101	2·6	74	733	..	5	30	3
				Central Group.					
Tribal . . .	177	421	2·37	311	739	17*	47*	79*	12*

* Age at marriage not recorded for 22 families.

Unfortunately no figures were recorded of the number of boys and girls separately in the above families. The figures in the preceding table show that in the whole of the Nicobars there are 3,708 males against 3,474 females or an excess of males over females, whereas from table No. VII showing the age groups one may surmise that actually more females are born. Thus in Kar Nikobar in the age group 0-6 there are 1,035 females against 1,007 males and in the Central Group, excluding Chaura where ages were not recorded there are 118 females against 106 males. Although the Nicobarese do not know their age it is extremely likely that the estimate in the lower age group from 0-6 is the most correct of all the groups and may be accepted. Accepting this figure one further arrives at the conclusion that the sex of the first born probably affects the number of each sex born thereafter. For instance on Kar Nikobar where the females in the lower group only exceed the males in the same group by about 3 per cent. only 754 females are born to 1,000 males, whereas in the Central Group the excess of females of the same age to male is 13 per cent. and 1,131 females are first born to 1,000 males. These figures are however not analogous ; in one case they are of a percentage of the population and in the other for the whole population.

These tables further bring out that the average number of children born per family of tribal religion is 3·2 whereas only 2·6 are born in those families which have been converted to Christianity and the number of surviving children is about 2·6 in the former case against 1·9 in the latter. While final conclusions cannot be drawn from these figures because the wives in Christian families have married on an average at a higher age and because of the introduction of Christianity only during the last few decades, the figures are perhaps significant and similar data in the future will require a careful analysis. With a survival rate of 1·9 per family the population would decrease. It must be taken into consideration that the introduction of Christianity has been held by some people to have had a similar effect in the Pacific Islands, various theories being ascribed to it. It may be that sex restraint of unmarried people which is universally insisted on by Christian missionaries affects a people who have been accustomed to unrestricted sexual intercourse and natural selection for perhaps thousands of years. Isolated cases are on record in the Nicobars where such restraint has created abnormal tendencies.

DIAGRAM SHOWING APPARENT MOVEMENT OF POPULATION

OF

CHAURA — TERESSA & BOMPOKA — CENTRAL GROUP — SOUTHERN GROUP

1901 – 1931

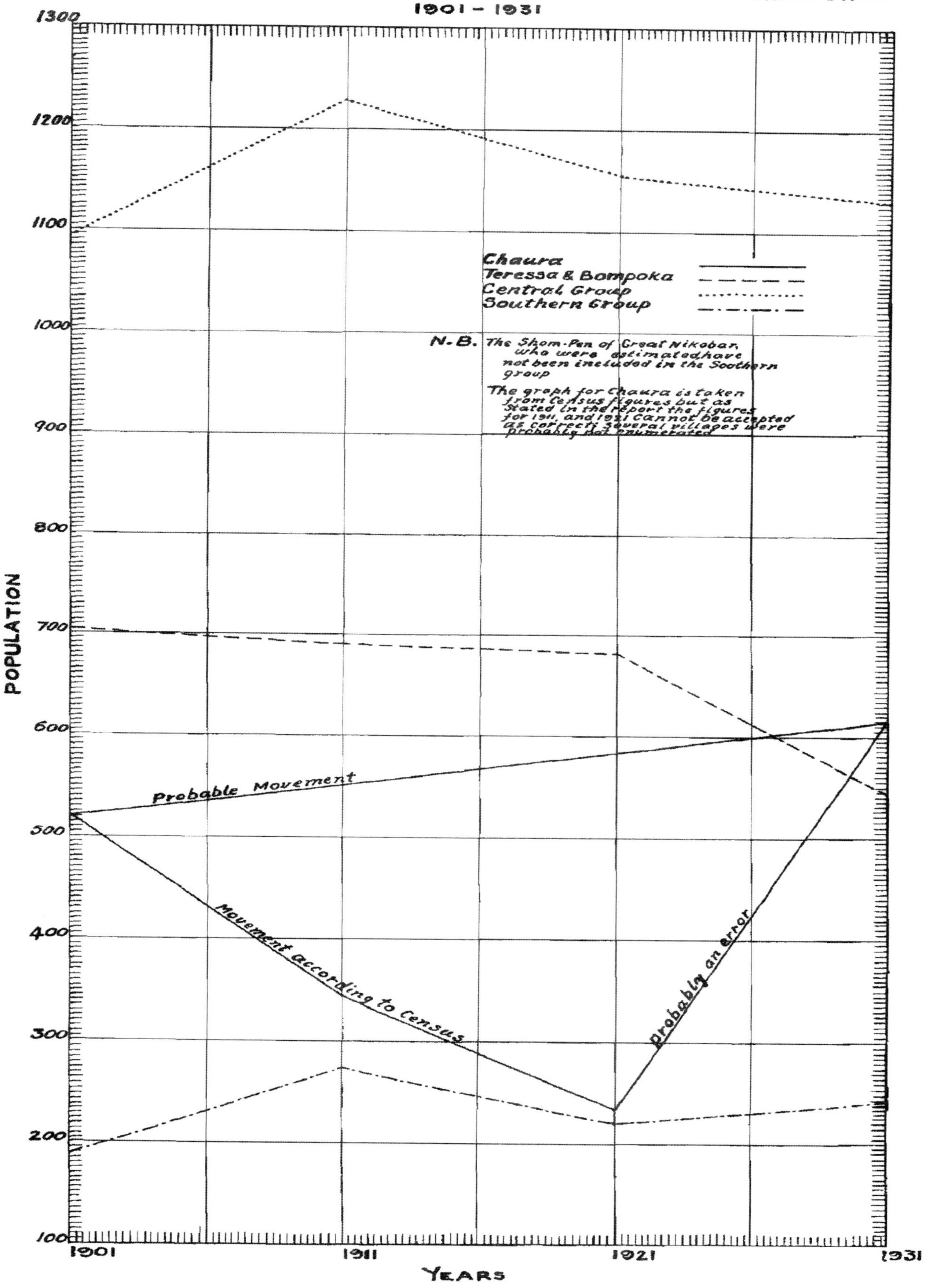

Chaura.—The Census figures show an increase from 234 to 615. It is not however believed that the figures of the last census were correct. Many of the Chaura men are absent from the island during a greater part of the fine weather season when they go trading to other islands or fetch clay from Teressa but this cannot be the explanation of the discrepancy in figures because only 93 females were shown on the last census against 271 in the present one and very few females leave the island even for temporary journeys. Mr. Lowis took the last Census and he thinks it possible that one or two of the villages were left out. The Chaura people have in the past shown great reluctance to allow strangers on their island and it is possible that the previous census party was not taken to one or two villages. The difference in huts, 142 against 82 of the previous census makes this very probable. The 1901 Census figures show 522 inhabitants and accepting these figures as correct there has been a small increase in the population.

Teressa and Bompoka.—There has been a steady decline in the population since 1901 when it stood at 702. Only 506 were found in 1931 amounting to a reduction of about 28 per cent. During the last decade the reduction has been 21 per cent. A casual visit to the islands convinces one that the decrease in population is entirely due to the prevalence of yaws. In Bengala village, the only one visited by the Superintendent of Census personally, dead and dying were found in several houses and it was pitiful to see so much suffering and so many disfigured. Several men were ashamed to show their faces. The islands have not been visited for many years except very occasionally by the Tahsildar. By the favour of the Senior Medical Officer, Dr. T. V. Damodharam Naidu accompanied the Superintendent of Census Operations and he diagnosed the disease while later Major D'Souza himself visited the island, and inoculated a number of sufferers. Unfortunately the S. S. "Shahjehan" could only stay at Teressa for a few hours so that only one village could be visited. Yaws is however prevalent throughout the Central Groups and a thorough investigation and treatment is necessary to eradicate the disease. This can only be done if special communication is provided for 2 or 3 months during the fine weather.

The Central Groups.—This includes Kachal, Kamorta, Nankauri, and Trinkat. The population shows a slight decline, that is from 1,071 in 1921 to 1,041 in 1931. Nothing very much is known of the condition of the people. The Census was taken by the Tahsildar of Nankauri. Cases of yaws were however found in Nankauri. It is difficult for the Tahsildar to visit the various islands owing to lack of communication. The steam cutter which is at his disposal is not sufficiently seaworthy to leave Nankauri harbour at most times of the year and in any case her steaming radius is very small.

The fertility tables of the various islands of the Central Group were combined for the whole group including Kamorta, Trinkat, Nankauri, Katchal, Chaura and Teressa and Bompoka. About 38 per cent. of the total families were examined and the average number of children born per family amounted to 2·37 while the number of children surviving per family amounted to less than 1·8 only or just a little less than the average of the survivals among children of Christian families on Kar Nikobar.

Southern Groups.—There is a slight increase of the population of the Southern Group, *i.e.*, from 216 to 240. A short visit certainly indicated that disease was less prevalent than in the Central Group.

Of the Shompen sufficient is not known to give an even nearly accurate estimate. The present estimate of 200 gives a reduced figure and is made on hearsay. The coastal population gave the names of the people in 5 different septs said to inhabit the banks of the three rivers Galatea, Alexandra and Dagmar and 2 inland septs one near Laful and the other between Galatea river and Laful, and only the number of population thus given has been accepted. The writer has explored considerable portions of the island and has not come across any other septs. It is however possible that the estimate is too low.

Nicobar Islands.

Total Population	10,240	
Tribal—		
(*a*) Shompen	200	1·95%
(*b*) Other Tribal Nicobarese	9,281	90·63%
Christians	338	3·30%
Muslims	285	2·78%
Confucians	111	1·08%

Besides these are 15 Hindus and 10 Buddhists who have not been indicated by colour.

The following are the principal mother tongues of the population of the Nicobars :—

Language.	Number of persons.	Percentage to the total population.
Nicobarese	9,885	96·53%
Others	355	3·46%

The indigenous languages of the Nicobars have been shown as one language. There are however distinct differences in dialect in the various groups, (Kar Nikobar, the Central Groups and the Southern Group) while the language of the Shompen differs altogether and is only understood by the Shompen and a few Great Nikobar coastal Nicobarese. The Nicobarese have a considerable gift for acquiring foreign languages and the following languages thus acquired from traders who visit the islands are recorded against the different groups :—

Island Groups.	Number of Nicobarese who can speak Hindi.	Number of Nicobarese who can speak Malay.	Number of Nicobarese who can speak Burmese.
Kar Nikobar	559	..	157
Central Group	5	372	1
Teressa and Bompoka	..	387	..
Southern Group	..	34	

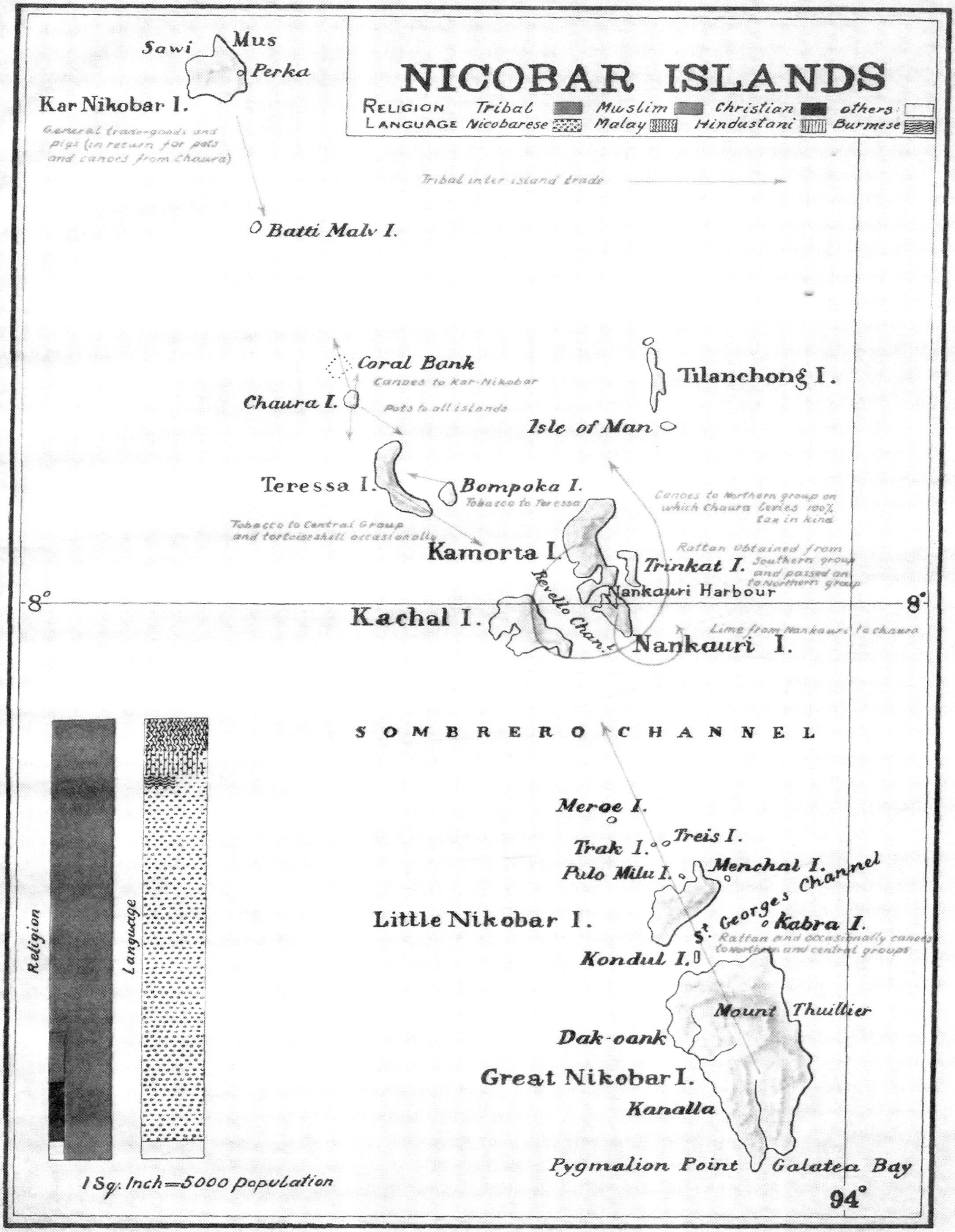

Reg. No. 2519. E. 31. 850.

Helio. S.I.O Calcutta.

APPENDIX A.

The Shom-Pen of Great Nikobar.

Contact with the Shom-Pen or inland tribe of Great Nikobar has been of an extremely desultory nature. With the exception of Mr. C. W. B. Anderson's exploration of Great Nikobar in 1905, no prolonged stay has ever been made among the people. Visits have always been short, limited to a day or two, and in reality little is known of their customs and habits, leaving an important field of research for the anthropologist of the future.

History.—The existence of an inland tribe in Great Nikobar was first mentioned by Pastor Rosen, a Danish missionary in 1831. In 1846 Admiral Steen Bille paid the first recorded visit. When the islands were annexed by the British Government Mr. de Roepstorff, officer in charge, paid three visits, finding a temporary encampment, and was accompanied on one occasion in 1881 by the Chief Commissioner, Colonel Cadell. Mr. Man first visited them in 1884 and was subsequently much in contact with them. His researches together with those of Boden Kloss and Anderson afford the only available data.

The Shom-Pen are divided into a number of small communities or septs, each sept living within its own territory and rarely leaving it except when bent on a raiding expedition. Constant feuds have been maintained for generations between the coast people and these inland tribes, and have resulted in the evacuation of the East Coast of Great Nikobar by the Nicobarese. Ethnologically the Shom-Pen are a problem. They differ from the coast tribes both racially and linguistically, and among themselves present several distinct types. The researches of Boden Kloss show a dark skinned people with curly or wavy hair, indicating a Malay type with possible pre-Dravidian miscegenation. Man holds they were in no way allied to Negritos, being fairer than Malays. Observations made by the Census party, which encountered a village community on the Alexandra River, found no signs of curly or wavy hair, but a dark-skinned people, with features among adults reminiscent of the North American Indian, and features of young boys suggestive of possible pre-Dravidian affinities. Again on the Dagmar River, fair Shom-Pen were found with curly hair.

Concerning the internal organization of the Shom-Pen very little is known, but as far as could be judged the same communal spirit exists which is so marked among the other Nicobarese. In their habits they are as nomadic as the Andamanese and move from one place to another directly the supplies of game and fruit in their vicinity are exhausted ; yet they keep strictly within the territories of their sept.

Habitations.—Huts are of a far more primitive and coarser type than those found in the rest of the Nicobars. There are two species. The first a lean-to of the pent roof type, raised three or four feet from the ground and thatched with long leaves of the areca palm. These are only constructed when a stay of a short nature is intended. The second, the permanent nature, consists of an erection on posts some eight or nine feet from the ground lecess to which is obtained by means of a ladder. The village community found on the Alexano a river had thatched theirs with long leaves of the areca palm, but Man mentions in his monograph on the Shom-Pen that roofing is often made of the spathe of the bark of the *areca augusta*. In 1905 Anderson noticed that the sites for permanent habitation were always well chosen for defensive purposes and were surrounded by a slight stockade, which fact affords evidence of inter-sept warfare among the Shom-Pen who would never have worried about the possibilities of an attack by the coastal Nicobarese on the inaccessible villages in the interior. A third type of hut is also found built in trees and was noticed on the Dagmar river and by Boden Kloss on the Galathea River,

There is no segregation of sexes in the huts or at meal times. Within the huts reed mats were observed and short lengths of wood which probably served as pillows. All cooking is done either within the hut or in a neighbouring shelter constructed for the purpose. The cooking pot is made of stout bark, later identified by Dr. King as *Calophyllene*. Lengths of bamboo (*bambusa gigantia*) with pierced inter-nodes are used for the storage of water. Beneath the hut a species of fencing is often erected to act as a cage for any wild pig captured, but of recent years owing to greater contact with the coastal people, domestic pig and dogs have found their way into Shom-Pen encampments.

["The family cooking pot of the Shom-Pen is ingeniously constructed from large strips of bark of two distinct kinds. One strip is folded lengthwise with the rough surfaces outwards to form a large trough, the folded ends being inserted into split stakes. The sides are then built up with the other strips, in pairs, and the open ends also inserted into split stakes, and the whole tightly bound, strips of cane being passed round from stake to stake, along the overlapping edges as well. The stakes are driven into the ground such a distance apart as to cause a bulge in the bark. The edges are bound with the leaves of *sterculia*. A small cane basket inserted into the bottom of the vessel completes the structure and serves the purpose of more easily lifting out the contents when cooked,"—C. W. B. Anderson *Exploration of Great Nicobar*, 1905.]

Dress.—Both men and women are now in possession of loin-cloths obtained from the trader through the coast inhabitants, but formerly both sexes wore a species of bark-cloth around the loins. The bark of '*celtis vestimentaria*' is obtained and subjected to repeated blows with a large stick. The substance is then immersed continually in water till all the hard substances are removed. When thoroughly pliable, it is stretched out to dry, presenting a fine tissue.

The length of the bark used by the women as a skirt is from 6 ft. to 8 ft. long and from 2 ft. to 2¼ ft. broad—(*Women of the Mintira Gunong Burmen*, Jour. Indian Archipelago, 1847, page 253). The holes of the ear are pierced and enormously distended, as strips of bamboos as much as 5" in circumference are inserted, and act as a receptacle for betel leaf and other odds and ends. Bead necklets and armlets are also much worn. A spathe band or piece of cloth is bound round the head to keep the hair in position.

Cultivation.—Cultivation is of an extremely crude and primitive type, reminiscent of that of the Tapiros of New Guinea. A sharp stake with the point hardened in the fire, serves as the sole agricultural implement.* Yams, edible roots, a coconut tree or two, pandanus, areca and plantain trees are planted, small fences being erected around the yams and edible roots to protect them from the depredations of both wild and tame pig. Betel is much chewed by both sexes, causing a prognathic deformation and blackening of the teeth. Lime is obtained by burning shells collected on the sea-shore.

Death.—The dead are buried in a sitting posture with the hands lashed together near the mouth in which pulp of pandanus is placed. The body is not subsequently disinterred as among other Nicobarese. According to Anderson, a year later a large feast accompanied by dancing is held, lasting some six to eight days to which all neighbouring septs are invited. The camp is immediately deserted and never occupied again, all septs being informed of the fact, it is however re-visited so that any ripe fruit from the plantations may be collected.

Marriage.—Very little is known about customs relating to marriage, religion and death. Anderson mentions the existence of a '*meluana*' or witch doctor, which he ascribes to the influence of the coast people. Marriage as a rule is arranged by the parents, and the girl is handed over to the parents-in-law after she is weaned. This lends great support to information gathered by the Census party that the Shom-Pen sell their children to the coast people for a dah and three fathoms of cloth per child. The child grows up with the family but assumes the position of a servant and in most cases subsequently marries into the family.

Canoes.—The Shom-Pen have small canoes made by themselves from 6 to 10 ft. in length; but they only use them on the rivers and never venture out to sea. Occasionally they help the coast people in the construction of a canoe. The canoes are roughly made possessing neither the technique nor the finish of those made by the coast people.

Weapons.—Neither the bow nor the Nicobarese cross-bow is known among the Shom-Pen. The only weapon is a wooden pointed spear (*hin-yuan*) of areca wood which is notched on the upper parts to serve as barbs. Of late years iron has been obtained to make these spear heads, and dahs are also obtained by trading. The chief diet of the Shom-Pen is turtle, snakes, frogs, birds, lizards, crocodiles, fresh-water fish, shell-fish, honey, yams, bulbs of the *caladium*, spathes of the areca, fruit of the *nipa* palm, plantain, pandanus, coconut and above all wild pig. Pigs are either staked and speared or hunted down with dogs, while birds such as the megapod are snared. Fish are either speared or caught by means of a network of bamboo placed across the stream at low tide, enabling the fish to be easily secured. Another very common method is to poison the water with the bruised bark of a forest climber, thus stupefying the fish. Anderson was told that bird-lime was used for catching birds.

Relations with the Coast tribes.—As has been said the constant feuds between the Shom-Pen and the coast tribes have caused the latter to evacuate the east coast of Great Nikobar; of recent years however no attacks have come to the notice of the Administration, although the inland tribes are to be trusted at no time. The aggressive party were always the Shom-Pen who came to the coast in search of iron and cloth, attacking any village when the menfolk were away, killing the remaining inhabitants, and plundering the huts. Each village is however on friendly terms with some sept of the Shom-Pen with whom they barter for rattan and obtain permission to make canoes in the jungle.

In this they are often helped by the inland sept who expect both payment for their labours and an extra present for the permission to make the canoe, this present being a form of royalty. The rattan is purchased in bundles from the Shom-Pen and forms the chief export of Great Nikobar not only to the rest of the Nicobars but to Penang and Singapore where it commands a high price. The practice of selling their children has caused the tribe to come much more in contact with the coast people of recent years, and it is not unusual to find several Shom-Pen at Kondul and in the coast villages of Great Nikobar. The children appeared to be quite happy and beyond having to perform numerous domestic duties are treated as one of the family. There is however a danger of their being exploited, as the Chinese captain of a junk at Nankauri said he could easily procure them.

Conclusion.—So far there is very little known either of the economic prospects of Great Nikobar or of the anthropology of its inland tribe. An untouched field of research awaits the future investigator, who, by staying among the people for many months, might be able to learn their language and record a great deal of valuable anthropological data.

**Note by Census Commissioner for India.*—This is also the case with some of the (?) proto-Australoid tribes in the hills of Southern India, whose sole implement is a digging stick with its point hardened in the fire.—J. H. H.

APPENDIX B.

Religion of Kar Nikobar.

With the exception of a small body of Christians and some Moslems and Buddhists the people of Kar Nicobar are animists.

People who write about them tend to say that they have no conception of a Supreme Being, but *during one of their festivals in which the witch-doctors to-miluo-no, who deal with the spirits* of the dead and the evil spirits, take no part at all unless as laymen. On the day of "taking food", *kia-la*, in all the houses offerings of food in pots, coconuts and fruits of several kinds are hung up and the people make supplication: "Let our houses be always supplied with plenty to eat; let us have many things to eat from other villages; let there come new girls to our villages; grant us to be happy".

Their conception of a Supreme Being may be very vague and undefined, but this supplication seems to be addressed to some being or beings apart from the spirits of the dead and the evil spirits and who supposedly can hear prayer.*

Origin of the Kar Nicobarese.—What might be called the Kar Nicobarese Creation Legend is as follows: "There was once a great flood in the land and all the surface of the earth was covered by water. One man was lucky enough to swim to a big tree which was not entirely covered by the water. He lived among its branches until the floods went down, existing on coconuts and dead animals that were floating by his tree. When the waters were dried up he found no other living human being at all, but in the branches of another tree he found a bitch *with her ear spiked to the tree by a great thorn. He climbed up the tree, released the animal* and made her his wife. They lived together and had offspring that were human. So in these parts the people copy the dog in wearing the *ki-sat* (a very narrow loin-cloth with the ends hanging down behind) for it has tails hanging down like dog's tail. The head-dress worn by the man (*ta-chokla*—a band made of the spathe of the betel-palm with its ends crossed) is symbolic of the ears of their first mother and all dogs are treated kindly and are never beaten".

There is hardly much reason to suggest that this tale is a remnant of former missionary teaching; it is more likely a form of the Flood legend which is common over Indonesia.

NOTE.—Prehistoric Egyptian chiefs sometimes wore as a war dress a short kilt and a tail, said by the British Museum to be a jackal's tail.

The *Khamis* in the Arakan District of Burma have villages in the plains opposite Kyauktaw and elsewhere but they are a timid naked people and the population fled from the only village I entered as soon as they saw me. Khami women wear only a very short skirt and a triangular bit of cloth over the left breast—the breast specially dedicated to the husband. The men wear nothing but a quite inadequate waistband of very narrow cloth, and are said to regard nakedness as a sign of manhood. The ends of the loin-cloth hang down before and behind like tails and for this reason the Arakanese have corrupted the name. Khami into Kwe-mi (Dog's tail). From *A Burmese Wonderland*, C. M. Enriquez.

The Mono-Alu of the Solomons have a tale of a chief who married a bitch's daughter. The Angami Nagas have a story of descent from a white dog and a woman who floated away on a raft, while according to Purchas's *Pilgrimage* the Peguans ascribe their origin to a dog and a China-woman who escaped shipwreck. The Ao-Nagas again have a dog clan, the Azukamr, who claim relationship with and the characteristics of dogs. (J. H. Hutton.)

Spirits.—The Kar Nicobarese have an intense belief in evil spirits *sio-ta-choich*, who are the unseen enemies of mankind. They never bring happiness or prosperity but only sickness and misfortune of all kinds.

The spirits of the dead *ma-a-la-ha* are distinguished from these evil spirits. The spirits of the dead maintain to a great extent the kindly temperament that they had in life and are ready to do good service to those who are still alive. Many of them, however, miss the friends and companions of their life on earth and this desire for their company will cause them to bring sickness to these friends so that they too may die and join the spirits in the spirits' world. So this friendly intentioned sickness has to be guarded against as well as the sickness caused by the evil spirits.

When a Kar Nicobarese dies his spirit is seized by the evil spirits and is carried about with great rejoicing.

The spirits of the dead then intervene and there is a struggle for the dead man's spirit. The struggle always ends in the victory of the spirits of the dead, who rescue their fellow and take him away to the Spirit world, a place, *El-ki-tel-ko-re*, which means "Mid-air", and there he lives on, very much as he did when alive on the earth.

Though these spirits of the dead live in "Mid-air", they can localize themselves and every village in Kar Nicobar has a place near it—avoided by all except the witch doctors called *panam-sio* (the place of the spirits) and there the witch doctors claim that they can meet and converse with the departed spirits.

Every year in July after the driving away of the evil spirits from the island the living provide food and clothing for the spirits of their relatives. When a man dies his belongings should also be destroyed as he will need them in the spirit-world, but often a pretence at doing this is enough.

*All the same it is probably a spell rather than a prayer, and magic rather than religion.

J. H. H.

The Driving away of the Evil Spirits.—Twice a year, in July and in November, the evil spirits are driven out of the villages.

During the day bamboos are got ready and decorated with bunches of leaves tied on them and all are daubed with soot and red paint. In the evening these are erected on the beach (*el panam*) and after sunset the people meet in the "Village Hall" and sing *ma-a-fai* songs; the lights are turned down and shaded with the spathe of the giant palm, because the evil spirits dread the light. The witch doctors then spear the devils with their magic spears made of a light, brittle wood—the devils squirm and squeak, making a noise such as one could make with a leaf between one's lips and drawing in one's breath. The captured spirits are tied up with a kind of creeper common in the island. The people help the witch doctors in wrestling and capturing the spirits, after these are speared. This goes on for three nights, if necessary, until all the spirits possible are captured, and on the fourth evening the doctors go round all the houses in the village, and those on *el-panam*, spearing and capturing until no more can be caught. Meanwhile by day rafts have been got ready by the young men and women, as many in number as will be necessary to ship away the captured spirits. These rafts are equipped with sails of palm-leaves, dry palm leaf torches and bunches of evil spirit expelling leaves.

NOTE.—The Malays, who regard diseases as caused by spirits have the custom of setting a boat afloat sometimes with a man in charge and loaded with eatables apparently to take away the disease, and in Borneo the soul of the dead with an effigy of the dead man, and formerly sometimes a female slave fastened to the raft, is set afloat, while in Oceania generally the custom appears sporadically, sometimes having taken the form of sending the embalmed body of the dead adrift in a canoe. This again is clearly associated with the use of canoe coffins and inasmuch as it is frequently the spirits of the dead who cause the disease these treatments of evil spirits and of the ghosts or souls of the dead are probably intimately connected.—J. H. H.

The tied-up spirits are placed on the rafts, and each raft is put in charge of a spirit of the dead, represented by a leaf-made figure about four feet high. The rafts are towed out beyond the breaking surf, those engaged in this task keeping the spirit-expelling leaves in their hands, and finally with great rejoicing the rafts are carried off by wind and tide.

The bamboos are then taken down and any evil spirits that happen to have been overlooked before are speared and thrown into the sea.

After this follow the feasts for the dead, referred to above. This feeding and clothing of the departed spirits is done partly because they will need these things in the spirit world and partly because they have helped in the driving away of the evil spirits.

Another expulsion of the evil spirits takes place in November but this time they are thrown into the sea only and not placed on rafts, as the wind is from the north-east, neither is there any feast for the dead.

At other times when an accident happens such as a man falling from a coco-palm and killing himself, the evil spirits in the place of the accident are driven down to the beach and deported or thrown into the sea.

Marriage, Birth, etc.—There is no marriage ceremony. The young man who desires to marry a girl makes friends with her family, helps her in her daily work and sleeps for a time in whatever house she may occupy.

During the night he seeks the girl, who will be sleeping among other girls, and by blowing on the lighted end of a cigarette he obtains light enough to discriminate. If the girl does not care for him she will resist with blows and scratches.

This will continue for several nights until, if she is willing to have him for a husband, she yields herself. When they begin living as man and wife both live with the girl's parents and he works for them. No dowry is given and no marriage settlements made. Formerly it was a crime punishable by death for either to commit adultery, but now a fine of three pigs is the penalty.

When the wife is pregnant—during the last two months—both parents must abstain from certain foods and certain kinds of actions as also for some time after birth. When the mother-to-be goes down to a birth-house on *el-panam* her husband goes with her. The birth of a child must take place in a birth-house for if it took place in a ceremonially clean house, that house would have to be destroyed.

When the young mothers living on *el-panam* (the parents of a child do not usually go back to their houses until three months after its birth) hear that the labour pains have come, they will arrive to massage the woman and the inexperienced will be taught the art of midwifery by the experienced. If the delivery is delayed it means that the child is being held back by something closed or knotted about the house and though care has been taken beforehand to see that no belongings of the parents are boxed up or knotted in any way, a new search is made and care is taken that the door of the hut and the lids of any boxes are left open so that the delivery of the child may not be hampered in any way. The men will lift up the racing canoes of the village an inch or two and let them down again, and if there are any logs or heavy articles lying about they will turn them over.

While the woman is pregnant neither she nor her husband must make anything tight, such as nailing a board or tying knots, for fear the spirit of the unborn child should get fastened up in these and delivery be rendered impossible.

After the birth of the child the mother and baby are rubbed over with saffron and their clothes dyed with it. The mother is for some time ceremonially unclean and may not feed herself nor touch her food with her fingers.

The husband looks after the mother, supplying all her needs and he may not do any heavy work nor walk in the sun nor bathe in the sea until the child is a month old, so that it may not get sick.

Another reason for his not walking in the sun is given also. If the child is born light-skinned the husband may not go out in the sun without an umbrella, lest the child's skin should become dark.

When the child is two or three months old it is well rubbed over with fowl's blood mixed with certain crushed leaves supplied by a witch doctor or other experienced person and also with the crushed shells of young coconuts and saffron. This is repeated monthly until the child can walk.

When the baby is three months, and in some cases not till it is six months old, the parents and child will return to their village but they must leave behind them all cooking pots, clothing, mats, etc., which they have been using for these are ceremonially unclean and will render unclean any house they are brought into.

The child's first food, other than its mother's milk, will be the tender part of the green coconut—the part nearest the shell. This is mixed with pandanus paste and warmed over a fire. It may not eat fish until it is over five years old.

If there are in the parents' opinion too many children in the family they will often give one away to another husband and wife who have too few children or are childless. Children handed over in this way are rarely claimed again.

If twins were born one of the twins used to be killed. A child born deformed was put to death also, as births of this kind (twins or deformities) were regarded as entirely abnormal, in fact contrary to nature. This is not done now, but the parents and those in attendance are horrified when such births take place.

The child, if a boy, as he grows up looks forward to the time when he can go to Chaura. This happens usually about the age of six or seven, and when he has done this he has won his spurs and can regard himself as a man.

Death and Burial, etc.—Death is feared among the Kar Nicobarese and even the word will not be mentioned. When a man is about to die he is usually brought to a "Death house" on the beach (*el-panam*) and there is left to die, the leaves which are said to keep away evil spirits having been placed around his bed.

When he is dead each group of houses in his village provides two yards of red cotton cloth and two yards of white in which the corpse is wrapped after having been washed with coconut water. If the deceased is wealthy he may be adorned with silver wire and necklaces of coins. When the time for the funeral comes the corpse is lifted by two men and brought down the ladder in as upright a position as possible to the relatives waiting below, where it is bound to pieces of old canoe to make it rigid and easier to carry to burial. The relatives weep and wail and pretend not to want the corpse buried but brought back to his own house in the village. The rest of the community wish it to be buried, so there is a struggle about the corpse (which sometimes suffers in the struggle), the relatives trying to take it towards the village, the others towards the burial ground.

It never reaches the village partly because those for burying are in the majority and also because if brought into the village it would render it ceremonially unclean.

When the burial ground, also on *el-panam*, is reached the corpse is put into the grave prepared for it, the wrappings over the region of the heart of the deceased are pulled aside and chickens and sometimes young pigs are stabbed and the blood allowed to drip on the body over the heart of the deceased.

These are then thrown into the grave and buried with the corpse. All the bedding, wraps, etc., used by the deceased while sick are burned and vessels, etc., are broken in pieces and the ashes and pieces are thrown into the sea.

A feast is then provided by the people living in the same group of houses as the deceased used to live in. The mourners rest next day and after a certain number of days—there seems to be no special number of days except that the number must be odd not even, there is a purification of the deceased and a chicken is burnt over the grave. Until this ceremony has been performed the mourners must not sing or laugh or dance, nor eat any fruit except coconut and bread-fruit (pandanus). Those who have handled the corpse are unclean for a month or two and may not touch their food with their fingers or hands, though they may use a small skewer. They may not do any "clean" work, such as that concerned with the preparation of food or building, nor may they enter any house. When this period of uncleanness is over they may return to their work and houses without any purification ceremony.

At the purification festival mentioned above the memorial post of the deceased is set up. This is a round log about a foot in diameter buried until about two to three feet of it is above the ground. A short distance from the top there is a hole cut through and while the feast is being kept a stick is put through the hole and spoons and forks are hung on the stick. These spoons and forks are removed later, but sometimes other spoons and coins are nailed on the post and those are not removed. There is a feast also at this purification festival held generally in the "Village Hall" after sunset, and a basket of pork is provided for the deceased and hung up for the night in the door of the house. Next morning the basket and its contents are thrown into the sea and the memorial post is set over the grave. Again there is a feast in the village hall in the morning and this finishes the whole burial ceremony.

Nowadays some of the richer people have coffins for their dead relatives, an imitation of European custom and sometimes the body is carried to the burial ground in a canoe, which is said to be an old custom at the burial of rich people. The canoe is afterwards cut up and broken to pieces.

After the burial ceremony the name of the deceased is not mentioned and if another man in the same village has the same name as deceased he will change it, or if the deceased bore a name like fire or water the relatives will henceforth use a synonym for this when mentioning it.

Feast for the Dead.—Once in 3 or 4 years a feast for the departed is held in a village. The villagers some ten months beforehand have agreed on the time about which it will be held and preliminary invitations are sent out to other villages. After these invitations are sent out, a tree of about 60 feet high is cut down and holes are bored at intervals all along the stem after the branches have been removed, and pegs are driven into the holes. When this has been done the post is set up in an arranged spot, with posts fixed alongside it, to which it is tied in order to steady it. A man climbs the post with the end of a rope in his hand. Fruit, baskets of pork, etc., are drawn up by this rope and fastened on the pegs, until sometimes there is a great array of food.

If the villagers are poor this post may not be set up. Bamboo cages able to hold about a dozen pigs are made in the village about the same time. Canoes are decorated and set up in front of their own houses. The graveyard on *el-panam* and part of the beach around it are tidied up and kept tidy. All this takes about three months and during that time no pigs may be killed in the village. Then the date is definitely fixed and special invitations are sent out saying that on the day after tomorrow the houses will be decorated, on the third day the pigs will be put into the cages and on the fourth day they will be killed.

This date may fall at any time of the year except that for convenience's sake the wet season is avoided and the months of November and December are chosen which are cold.

Pigs are brought into the village from outside having their legs tied to a pole and they are carried round the village before being put into the cages.

Soon after the special invitations are sent out the nearest visitors begin to arrive. These visitors will dance all night by the group of houses where the post with the food on it has been erected. Next morning the post is cut down and the food, putrid or fresh, is thrown into the jungle. A pig is taken and sacrificed and the intestines and some of the flesh are placed on coconut leaves over the place where the post stood.

Then the pigs for the feast are slaughtered near the village and singed over the flames of palm leaf torches. After a mid-day feast the visitors all receive a portion of pork. Every part of a pig except the lungs and lower jaw bone is given away. After this distribution some of the visitors return home, though many wait for the pig-wrestling.* Some of the most savage pigs are let out of the cages in the late afternoon and men who are skilled in the sport seize these pigs by the ears and hold them. Sometimes a man is bitten or gored by the tusks of the pigs; any pig that injures a man is speared at once. Young folk may not eat the flesh of such a pig, only the older people. No reason is given for this except that it is the custom. After this is over more of the guests will return home.

Next day the fat pigs are reduced to lard, which is stored in coconut shells. There will be dancing through the night by the villagers and any visitors who have stayed on.

On the following days preparations are made for digging up the bones by the deceased's friends. Water is drawn from wells and covered over with leaves. The women squat by the memorial posts at the graves and lament. A fence of palm leaves is made right round the burial ground, except for one exit near the unclean place in the jungle where the bones are thrown away.

Then the bones of those who have been dead for two years or more are dug up, a witch doctor standing by each grave and keeping evil spirits away by waiving a bunch of the leaves that keep away evil spirits. If by chance the bones are found to have flesh on them they are put back and covered over again to await the next festival. Otherwise the skull is wiped clean by hand, wrapped in white calico and placed on a spathe of palm. The other bones are taken out one by one and placed on the same spathe. This is then carried to the Dead House on *el-panam* and placed on top of big yams that are scattered under the Dead House for this purpose.

Then this spathe containing all the bones is wrapped round with white and red calico. When all the digging is completed and the bones wrapped up, the bundles containing the bones of more important people are re-interred in the grave from which they were taken, the others are carried to the unclean place in the jungle and the bones are scattered there and the cloth torn to rags.

After all this the grave diggers go down to the sea and wash their hands and legs or bathe.

Witch Doctors.—In Kar Nicobar only of these islands is there a novitiate to the School of Witch Doctors. These novices are called *ma-a-fai* and they may be of either sex, though female applicants are very rare. If a man or boy is of a sickly nature the witch doctors usually want him as a novice and at night will throw into the house where he resides some leaves such as they use for their charms and perhaps one or two chickens with their legs tied together. When these are found the sickly man's friends know that the spirits are calling him and he must become a novice. A day is fixed for his novitiate and just before sunset the witch doctors and friends of the man or boy thump the ground under the house with stems of the coconut leaf, each one holding in his hand a bunch of evil-spirit-expelling leaves.

---

* Similarly the Ao Nagas of Assam wrestle with the mithan (gayal) bulls which are to be sacrificed.

J. H. H.

The novice is meanwhile lying on his back on the floor of the house. Then the people all go up and spread over him several large banana leaves. To each leaf several wing feathers of a fowl are fastened and singed. Soon after the leaves are removed and a witch doctor finds several small lizards which are presumed to have come out of the novice's body and to have been the cause of his sickness.

Early next morning the novice is decked out with the jewellery of the witch doctors as well as with other jewellery lent by friends. His arms and legs are covered with silver wire and round his neck are necklets of two-anna pieces. A throne is made for him on which he is seated and he is given a magic spear and a sceptre. In this chair he may afterwards be carried from village to village, though this is rarely done.

After a few days he goes with his friends to the edge of the jungle where *pa-nam sio* (the place of the spirits) is. The friends remain behind and he goes with the witch doctors and is introduced to the spirits.

Then all go to the novice's house where dancing takes place and songs are sung. This singing and dancing takes place frequently during the novitiate of the person, which lasts about a year. During that novitiate he may do no work of any kind and may not even touch a dah. He may remain all his life a *ma-a-fai* if he wishes, or he may resign, for which there is a special ceremony, but if he wishes to carry on he is promoted to the ranks of the *to-mi-luo-no*, and then may work if he chooses.

These *to-mi-luo-no* deal with the evil spirits that are such a terror to the ordinary man and which bring sickness and all kinds of misfortune.

Eclipses.—These may perhaps come under the head of religion, though in this case evil spirits are not the cause of the eclipse but a python who according to the Island folk-tales was a man at one time.

This python now and again starts swallowing up either the sun or moon. When this begins the people collect and beat tins or anything that will make a noise and shout " Vomit it out ". The python pays no heed to their calls but goes on swallowing. Then as the sun or moon is swallowed the cry changes to " Evacuate it " and to this cry the python does pay heed and the people get back their sun or moon again.

Christianity.—The first attempt to Christianise the people of Kar Nicobar was made by Jesuit missionaries in 1711, but the settlers succumbed to the effects of the climate and all traces of their work soon disappeared.

About 1834 or 1835 two Roman Catholic missionaries arrived on the island from Malacca. These were expelled from the island and went on to Teressa and Kamorta, where one died and the other left.

Captain Gardener in the Singapore Review, Volume II, gives an account of two Moravian missionaries being expelled in 1851.

" Having converted a few natives ", he says, " dispute arose between them and their heathen countrymen. They were of such a serious nature that it was determined to hold a general council of delegates from every village to consider a remedy for the evil. They came to the conclusion, that, as they had always lived in love and amity with each other before the arrival of the missionaries, with their strange story of the first woman stealing the orange, etc., the obvious remedy was to send them away. Accordingly the missionaries were waited upon, and told respectfully that they must leave at the first opportunity, that the natives were not to be joked with, and must be obeyed.

The Mission house was then burned down and a fence erected around the spot, inside which no native will step. It is unholy ground, they say, where the devil first landed ; for until the missionaries brought him with them, he had never been in the island or knew where it was. I was told that a day is now set apart in the year when all the inhabitants assemble to drive the devil out of the island ".

In 1886 Mr. V. Solomon, a Madrassi of the Anglican Communion, became Agent in the island. He acted also as School master and Catechist, and under him for the first time in the island's history Christianity made some progress.

Of him, Sir R. C. Temple, the Chief Commissioner, in a lecture given in 1899 before the Indian Section of the Society of Arts said : " He is imbued with an untiring enthusiasm resting on a foundation of much common sense, and by the exercise of these qualities he has acquired a remarkable ascendancy over the people, used for their good . . . . Mr. Solomon's efforts to keep up peace and goodwill between village and village are practical ".

The first Christian to be baptized was Rose, a female, on the 24th of July 1900 and since then the number of Christians has been slowly increasing.

There is no resident Chaplain on the island. The Rev. George Whitehead lived amongst the people for some years and put their language into writing with the assistance of Mr. J. Richardson, the Nicobarese Headmaster of the school, and produced a Prayer Book and some reading books comprised mainly of legends common to the people as well as extracts from the Old and New Testaments. With this exception the Nicobarese Christians as Catechist and teachers and members of the Church Committee carry on the spiritual and educational work themselves with occasional visits (about five times a year) from the Chaplain at Port Blair, who administers the small grant given by the Indian Government for educational and hospital work, on the island and supervises the work of the hospital and the five schools that are there.

G. S.

APPENDIX C.

Nicobars.

ABSTRACT FROM A LECTURE DELIVERED AT THE CLINICAL SOCIETY OF PORT BLAIR ON 13TH FEBRUARY 1932.

Yaws in the Nicobar Islands by Major A. J. D'Souza, I.M.S., Senior Medical Officer, Port Blair.

Incidence of Yaws in the Nicobar Islands is not mentioned in standard books on Tropical Medicine (Manson and Castellani). I have received reports from time to time, since my arrival in Port Blair, that syphilis is very prevalent in the Nicobars, causing severe disfiguration of the inhabitants and threatening the extinction of the race. Two typical cases of yaws in the secondary stage were noticed by me among Nicobarese who were sent to Port Blair for a trial for murder and were cured with 2 injections of N. A. B. (O. 6 & O. 9 Grms.) in 1930 : and it transpired that the cases reported to be suffering from syphilis in the Nicobars may be cases of yaws. I understand that Lt.-Col. Barker, I.M.S., S. M. O. in Port Blair, in 1924 brought a case of yaws from the Nicobars and demonstrated the lesions at a meeting of the Clinical Society, but I fail to find any record of the prevalence of this disease in the Nicobars. An opportunity occurred for investigation, when the Census Superintendent for the Andaman and Nicobar islands required the services of a Sub-Assistant Surgeon to record the anthropological measurements of the Andamanese and Nicobarese in connection with his report for these islands. Dr. Naidu was deputed for this work, and after receiving preliminary instructions in the use of instruments for taking these measurements in Calcutta, he proceeded to Nicobars on 7th February 1931. I sent him well equipped with what I considered an adequate supply of N. A. B. in the hope of temporarily ameliorating the condition of people and awaiting a report from him as to any further steps to be taken to combat the disease. I may mention that the Andaman islands are free from yaws, while syphilis and gonorrhœa are common and are principally responsible for undermining the fertility of the Andamanese. Dr. Naidu worked under difficult conditions with regard to language and time limit and the discomfort of a camp life from 7th February 1931 to 18th March 1931. From his report it would appear that an interesting study of tropical diseases could be made in these islands. His time was limited for a study of the local conditions, as well as of the diseases prevalent among the inhabitants living in the various villages. The principal diseases prevalent in both the Great and Little Nicobar as well as the Central Group are yaws and elephantiasis. Altogether he treated 60 cases of yaws :—

		Nos.
Little Nicobar.—	Pulo Milo	1
Great Nicobar.—	Kondul	2
	Pulobabi	3
	Shompen camp Alexandra river	1
Central Group.—	Bompoka	4
	Nankauri	7
	Chaura	9
	Teressa	33
	Total	60

He also noticed that at Chaura, out of a total population of about 600, 35 were showing visible signs of elephantiasis. During the course of his whole journey he came across only two cases of syphilis—one contracted at Nankauri and the other at Kar Nikobar—both trading centres for the outside world with a floating population of eastern nationals. He had a large out-patients' attendance wherever he camped. The people from different islands appreciated the treatment given and expressed a desire to Mr. Bonington, Census Superintendent, and to Dr. Naidu that they wanted the whole-time services of a doctor for the island. If a doctor could be appointed for them, Teressa or Camorta would be a central place for a hospital or dispensary. As regards medical facilities for the Nicobars, a doctor appointed by the Kar Nikobar Mission (subsidised by the local Government) is stationed at Kar Nikobar in charge of a hospital and a small dispensary in charge of a compounder is established at Nankauri ; but there are no amenities for treatment at any of the other islands, unless the inhabitants can go in fine weather to either of these centres. Dr. Naidu exhausted his stock of N. A. B. in treating cases of yaws before he returned. On receiving his report I proceeded to the Nicobars with Dr. Naidu in April 1931 with a plentiful supply of N. A. B. We took the opportunity of examining some of the cases that had received an injection two months previously. The inhabitants were so impressed with the efficacy of the treatment that more cases eagerly sought treatment and the following number was treated :

Central Group :—

Chaura	10
Teressa	35
Nankauri	2
Total	47

This number would have been considerably higher if it had been possible to send information beforehand to the various villages of our impending visit. The cases that had received an injection in February or March had all healed up with the exception of two who still manifested latent infection and indolent sores. These were given a second injection each. We studied together the disease, local peculiarities and notions of the disease which are given under their appropriate headings in the lecture.

Injections.—Conditions under which they were given were not ideal. No previous preparation of the patient was possible and sterilization and preparation of solution and administration of injection were all performed in the centre of a group of anxious and expectant patients and their friends and relations either on the deck of the boat or on a sandy shore. There were no accidents or ill effects and pain was negligible. As even the three children who were given the injections did not cry nor make a noise to resent the treatment. It was useless to advise them to rest after the injections ; but they departed happily hoping to be cured of the disease in the same way as their friends were on the previous occasion. I am also showing a few photographs of typical cases. No photographer was available, my servant acted as my photographer and although the prints are not of the best quality they depict the principal lesions of interest we found in the islands.

*Yaws (**Framboesia**).*

Island.	Local synonyms for yaws.	For syphilis.
Teressa	*Aiyoke*	*Thannoi.*
Chaura	*Aiyak*	*Sakayee.*

Although they do not bear any relation to the native names mentioned by Manson or Castellani, there is a resemblance in phonation in the local synonyms for yaws in the two islands, while it is noteworthy that the names for syphilis are distinct and definite without any such similarity.

Definition.—Yaws is a chronic contagious inoculable disease of a granulomatous type with an indefinite and lengthy incubation period, which is followed by constitutional symptoms such as fever, malaise, pains in muscles and bones and joints, subsiding with the development of granuloma. In its progress there are three well defined stages, the granulomata varying in each stage in sites, number and extent.

Geographical distribution and endemicity.—The Nicobar islands may be regarded as a continuation of the chain of islands of the Malay Archipelago and is adjacent to the endemic areas of yaws, *viz.*, Upper Burma, Assam, Siam, Ceylon, Java, and Sumatra. As the sanitation is primitive and conditions are ideal for the maintenace of infection, in the way of primitive huts whose floors and walls may be impregnated with infection and where human beings, dogs and pigs live together, it is easy to understand how this endemic disease may rapidly take on an epidemic form ; although it has not been possible to trace any epidemicity to this disease in any of the islands where intelligible information has been available. We have not been able to trace any cases to house infection nor to direct insect bites. We are of opinion that infection is most likely conveyed by insects, *e.g.*, flies from a yaws sore infecting a pre-existing sore such as an ordinary sore or itch pustules or scratches or breaches on the skin, which are numerous, owing to the jungle life the people lead. It is quite possible that house infection is important judging by the habits of the people but our conclusion is based on the innumerable flies we saw settling on yaws sores and it is easily conceivable how such flies can convey the spirochoetes to pre-existing breaches of skin. Principal occupations of the people are cultivation of coconut and tobacco, pig breeding and fishing. While it has been observed by authorities on yaws that the disease has a predilection for certain native races, particularly of the negro or negrito stock, it is not known among the Andamanese who belong to the Negrito stock, although syphilis is very common among them, and yaws exists endemically within 150 miles of these islands.

Symptoms . . . . 3 stages are differentiated.

(1) Primary stage of infiltrated nodule.

(2) Secondary stage of granulomatous eruptions.

(3) Tertiary stage of deep ulcerations and gummatous nodules and bone lesions.

There is no para stage corresponding to syphilis.

Primary stage.—" Madre Buba or Mother Yaws ". An infiltrated papule develops at the site of inoculation or a granuloma in an old skin lesion such as an ulcer, itch pustule or insect bite or any abrasion and scratch incidental to a jungle life. In the initial stage, they complained of intense itching lasting for about a week.

Secondary stage or stage of generalized eruptions.—The onset of this stage corresponds with the decline of constitutional symptoms and most of our cases treated were well advanced in the secondary stage. Generalised eruption is ushered in as follows :—Minute roundish papules of the size of a pin head are seen with a yellow crust at the apex usually three months after the primary lesion, lasting a few weeks and leaving when they disappear furaceous patches ; these patches are circular and show a fine sand-colored desquamation as if the skin has been dusted over with flour or atta. This condition was only noticed in one of our cases. Some papules coalesce enlarge and skin gets proliferated or hyperkeratoid.

Tertiary stage.—This is a stage of gummatous nodules and deep ulcerative processes. The transition period between secondary and tertiary stages differs widely from that of syphilis. Instead of getting absorbed and healing, yaws may spread marginally as well as deeply and leading to extensive ulcers which may last for years. Such ulcers may involve deep structures producing necrosis of bone or cartilage or give rise to cicatricial contractures in the process of healing or from immobility of joints, and it is said that in such cases (8 per cent. according to Manson) typical lesions of yaws disappear and the ulcer is non-infective.

Feet, Crab Yaws and Clavus.—Yaws in the soles of feet is limited by thick skin. Like an abscess in this region, it is under high tension. It attains a large size before it bursts and is therefore very painful. When the thick epidermis gives way, yaws is converted into a fungating ulcer and although painful to the touch is not painful to the same degree as it was before it burst through skin. This ulcer, after the pent up secretion oozes out, appears like the section of a pomagranate cut through with a knife.

" Gangosa ".—This is a destructive disfiguring process with deep ulceration of the nose and pharynx and is said to commence as an ulcer of the soft palate. It spreads slowly and leads to complete destruction of hard palate, soft parts, cartilage and bones of nose ; in some cases sparing the upper lip as a bridge, in other cases leading to its partial destruction. A great cavity is left with the tongue as the floor, which remains unaffected.

Bone Lesions.—These are common in the tertiary stage. As in syphilis painful nodes on the anterior surfaces of long bones such as tibia, radius, ulna and clavicle, hard, tender and painful in the beginning remain as thickenings when acuteness subsides.

The characteristic sabre-shaped deformity of long bones affecting tibia, forearms, arms, and clavicle and digits was noticed in the case which is photographed.

General Health.—Yaws is a chronic disease which does not appear to incapacitate its victims from carrying on their vocation or occupation so far as the Nicobar Islands are concerned. Perhaps the early constitutional disturbances may restrict their movements, although from the information gathered not to any appreciable extent.

In spite of their animistic ideas of religion, they appear to be grateful for western methods of treatment and need no persuation to be injected, as they have gained faith after the first course of injections given as to the efficiency of our means of curing the disease.

They believe that it is a chronic disease but not fatal disease. Although at Teressa many adults are reported to have died of the disease, only 3 children under 10 have died at Chaura from yaws within the last 3 years. We have to take into consideration an outbreak of small-pox which may have been responsible for the large number of deaths reported at Teressa.

Treatment.—With limited time at our disposal the only treatment tried was injections of Novarsenobillon,

0·9 grms. for adults.

0·6 grms. for young adults.

0·3 grms. for children up to 10 years of age.

One injection appears to have cured most of the cases, although this needs confirmation by a second visit to the islands to examine the cases that have been injected.

Treatment adopted by the Nicobarese.—At Chaura, application of certain leaves (*rafab*) according to them appears to check the disease. At Teressa the ulcers are rubbed with sand and then washed in sea water, which is supposed to irritate the ulcers and assist cleaning, and a paste of leaves (*ramintho*) made by boiling and grinding is then applied. Ulcers are said to disappear in a few cases after a series of applications. The inhabitants appear healthy and well nourished and yaws did not affect their general health, so that the prescription of tonics, good food as general treatment was not necessary in them.

Prophylaxis.—To prevent contagion and spread of this disease, it would be necessary to isolate and segregate infected cases and give them N. A. B. injections—one, two or three according to the response and keep them under observation. House infection cannot be eliminated unless the thatched houses are burnt down, and sanitation in and around inhabited houses improved, but such measures are impracticable in an uncivilised country. In my opinion the only way of adopting prophylactic measures for the eradication of the disease is to appoint a medical officer with a steam launch at his disposal for one year so that he can visit all islands in turn periodically and give appropriate treatment where necessary. Each endemic area needs to be visited at least once in three months.

In concluding this lecture I wish to express my thanks to Dr. D. Naidu for his loyal co-operation and help in collecting statistics and local information and in treating cases under adverse conditions.

Note by the Census Superintendent.—This appendix abstracted from a paper written by Major A. J. D'Souza, I.M.S., is of value as indicating the extent of yaws in the Nicobars. It shows that the disease is prevalent throughout the Central and Southern groups and was found to exist even among the Shom-Pen. It is particularly virulent in Teressa where out of 17 villages only one was visited in the 24 hours spent on the island while a few patients came on board from another village. Yet 68 persons were treated at Teressa. There are only 437 persons on the island so it seems not too high to estimate that about half of the inhabitants are infected with this dreadful disease which without modern treatment takes a course almost identical to that of syphilis when not treated, and as Major D'Souza says it threatens to exterminate the inhabitants. I am grateful to Major D'Souza for his kind co-operation in placing Dr. Damodaram Naidu at my disposal during my visit to these islands for without this co-operation the extent of the disease would not have come to light. Dr. Naidu having been previously in East Africa where the disease is not uncommon, recognized it at once. It is to be regretted that owing to the difficulty of keeled transport and the short time at our disposal we were unable to visit all the outlying villages of the different groups. It is however desirable that an extensive visit be made in the near future by a medical officer so that the disease may at any rate be kept within limits if not entirely exterminated. The number of small coffins with the remains of the bones of deceased relatives in the different huts, 6 to 12 in number, also indicate the high death rate, most of them had probably died within the last year or two, for it is usual for the remains to be thrown into a common ossuary periodically at the ossuary feast.

M. C. C. BONINGTON.

Part II
TABLES.

A.—*Imperial Tables.*

B.—*Provincial Table.*

Tables IV and V were not compiled for the Andamans and Nicobars as there are no towns. Table XI was not compiled as the castes of convicts have little choice as to the occupation followed. Table XII was not compiled as there are no educated persons unemployed in the Andaman or Nicobar Islands. Table XIV was not compiled as the numbers of different castes are so small that their figures of literacy carry no significance.

TABLE I.—AREA, HOUSES AND POPULATION.

Administrative unit.	Area in square miles.	Towns.	Villages.	Occupied Houses.			Population.								
				Total.	In Towns.	In villages.	Persons.			Males.			Females.		
							Total.	Urban.	Rural.	Total.	Urban.	Rural.	Total.	Urban.	Rural.
1	2	3	4	5	6	7	8	9	10	11	12	13	14	15	16
Andaman and Nicobar islands	3,143	Nil	239	5,710	Nil	5,710	29,463	Nil	29,463	19,702	Nil	19,702	9,761	Nil	9,761
Andamans	2,508	"	90	4,267	"	4,267	19,223	"	19,223	14,258	"	14,258	4,965	"	4,965
Port Blair	473	"	74	3,863	"	3,863	17,345	"	17,345	12,715	"	12,715	4,630	"	4,630
Rest of Andamans	2,035	"	16	404	"	404	1,878	"	1,878	1,543	"	1,543	335	"	335
Nicobars	635	"	149	1,443	"	1,443	10,240	"	10,240	5,444	"	5,444	4,796	"	4,796

TABLE II.—VARIATION IN POPULATION DURING LAST FIFTY YEARS.

Administrative unit.	Persons.						Variation: Increase (+), Decrease (—).					Net variation in period 1881 to 1931 Increase +, Decrease —.
	1931.	1921.	1911.	1901.	1891.	1881.	1921 to 1931.	1911 to 1921.	1901 to 1911.	1891 to 1901.	1881 to 1891.	
1	2	3	4	5	6	7	8	9	10	11	12	13
Andaman and Nicobar islands	29,463	27,086	26,459	24,649	15,609	14,628	+2,377	+627	+1,810	+9,040*	+981	+14,835
Andamans	19,223	17,814	17,641	18,138	15,609	14,628	+1,409	+173	—497	+2,529	+981	+4,595
Port Blair	17,345	15,675	16,324	16,256	15,609	14,628	+1,670	—649	+68	+647	+981	+2,717
Rest of Andamans	1,878	2,139	1,317	1,882	..	..	—261	+822	—565	..	..	..
Nicobars	10,240	9,272	8,818	6,511	..	..	+968	+454	+2,307	..	..	..

Administrative unit.	Males.						Females.					
	1931.	1921.	1911.	1901.	1891.	1881.	1931.	1921.	1911.	1901.	1891.	1881.
1	14	15	16	17	18	19	20	21	22	23	24	25
Andaman and Nicobar islands	19,702	20,793	19,570	18,695	13,375	12,640	9,761	6,293	6,880	5,954	2,234	1,988
Andamans	14,258	15,551	14,737	15,158	13,375	12,640	4,965	2,263	2,904	2,980	2,234	1,988
Port Blair	12,715	13,747	14,109	14,122	13,375	12,640	4,630	1,928	2,215	2,134	2,234	1,988
Rest of Andamans	1,543	1,804	628	1,036	..	..	335	335	689	846	..	..
Nicobars	5,444	5,242	4,833	3,537	..	..	4,796	4,030	3,985	2,974	..	..

* Increase due to Census of Nicobars not having been taken in previous years.

TABLE III.—TOWNS AND VILLAGES CLASSIFIED BY POPULATION.

Administrative unit.	Total number of inhabited towns and villages.	Population.	Under 500		500—1,000		1,000—2,000		2,000—5,000		Boats and Steamship population unclassified.
			Number.	Population.	Number.	Population.	Number.	Population.	Number.	Population	
1	2	3	4	5	6	7	8	9	10	11	12
Andaman and Nicobar islands	239	29,463	224	14,886	12	8,049	2	2,209	1	3,988	331
Andamans	90	19,223	84	10,279	3	2,431	2	2,209	1	3,988	316
Port Blair	74	17,345	69	9,197	2	1,635	2	2,209	1	3,988	316
Rest of Andamans	16	1,878	15	1,082	1	796	..	..	..	..	..
Nicobars	149	10,240	140	4,607	9	5,618	..	..	..	..	15

TABLE VI.—BIRTH-PLACE.

Province, State or Country where born.	Andaman and Nicobar Islands.			Andamans.			Nicobars.		
	Persons.	Males.	Females.	Persons.	Males.	Females.	Persons.	Males.	Females.
1	2	3	4	5	6	7	8	9	10
Total Population	29,463	19,702	9,761	19,223	14,258	4,965	10,240	5,444	4,796
A.—BORN IN INDIA	28,973	19,241	9,732	18,845	13,902	4,943	10,128	5,339	4,789
(a) BORN WITHIN THE PROVINCE	14,718	7,754	6,964	4,704	2,519	2,185	10,014	5,235	4,779
(b) PROVINCES OR STATES IN INDIA BEYOND THE ANDAMANS AND NICOBARS	13,552	10,914	2,638	13,442	10,813	2,629	110	101	9
Ajmer-Merwara	24	24	..	24	24	..	..	..	..
Assam	152	134	18	152	134	18	..	..	..
Baluchistan	20	20	..	20	20	..	..	..	..
Bengal	967	814	153	949	797	152	18	17	1
Bihar and Orissa	620	565	55	619	564	55	1	1	..
Bombay	537	477	60	495	435	60	42	42	..
Burma	2,971	2,453	518	2,953	2,439	514	18	14	4
Central Provinces and Berar	433	373	60	426	366	60	7	7	..
Coorg	7	7	..	7	7	..	..	..	..
Delhi	8	6	2	8	6	2	..	..	..
Madras including Laccadives	2,747	1,896	851	2,727	1,880	847	20	16	4
North-West Frontier Province	398	335	63	397	334	63	1	1	..
Punjab	1,983	1,598	385	1,983	1,598	385	..	..	..
United Provinces of Agra and Oudh	2,434	2,010	424	2,431	2,007	424	3	3	..
Baroda State	19	17	2	19	17	2	..	..	..
Central India Agency	54	39	15	54	39	15	..	..	..
Gwalior State	34	32	2	34	32	2	..	..	..
Hyderabad State	7	6	1	7	6	1	..	..	..
Jammu and Kashmir State	14	11	3	14	11	3	..	..	..
Cochin State	15	9	6	15	9	6	..	..	..
Travancore State	12	8	4	12	8	4	..	..	..
Mysore State	29	22	7	29	22	7	..	..	..
Rajputana Agency	67	58	9	67	58	9	..	..	..
(c) INDIA UNSPECIFIED	703	573	130	699	570	129	4	3	1
B.—BORN IN OTHER ASIATIC COUNTRIES	328	317	11	217	213	4	111	104	7
Ceylon	8	8	..	5	5	..	3	3	..
China	179	168	11	73	69	4	106	99	7
Honkong	1	1	..	1	1	..	..	..	..
Japan	135	135	..	135	135	..	..	..	..
Nepal	3	3	..	3	3	..	..	..	..
Straits Settlement	2	2	..	..	..	..	2	2	..
C.—BORN IN EUROPE	148	136	12	147	135	12	1	1	..
United Kingdom	145	133	12	144	132	12	1	1	..
Germany	1	1	..	1	1	..	..	..	..
Sweeden	2	2	..	2	2	..	..	..	..
D.—BORN IN AFRICA	3	..	3	3	..	3	..	..	..
E.—BORN IN AMERICA	3	2	1	3	2	1	..	..	..
F.—BORN IN AUSTRALASIA	8	6	2	8	6	2	..	..	..
(1) British Dominions Fiji Islands	8	6	2	8	6	2	..	..	..

TABLE VII.—Age, Sex and Civil Condition.

Andamans.

Age Group.	Population.			Unmarried.			Married.			Widowed.		
	Persons.	Males.	Females.	Persons.	Males.	Females.	Persons.	Males.	Females.	Persons.	Males.	Females
1	2	3	4	5	6	7	8	9	10	11	12	13
0—1	*433*	*225*	*208*	*433*	*225*	*208*	..	..	..	..	..	..
1—2	*359*	*182*	*177*	*359*	*182*	*177*	..	..	..	..	..	..
2—3	*415*	*213*	*202*	*415*	*213*	*202*	..	..	..	..	..	..
3—4	*355*	*185*	*170*	*355*	*185*	*170*	..	..	..	..	..	..
4—5	*276*	*142*	*134*	*276*	*142*	*134*	..	..	..	..	..	..
0—5	1,838	947	891	1,838	947	891	..	..	..	..	..	..
5—10	1,193	638	555	1,164	628	536	27	10	17	2	..	2
10—15	1,044	581	463	934	559	375	107	21	86	3	1	2
15—20	1,315	868	447	684	617	67	605	234	371	26	17	9
20—25	2,040	1,502	538	873	844	29	1,100	608	492	67	50	17
25—30	2,911	2,419	492	867	861	6	1,866	1,399	467	178	159	19
30—35	2,813	2,389	424	617	614	3	1,946	1,546	400	250	229	21
35—40	1,997	1,731	266	347	342	5	1,413	1,177	236	237	212	25
40—45	1,488	1,281	207	250	245	5	1,035	866	169	203	170	33
45—50	859	715	144	112	110	2	589	485	104	158	120	38
50—55	580	475	105	84	72	12	368	308	60	128	95	33
55—60	262	203	59	26	20	6	161	134	27	75	49	26
60—65	187	134	53	21	12	9	107	90	17	59	32	27
65—70	93	47	46	15	5	10	38	32	6	40	10	30
70 and over	143	78	65	17	12	5	38	36	2	88	30	58
Total	18,763	14,008	4,755	7,849	5,888	1,961	9,400	6,946	2,454	1,514	1,174	340

No age was recorded for the Andamanese population of 460 (males 250, females 210).

Nicobars.

Age Group.	Persons.	Males.	Females.	Persons.	Males.	Females.	Persons.	Males.	Females.	Persons.	Males.	Females
0—1	*380*	*162*	*218*	*380*	*162*	*218*	..	..	..	..	..	..
1—2	*277*	*124*	*153*	*277*	*124*	*153*	..	..	..	..	..	..
2—3	*381*	*184*	*197*	*381*	*184*	*197*	..	..	..	..	..	..
3—4	*393*	*207*	*186*	*393*	*207*	*186*	..	..	..	..	..	..
4—5	*339*	*188*	*151*	*339*	*188*	*151*	..	..	..	..	..	..
0—5	1,770	865	905	1,770	865	905	..	..	..	..	..	..
5—10	1,216	686	530	1,216	686	530	..	..	..	..	..	..
10—15	951	535	416	904	527	377	47	8	39	..	..	..
15—20	603	279	324	305	206	99	288	71	217	10	2	8
20—25	649	321	328	135	114	21	491	202	289	23	5	18
25—30	774	403	381	63	59	4	677	332	345	34	12	22
30—35	737	382	355	49	45	4	643	320	323	45	17	28
35—40	628	320	308	42	39	3	544	267	277	42	14	28
40—45	553	290	263	35	32	3	486	247	239	32	11	21
45—50	419	261	158	19	16	3	363	230	133	37	15	22
50—55	332	204	128	20	17	3	269	171	98	43	16	27
55—60	196	123	73	21	17	4	132	95	37	43	11	32
60—65	146	96	50	16	12	4	91	73	18	39	11	28
65—70	60	34	26	3	2	1	31	24	7	26	8	18
70 and over	146	78	68	3	2	1	64	46	18	79	30	49
Total	9,180	4,877	4,303	4,601	2,639	1,962	4,126	2,086	2,040	453	152	301

Ages of 1,060 persons (567 males and 493 females) on the islands of Chaura and of the Southern Group have not been recorded.

TABLE VIII.—Civil Condition by Religion and Age.

Andamans.

Religion.	Sex.	Population dealt with.	Unmarried. Total.	0—6.	7—13.	14—16.	17—23.	24—43.	44 and over.	Married. Total.	0—6.	7—13.	14—16.	17—23.	24—43.	44 and over.	Widowed. Total.	0—6.	7—13.	14—16.	17—23.	24—43.	44 and over.
1	2	3	4	5	6	7	8	9	10	11	12	13	14	15	16	17	18	19	20	21	22	23	24
Hindus	Males	5,442	2,286	532	429	148	295	734	148	2,539	..	7	13	172	1,699	648	617	..	..	3	12	345	257
	Females	2,161	861	843	299	53	13	9	4	1,195	..	21	71	259	610	144	195	..	1	1	7	43	143
Brahmanic Hindus	*Males*	*5,297*	*2,265*	*527*	*426*	*146*	*292*	*726*	*148*	*2,519*	..	*7*	*13*	*169*	*1,687*	*643*	*613*	..	..	*3*	*12*	*343*	*255*
	Females	*2,116*	*839*	*469*	*294*	*51*	*12*	*9*	*4*	*1,086*	..	*21*	*68*	*251*	*604*	*142*	*191*	..	*1*	*1*	*7*	*41*	*141*
Arya	*Males*	*45*	*21*	*5*	*3*	*2*	*3*	*8*	..	*20*	..	..	..	*3*	*12*	*5*	*4*	..	..	..	..	*2*	*2*
	Females	*45*	*22*	*14*	*5*	*2*	*1*	..	..	*19*	..	..	*3*	*8*	*6*	*2*	*4*	..	..	..	..	*2*	*2*
Sikhs	Males	503	284	55	39	14	52	115	9	185	..	..	1	11	129	44	34	..	..	..	1	24	9
	Females	146	60	41	17	..	..	2	..	80	..	..	2	21	54	3	6	..	..	..	..	3	3
Buddhists	Males	2,502	889	108	652	18	180	469	52	1,457	..	2	..	60	1,249	146	156	..	..	..	8	111	37
	Females	400	174	95	59	10	14	4	..	212	..	..	3	45	139	25	14	..	..	..	2	4	8
Zoroastrian	Males	1	..	..	..	..	..	..	..	1	..	..	..	..	1	..	..	..	..	..	..	..	..
Muslims	Males	4,722	2,017	455	314	112	341	714	81	2,871	..	4	5	199	1,738	425	334	..	..	..	8	237	89
	Females	1,712	705	398	251	37	11	7	1	900	..	12	65	226	524	73	107	..	..	..	8	17	82
Christians	Males	797	401	70	82	18	117	154	10	364	..	..	2	58	247	57	32	..	..	..	1	17	14
	Females	326	169	83	42	15	18	10	1	138	..	1	1	31	81	24	19	..	..	..	..	2	17
Tribal	Males	255*	..	..	..	..	..	..	..	5	..	..	..	5	..	..	..	..	..	..	..	..	..
	Females	219†	..	..	..	..	..	..	..	9	..	..	..	5	4	..	..	..	..	..	..	..	..
Shintoists	Males	36	3	..	..	..	1	2	..	33	..	..	..	..	30	3	..	..	..	..	..	..	..
	Females	1	..	..	..	..	..	..	..	1	..	..	..	..	1	..	..	..	..	..	..	..	..
Total	..	19,223	7,849	2,320	1,544	425	1,034	2,220	306	9,400	..	47	163	1,002	6,506	1,592	1,514	..	1	4	47	803	659

No age was recorded for aboriginal population of 460 (males *250, females †210).

Nicobars.

Religion.	Sex.	Population dealt with.	Unmarried. Total.	0—6.	7—13.	14—16.	17—23.	24—43.	44 and over.	Married. Total.	0—6.	7—13.	14—16.	17—23.	24—43.	44 and over.	Widowed. Total.	0—6.	7—13.	14—16.	17—23.	24—43.	44 and over.
Hindus	Males	13	11	1	..	..	3	5	2	2	..	..	..	..	1	1	..	..	..	..	..	..	..
	Females	2	1	1	..	..	..	..	..	1	..	..	..	..	1	..	..	..	..	..	..	..	..
Buddhists	Males	8	5	..	..	..	..	3	2	3	..	..	..	..	2	1	..	..	..	..	..	..	..
	Females	2	..	..	..	..	..	..	..	2	..	..	..	..	1	1	..	..	..	..	..	..	..
Muslims	Males	244	131	18	17	28	28	35	5	103	..	..	1	2	71	29	10	..	..	..	..	6	4
	Females	41	21	11	9	..	1	..	..	20	..	..	..	4	1	15	..	..	..	..	..	..	..
Christians	Males	187	108	37	47	16	7	1	..	74	..	..	..	8	53	18	5	..	..	..	..	2	3
	Females	151	76	40	26	5	4	1	..	66	..	..	3	7	48	8	9	..	..	..	..	4	5
Tribal	Males	4,889*	2,251	1,032	762	205	116	92	44	1,938	..	5	5	130	1,124	669	138	..	..	..	4	50	84
	Females	4,592*	1,908	1,113	569	141	47	21	17	1,899	..	6	63	366	1,106	358	292	..	..	..	15	89	188
Confucian	Males	103	72	2	..	5	..	48	17	30	..	..	..	..	20	10	1	..	..	..	..	..	1
	Females	8	3	2	1	..	..	..	..	5	..	..	..	..	5	..	..	..	..	..	..	..	..
Total	..	10,240	4,587	2,257	1,431	400	206	206	87	4,138	..	11	72	517	2,433	1,105	455	..	..	..	19	151	285

*Ages of 1,060 persons (567 males and 493 females) on the islands of Chaura and of the Southern Group have not been recorded.

TABLE IX.—INFIRMITIES—PART I— DISTRIBUTION BY LOCALITY.

Andaman and Nicobar Islands.

Locality.	Population afflicted.			Insane.			Deaf—Mutes.			Blind.			Lepers.		
	Persons.	Males.	Females.	Persons.	Males.	Females.	Persons.	Males.	Females.	Persons.	Males.	Females.	Persons.	Males.	Females.
1	2	3	4	5	6	7	8	9	10	11	12	13	14	15	16
Andaman and Nicobar Islands	26	17	9	7	6	1	8	6	2	9	4	5	2	1	1
Andamans	21	13	8	5	4	1	7	5	2	7	3	4	2	1	1
Nicobars	5	4	1	2	2	..	1	1	..	2	1	1	..	..	..

No dual infirmity has been recorded.

TABLE IX.—INFIRMITIES—PART II—DISTRIBUTION BY AGE.

Andaman and Nicobar Islands.

Age.	Population afflicted.			Insane.			Deaf—Mutes.			Blind.			Lepers.		
	Persons.	Males.	Females.	Persons.	Males.	Females.	Persons.	Males.	Females.	Persons.	Males.	Females.	Persons.	Males.	Females.
1	2	3	4	5	6	7	8	9	10	11	12	13	14	15	16
0—5	..	..	..	..	..	..	..	..	..	..	..	..	..	..	..
5—10	2	2	..	2	2	..	..	..	..	..	..	..	..	..	..
10—15	1	..	1	..	..	..	..	..	..	1	..	1	..	..	..
15—20	2	1	1	..	..	..	..	..	..	2	1	1	..	..	..
20—25	..	..	..	..	..	..	..	..	..	..	..	..	..	..	..
25—30	1	1	..	1	1	..	..	..	..	..	..	..	..	..	..
30—35	2	1	1	..	..	..	1	1	..	..	..	..	1	..	1
35—40	5	5	..	2	2	..	2	2	..	..	..	..	1	1	..
40—45	2	1	1	..	..	..	2	1	1	..	..	..	..	..	..
45—50	3	2	1	1	1	..	1	..	1	1	1	..	..	..	..
50—55	1	..	1	1	..	1	..	..	..	..	..	..	..	..	..
55—60	..	..	..	..	..	..	..	..	..	..	..	..	..	..	..
60—65	4	2	2	..	..	..	1	1	..	3	1	2	..	..	..
65—70	2	1	1	..	..	..	..	..	..	2	1	1	..	..	..
70 and over	1	1	..	..	..	..	1	1	..	..	..	..	..	..	..
Total	26	17	9	7	6	1	8	6	2	9	4	5	2	1	1

TABLE X.—OCCUPATION OR MEANS OF LIVELIHOOD—GENERAL TABLE.

	Andaman and Nicobar Islands.	Andamans.	Nicobars.
Total Earners	14,258	11,624	2,634
Total Working Dependants	6,677	483	6,194
Total Non-working Dependants	8,528	7,116	1,412
Total Population	29,463	19,223	10,240

Group number.	Occupations.	Andaman and Nicobar Islands. Total following occupation.	As principal occupation. Males.	As principal occupation. Females.	As Working Dependants. Males.	As Working Dependants. Females.	As subsidiary to other occupation. Males.	As subsidiary to other occupation. Females.	Andamans. Total following occupation.	As principal occupation. Males.	As principal occupation. Females.	As Working Dependants. Males.	As Working Dependants. Females.	As subsidiary to other occupation. Males.	As subsidiary to other occupation. Females.	Nicobars. Total following occupation.	As principal occupation. Males.	As principal occupation. Females.	As Working Dependants. Males.	As Working Dependants. Females.	As subsidiary to other occupation. Males.	As subsidiary to other occupation. Females.
1	2	3	4	5	6	7	8	9	10	11	12	13	14	15	16	17	18	19	20	21	22	23
	A																					
	PRODUCTION OF RAW MATERIALS.	11,423	4,851	114	3,368	2,972	113	5	2,952	2,634	54	42	104	113	5	8,471	2,217	60	3,326	2,868	..	..
	I.—EXPLOITATION OF ANIMALS AND VEGETATION.	11,423	4,851	114	3,368	2,972	118	5	2,952	2,634	54	42	104	118	5	8,471	2,217	60	3,326	2,868	..	..
	1. Pasture and Agriculture	11,349	4,785	114	3,368	2,972	105	5	2,878	2,568	54	42	104	105	5	8,471	2,217	60	3,320	2,868	..	..
	(a) Cultivation	*1,786*	*1,519*	*53*	*40*	*104*	*68*	*2*	*1,786*	*1,519*	*53*	*40*	*104*	*68*	*2*	..	..	..	..	..	..	..
4	Rent collectors, clerks, etc.	6	6	..	..	..	..	..	6	6	..	..	..	..	..	..	..	..	..	..	..	..
5	Cultivating owners	401	358	28	1	..	14	..	401	358	28	1	..	14	..	..	..	..	..	..	..	..
6	Tenant Cultivators	1,142	950	24	36	104	26	2	1,142	950	24	36	104	26	2	..	..	..	..	..	..	..
7	Agricultural Labourers	237	205	1	3	..	28	..	237	205	1	3	..	28	..	..	..	..	..	..	..	..
	(b) Cultivation of special crops, fruit, etc. (planters, managers, clerks, and labourers).	*8,598*	*2,334*	*61*	*3,326*	*2,868*	*7*	*2*	*127*	*117*	*1*	..	..	*7*	*2*	*8,471*	*2,217*	*60*	*3,326*	*2,868*	..	..
10	Coconut	8,530	2,266	61	3,326	2,868	7	2	59	49	1	..	..	7	2	8,471	2,217	60	3,326	2,868	..	..
11	Coffee	4	4	..	..	..	..	..	4	4	..	..	..	..	..	..	..	..	..	..	..	..
16	Market Gardeners, flower and fruit growers.	64	64	..	..	..	..	..	64	64	..	..	..	..	..	..	..	..	..	..	..	..
	(c) Forestry	*893*	*862*	..	..	..	*30*	*1*	*893*	*862*	..	..	..	*30*	*1*	..	..	..	..	..	..	..
17	Forest officers, Rangers, Guards, etc.	362	361	..	..	..	1	..	362	361	..	..	..	1	..	..	..	..	..	..	..	..
18	Woodcutters and charcoal burners	1	1	..	..	..	..	..	1	1	..	..	..	..	..	..	..	..	..	..	..	..
19	Collectors of Forest produce	530	500	..	..	..	29	1	530	500	..	..	..	29	1	..	..	..	..	..	..	..
	(d) Stock Raising	*72*	*70*	..	*2*	..	..	..	*72*	*70*	..	*2*	..	..	..	..	..	..	..	..	..	..
21	Cattle and buffalo breeders and keepers	72	70	..	2	..	..	..	72	70	..	2	..	..	..	..	..	..	..	..	..	..
	2. Fishing and Hunting	74	66	..	..	..	8	..	74	66	..	..	..	8	..	..	..	..	..	..	..	..
27	Fishing and Pearling	74	66	..	..	..	8	..	74	66	..	..	..	8	..	..	..	..	..	..	..	..
	B																					
	PREPARATION AND SUPPLY OF MATERIAL SUBSTANCES.	3,080	2,710	10	16	11	323	4	2,782	2,419	9	16	11	323	4	298	297	1	..	..	..	..
	III.—INDUSTRY	1,342	1,059	9	14	7	250	3	1,335	1,052	9	14	7	250	3	7	7	..	..	..	..	..
	5. Textiles	227	1	4	..	1	221	..	227	1	4	..	1	221	..	..	..	..	..	..	..	..
42	Cotton ginning, cleaning and pressing	1	..	1	..	..	..	..	1	..	1	..	..	..	..	..	..	..	..	..	..	..
45	Rope, twine, string and other fibres	226	1	3	..	1	221	..	226	1	3	..	1	221	..	..	..	..	..	..	..	..
	6. Hides, Skins and hard materials from the animal kingdom.	4	4	..	..	..	..	..	4	4	..	..	..	..	..	..	..	..	..	..	..	..
58	Bone, ivory, horn, shell, etc., workers (except buttons).	4	4	..	..	..	..	..	4	4	..	..	..	..	..	..	..	..	..	..	..	..
	7. Nicobars	480	448	1	14	..	17	..	474	442	1	14	..	17	..	6	6	..	..	..	..	..

No.	Occupation																					
54	Sawyers	30	19	..	..	..	11	..	30	19	..	..	..	11	..	..	..	..	..	..	..	..
55	Carpenters— turners and joiners	428	422	..	..	..	6	..	422	416	..	..	..	6	..	6	6	..	..	..	..	..
56	Basket makers and other industries of woody materials, including leaves, and thatchers and builders working in bamboo, reeds or similar materials.	22	7	1	14	..	..	..	22	7	1	14	..	..	..	..	..	..	..	..	..	..
	8. Metals	38	38	..	..	..	..	..	38	38	..	..	..	..	..	..	..	..	..	..	..	..
59	Blacksmiths, other workers in iron, makers of implements.	32	32	..	..	..	..	..	32	32	..	..	..	..	..	..	..	..	..	..	..	..
60	Workers in brass, copper bell-metal	6	6	..	..	..	..	..	6	6	..	..	..	..	..	..	..	..	..	..	..	..
	9. Ceramics	3	3	..	..	..	..	..	3	3	..	..	..	..	..	..	..	..	..	..	..	..
63	Potters and makers of earthenware	2	2	..	..	..	..	..	2	2	..	..	..	..	..	..	..	..	..	..	..	..
65	Other workers in ceramics	1	1	..	..	..	..	..	1	1	..	..	..	..	..	..	..	..	..	..	..	..
	10. Chemical Products properly so called and analogous.	110	107	..	..	..	3	..	110	107	..	..	..	3	..	..	..	..	..	..	..	..
66	Manufacture of matches, fire-works and other explosives.	103	103	..	..	..	..	..	103	103	..	..	..	..	..	..	..	..	..	..	..	..
67	Manufacture of aerated and mineral waters and ice.	5	2	..	..	..	3	..	5	2	..	..	..	3	..	..	..	..	..	..	..	..
68	Manufacture and refining of vegetable oils.	1	1	..	..	..	..	..	1	1	..	..	..	..	..	..	..	..	..	..	..	..
70	Others (Soap-making)	1	1	..	..	..	..	..	1	1	..	..	..	..	..	..	..	..	..	..	..	..
	11. Food Industry	22	21	..	..	..	1	..	22	21	..	..	..	1	..	..	..	..	..	..	..	..
73	Butchers	10	10	..	..	..	..	..	10	10	..	..	..	..	..	..	..	..	..	..	..	..
75	Sweet and condiment makers	1	1	..	..	..	..	..	1	1	..	..	..	..	..	..	..	..	..	..	..	..
78	Manufacturers of tobacco	3	3	..	..	..	..	..	3	3	..	..	..	..	..	..	..	..	..	..	..	..
81	Others (Bakers)	8	7	..	..	..	1	..	8	7	..	..	..	1	..	..	..	..	..	..	..	..
	12. Industries of dress and the toilet	254	284	4	..	6	7	3	253	283	4	..	6	7	3	1	1	..	..	..	..	..
82	Boot, shoe, sandal and clog-makers	16	16	..	..	..	..	..	16	16	..	..	..	..	..	..	..	..	..	..	..	..
83	Tailors, milliners, dress-makers and darners.	91	77	3	..	6	4	1	91	77	3	..	6	4	1	..	..	..	..	..	..	..
84	Embroiderers, hat-makers and makers of other articles of wear.	4	..	1	..	..	1	2	4	..	1	..	..	1	2	..	..	..	..	..	..	..
85	Washing and cleaning	80	80	..	..	..	..	..	79	79	..	..	..	..	..	1	1	..	..	..	..	..
86	Barbers, hair dressers and wigmakers	68	61	..	..	..	2	..	68	61	..	..	..	2	..	..	..	..	..	..	..	..
	14. Building Industries	40	39	..	..	..	1	..	40	39	..	..	..	1	..	..	..	..	..	..	..	..
90	Lime burners, cement workers; excavators and well sinkers; stone cutters and dressers; brick-layers and masons; builders (other than buildings made of bamboo or similar materials), painters, decorators of houses, tilers, plumbers, etc.	40	39	..	..	..	1	..	40	39	..	..	..	1	..	..	..	..	..	..	..	..
	15. Construction of Means of Transport.	12	12	..	..	..	..	..	12	12	..	..	..	..	..	..	..	..	..	..	..	..
91	Persons engaged in making assembling or repairing motor vehicles or cycles.	12	12	..	..	..	..	..	12	12	..	..	..	..	..	..	..	..	..	..	..	..
	16. Production and transmission of physical force.	7	7	..	..	..	..	..	7	7	..	..	..	..	..	..	..	..	..	..	..	..
94	Heat, light, electricity, motive power, etc., gas works and electric light and power.	7	7	..	..	..	..	..	7	7	..	..	..	..	..	..	..	..	..	..	..	..
	17. Miscellaneous and undefined industries.	145	145	..	..	..	..	..	145	145	..	..	..	..	..	..	..	..	..	..	..	..
95	Printers, engravers, book binders, etc.	27	27	..	..	..	..	..	27	27	..	..	..	..	..	..	..	..	..	..	..	..
97	Makers of clocks and surgical or scientific instruments.	1	1	..	..	..	..	..	1	1	..	..	..	..	..	..	..	..	..	..	..	..
98	Makers of jewellery and ornaments	12	12	..	..	..	..	..	12	12	..	..	..	..	..	..	..	..	..	..	..	..
100	Scavenging	105	105	..	..	..	..	..	105	105	..	..	..	..	..	..	..	..	..	..	..	..
	IV.—TRANSPORT	1,006	980	..	..	1	25	..	977	951	..	..	1	25	..	29	29	..	..	..	..	..
	19. Transport by water	586	582	..	..	..	4	..	570	566	..	..	..	4	..	16	16	..	..	..	..	..
102	Shipowners, boat owners and their employees, officers, mariners, etc., ships brokers, boatmen and towmen.	573	569	..	..	..	4	..	557	553	..	..	..	4	..	16	16	..	..	..	..	..
104	Labourers employed on harbours, docks, rivers and canals,	13	13	..	..	..	..	..	13	13	..	..	..	..	..	..	..	..	..	..	..	..

TABLE X.—Occupation or Means of Livelihood—General Table—*contd.*

	Andaman and Nicobar Islands.	Andamans.	Nicobars.
Total Earners	14,258	11,624	2,634
Total Working Dependants	6,677	483	6,194
Total Non-working Dependants	8,528	7,116	1,412
Total Population	29,463	19,223	10,240

Group number.	Occupations.	Andaman and Nicobar Islands. Total following occupation.	As principal occupation. Males.	As principal occupation. Females.	As Working Dependants. Males.	As Working Dependants. Females.	As subsidiary to other occupation. Males.	As subsidiary to other occupation. Females.	Andamans. Total following occupation.	As principal occupation. Males.	As principal occupation. Females.	As Working Dependants. Males.	As Working Dependants. Females.	As subsidiary to other occupation. Males.	As subsidiary to other occupation. Females.	Nicobars. Total following occupation.	As principal occupation. Males.	As principal occupation. Females.	As Working Dependants. Males.	As Working Dependants. Females.	As subsidiary to other occupation. Males.	As subsidiary to other occupation. Females.
1	2	3	4	5	6	7	8	9	10	11	12	13	14	15	16	17	18	19	20	21	22	23
	PREPARATION AND SUPPLY OF MATERIAL SUBSTANCES—*contd.* IV.—TRANSPORT—*contd.*																					
	20. Transport by Road	396	376	..	..	1	19	..	384	364	..	..	1	19	..	12	12	..	..	..	..	..
105	Persons (other than labourers) employed on the construction and maintenance of roads and bridges.	6	6	..	..	..	..	..	6	6	..	..	..	..	..	..	..	..	..	..	..	..
106	Labourers employed on roads and bridges.	2	2	..	..	..	..	..	2	2	..	..	..	..	..	..	..	..	..	..	..	..
107	Owners, managers and employees (excluding personal servants) connected with mechanically driven vehicles.	90	90	..	..	..	..	..	90	90	..	..	..	..	..	..	..	..	..	..	..	..
108	Owners, managers and employees (excluding personal servants) connected with other vehicles.	154	134	..	..	1	19	..	142	122	..	..	1	19	..	12	12	..	..	..	..	..
110	Pack elephant, camel, mule, ass and bullock owners and drivers.	127	127	..	..	..	..	..	127	127	..	..	..	..	..	..	..	..	..	..	..	..
111	Porters and messengers	17	17	..	..	..	..	..	17	17	..	..	..	..	..	..	..	..	..	..	..	..
	22. Post Office, Telegraph and Telephone Services.	24	22	..	..	..	2	..	23	21	..	..	..	2	..	1	1	..	..	..	..	..
114	Post Office, Telegraph and Telephone Services.	24	22	..	..	..	2	..	23	21	..	..	..	2	..	1	1	..	..	..	..	..
	V.—TRADE	732	677	1	2	3	48	1	470	416	..	2	3	48	1	262	261	1	..	..	..	..
	23. Banks, Establishments of credits, exchange and insurance.	3	3	..	..	..	..	..	3	3	..	..	..	..	..	..	..	..	..	..	..	..
115	Bank Managers, Money lenders, exchange and insurance agents, money exchangers and brokers and their employees.	3	3	..	..	..	..	..	3	3	..	..	..	..	..	..	..	..	..	..	..	..
	24. Brokerage Commission and export	4	2	..	..	..	2	..	4	2	..	..	..	2	..	..	..	..	..	..	..	..
116	Brokers, Commission Agents, Commercial Travellers, warehouse owners and employees.	4	2	..	..	..	2	..	4	2	..	..	..	2	..	..	..	..	..	..	..	..
	25. Trade in Textiles	2	2	..	..	..	..	..	2	2	..	..	..	..	..	..	..	..	..	..	..	..
117	Trade in piece-goods, wool cotton, silk, hair and other textiles.	2	2	..	..	..	..	..	2	2	..	..	..	..	..	..	..	..	..	..	..	..
	26. Trade in skins, leather and furs	3	3	..	..	..	..	..	3	3	..	..	..	..	..	..	..	..	..	..	..	..
118	Trade in skins, leather, furs, feathers, horn, etc., and the articles made from these.	3	3	..	..	..	..	..	3	3	..	..	..	..	..	..	..	..	..	..	..	..
	27. Trade in wood	2	2	..	..	..	..	..	2	2	..	..	..	..	..	..	..	..	..	..	..	..
119	Trade in wood (not firewood)	2	2	..	..	..	..	..	2	2	..	..	..	..	..	..	..	..	..	..	..	..
	31. Hotels, Cafés, Restaurants, etc.	50	50	..	..	..	..	..	50	50	..	..	..	..	..	..	..	..	..	..	..	..
126	Vendors of wine, liquors, aerated waters and ice.	3	3	..	..	..	..	..	3	3	..	..	..	..	..	..	..	..	..	..	..	..

127	Owners and managers of hotels, cook shops, serais, etc. (and employees).	47	47	..	..	..	..	..	47	47	..	..	..	..	..	..	..	..	..	..	..	..
	33. Other trade in food stuffs	161	137	..	2	1	21	..	161	137	..	2	1	21	..	..	..	..	..	..	..	..
130	Dealers in sweetmeats, sugar and spices	31	31	..	..	..	..	..	31	31	..	..	..	..	..	..	..	..	..	..	..	..
131	Dealers in dairy product eggs and poultry.	113	89	..	2	1	21	..	113	89	..	2	1	21	..	..	..	..	..	..	..	..
132	Dealers in animals for food	6	6	..	..	..	..	..	6	6	..	..	..	..	..	..	..	..	..	..	..	..
134	Dealers in other food stuffs	11	11	..	..	..	..	..	11	11	..	..	..	..	..	..	..	..	..	..	..	..
	34. Trade in furniture	3	3	..	..	..	..	..	3	3	..	..	..	..	..	..	..	..	..	..	..	..
139	Trade in furniture, carpets, curtains and bedding.	3	3	..	..	..	..	..	3	3	..	..	..	..	..	..	..	..	..	..	..	..
	35. Trade in building materials	1	1	..	..	..	..	..	1	1	..	..	..	..	..	..	..	..	..	..	..	..
141	Trade in building materials (other than bricks, tiles and woody materials).	1	1	..	..	..	..	..	1	1	..	..	..	..	..	..	..	..	..	..	..	..
	39. Trade in other sorts	508	474	1	..	2	25	1	241	213	..	..	2	25	1	262	261	1	..	..	..	..
150	General storekeepers and shopkeepers otherwise unspecified.	502	473	1	..	2	25	1	240	212	..	..	2	25	1	262	261	1	..	..	..	..
151	Itinerant traders, pedlars and hawkers (other than food, etc.).	1	1	..	..	..	..	..	1	1	..	..	..	..	..	..	..	..	..	..	..	..
	C																					
	PUBLIC ADMINISTRATION AND LIBERAL ARTS.	1,712	1,651	20	..	2	38	1	1,699	1,643	15	..	2	34	1	13	8	5	..	..	..	..
	VI.—PUBLIC FORCE	785	767	..	..	..	18	..	785	767	..	..	..	18	..	..	..	..	..	..	..	..
	40. Army	122	122	..	..	..	..	..	122	122	..	..	..	..	..	..	..	..	..	..	..	..
153	Army (Imperial)	111	111	..	..	..	..	..	111	111	..	..	..	..	..	..	..	..	..	..	..	..
154	Army (Indian States)	11	11	..	..	..	..	..	11	11	..	..	..	..	..	..	..	..	..	..	..	..
	43. Police	663	645	..	..	..	18	..	663	645	..	..	..	18	..	..	..	..	..	..	..	..
157	Police	636	636	..	..	..	..	..	636	636	..	..	..	..	..	..	..	..	..	..	..	..
158	Village watchmen	27	9	..	..	..	18	..	27	9	..	..	..	18	..	..	..	..	..	..	..	..
	VII.—PUBLIC ADMINISTRATION	734	720	..	..	..	14	..	730	716	..	..	..	14	..	4	4	..	..	..	..	..
	44. Public Administration	734	720	..	..	..	14	..	730	716	..	..	..	14	..	4	4	..	..	..	..	..
159	Service of the State	656	651	..	..	..	5	..	652	647	..	..	..	5	..	4	4	..	..	..	..	..
161	Municipal and other local (not village) service.	19	19	..	..	..	..	..	19	19	..	..	..	..	..	..	..	..	..	..	..	..
162	Village officials and servants other than watchmen.	59	50	..	..	..	9	..	59	50	..	..	..	9	..	..	..	..	..	..	..	..
	VIII.—PROFESSIONS AND LIBERAL ARTS.	193	164	20	..	2	6	1	184	160	15	..	2	6	1	9	4	5	..	..	..	..
	45. Religion	16	15	..	..	..	1	..	15	14	..	..	..	1	..	1	1	..	..	..	..	..
163	Priests, Ministers, etc.	8	8	..	..	..	..	..	7	7	..	..	..	..	..	1	1	..	..	..	..	..
164	Monks, Nuns, religious mendicants	3	3	..	..	..	..	..	3	3	..	..	..	..	..	..	..	..	..	..	..	..
165	Other religious workers	2	1	..	..	..	1	..	2	1	..	..	..	1	..	..	..	..	..	..	..	..
166	Servants in religious edifices, burial and burning grounds.	3	3	..	..	..	..	..	3	3	..	..	..	..	..	..	..	..	..	..	..	..
	46. Law	6	6	..	..	..	..	..	6	6	..	..	..	..	..	..	..	..	..	..	..	..
167	Lawyers of all kinds including Qazis, Law agents and Mukhtiars.	1	1	..	..	..	..	..	1	1	..	..	..	..	..	..	..	..	..	..	..	..
168	Lawyer's clerks, petition writers, etc.	5	5	..	..	..	..	..	5	5	..	..	..	..	..	..	..	..	..	..	..	..
	47. Medicine	82	68	8	..	2	3	1	79	67	6	..	2	3	1	3	1	..	..	..	..	..
169	Registered medical practitioners including oculists.	16	16	..	..	..	..	..	16	16	..	..	..	..	..	..	..	..	..	..	..	..
172	Midwives, vaccinators, compounders, Nurses, Masseurs, etc.	63	49	8	..	2	3	1	60	48	6	..	2	3	1	3	1	2	..	..	..	..
173	Veterinary Surgeons	3	3	..	..	..	..	..	3	3	..	..	..	..	..	..	..	..	..	..	..	..
	48. Instruction	77	63	12	..	..	2	..	72	61	9	..	..	2	..	5	2	3	..	..	..	..
174	Professors and teachers of all kinds	64	50	12	..	..	2	..	59	48	9	..	..	2	..	5	2	3	..	..	..	..
175	Clerks and servants connected with education.	13	13	..	..	..	..	..	13	13	..	..	..	..	..	..	..	..	..	..	..	..

TABLE X.—OCCUPATION OR MEANS OF LIVELIHOOD—GENERAL TABLE—*concld.*

Andaman and Nicobar Islands. Total Earners . . . 14,258; Total Working Dependants . . . 6,677; Total Non-working Dependants . . . 8,528; Total Population . . . 29,463

Andamans. Total Earners . . . 11,624; Total Working Dependants . . . 483; Total Non-Working Dependants . . . 7,116; Total Population . . . 19,223

Nicobars. Total Earners . . . 2,634; Total Working Dependants . . . 6,194; Total Non-Working Dependants . . . 1,412; Total Population . . . 10,240

Group number.	Occupations.	Andaman and Nicobar Islands. Total following occupation.	As principal occupation.		As Working Dependants.		As subsidiary to other occupation.		Andamans. Total following occupation.	As principal occupation.		As Working Dependants.		As subsidiary to other occupation.		Nicobars. Total following occupation.	As principal occupation.		As Working Dependants.		As subsidiary to other occupation.	
			Males.	Females.	Males.	Females.	Males.	Females.		Males.	Females.	Males.	Females.	Males.	Females.		Males.	Females.	Males.	Females.	Males.	Females.
1	2	3	4	5	6	7	8	9	10	11	12	13	14	15	16	17	18	19	20	21	22	23
	PUBLIC ADMINISTRATION AND LIBERAL ARTS—*contd.*																					
	VIII.—PROFESSIONS AND LIBERAL ARTS—*contd.*																					
	49. Letters, Arts and Sciences	12	12	..	..	..	..	..	12	12	..	..	..	..	..	..	..	..	..	..	..	..
176	Public scribes, stenographers etc.	2	2	..	..	..	..	..	2	2	..	..	..	..	..	..	..	..	..	..	..	..
177	Architects, surveyors, engineers and their employees (not being state servants).	4	4	..	..	..	..	..	4	4	..	..	..	..	..	..	..	..	..	..	..	..
178	Authors, editors, journalists and photographers.	2	2	..	..	..	..	..	2	2	..	..	..	..	..	..	..	..	..	..	..	..
183	Managers and employees of places of public entertainment, race courses, societies, clubs.	4	4	..	..	..	..	..	4	4	..	..	..	..	..	..	..	..	..	..	..	..
	D																					
	MISCELLANEOUS	12,534	11,854	329	270	38	43	..	12,488	11,808	329	270	38	43	..	46	46	..	..	..	..	..
	IX.—PERSONS LIVING ON THEIR INCOME.	13	8	3	..	1	1	..	13	8	3	..	1	1	..	..	..	..	..	..	..	..
	50. Persons living principally on their income.	13	8	3	..	1	1	..	13	8	3	..	1	1	..	..	..	..	..	..	..	..
185	Proprietors (other than of agricultural land), fund and scholarship holders and pensioners.	13	8	3	..	1	1	..	13	8	3	..	1	1	..	..	..	..	..		..	..
	X.—DOMESTIC SERVICE	809	736	29	3	37	4	..	765	692	29	3	37	4	..	44	44	..	..	..	..	..
	51. Domestic Service	809	736	29	3	37	4	..	765	692	29	3	37	4	..	44	44	..	..	..	..	..
187	Domestic Service (other than motor drivers).	809	736	29	3	37	4	..	765	692	29	3	37	4	..	44	44	..	..	..	..	..
	XI.—INSUFFICIENTLY DESCRIBED OCCUPATIONS.	4,155	3,970	148	..	..	37	..	4,153	3,968	148	..	..	37	..	2	2	..	..	..	..	..
	52. General terms which do not indicate a definite occupation.	4,155	3,970	148	..	..	37	..	4,153	3,968	148	..	..	37	..	2	2	..	..	..	..	..
188	Manufacturers, Business men and contractors otherwise unspecified.	48	33	..	..	..	15	..	48	33	..	..	..	15	..	..	..	..	..	..	..	..
189	Cashiers, Accountants, Book-keepers, clerks and other employees in unspecified offices and warehouses and shops.	18	18	..	..	..	..	..	17	17	..	..	..	..	..	1	1	..	..	..	..	..
190	Mechanics otherwise unspecified	137	131	..	..	..	6	..	137	131	..	..	..	6	..	..	..	..	..	..	..	..
191	Labourers and workmen otherwise unspecified.	3,952	3,788	148	..	..	16	..	3,951	3,787	148	..	..	16	..	1	1	..	..	..	..	..
	XII.—UNPRODUCTIVE	7,557	7,140	149	267	..	1	..	7,557	7,140	149	267	..	1	..	..	..	..	..	..	..	..
	53. Inmates of Jails, Asylums and Alms-houses.	7,555	7,139	148	265	..	..	..	7,552	7,139	148	265	..	..	..	..	..	..	..	..	..	..
192	Inmates of jails, asylums and alms-houses.	7,552	7,139	148	265	..	..	..	7,552	7,139*	148*	265	..	..	..	..	..	..	..	..	..	..
	54. Beggars, Vagrants, Prostitutes	2	..	1	1	..	..	..	2	..	1	1	..	..	..	..	..	..	..	..	..	..
193	Beggars and vagrants	2	..	1	1	..	..	..	2	..	1	1	..	..	..	..	..	..	..	..	..	..
	55. Other unclassified non-productive industries.	3	1	..	1	..	1	..	3	1	..	1	..	1	..	..	..	..	..	..	..	..
195	Other unclassified non-productive industries.	3	1	..	1	..	1	..	3	1	..	1	..	1	..	..	..	..	..	..	..	..

*7,139 male convicts and 148 female convicts who receive pay and whose labour is productive have already been shown against the occupation which they pursue; the sum of columns eleven and twelve will therefore exceed the number of total earners in the heading by 7,139 and 148.

TABLE XIII-A.—LITERACY BY AGE.

Locality.	Age.	Population. Total.			Population. Literate.			Population. Illiterate.			Literate in English.		
		Persons.	Males.	Females.	Persons.	Males.	Females.	Persons.	Males.	Females.	Persons.	Males.	Females.
1	2	3	4	5	6	7	8	9	10	11	12	13	14
Andamans . .	0—5	1,838	947	891	..	..	..	1,838	947	891	..	..	..
	5—10	1,193	638	555	53	33	20	1,140	605	535	15	10	5
	10—15	1,044	581	463	183	137	46	861	444	417	53	43	10
	15—20	1,315	868	447	260	208	52	1,055	660	395	112	102	10
	20 and over.	13,373	10,974	2,399	3,470	3,264	206	9,903	7,710	2,193	764	705	59
Total		19,223*	14,258	4,965	3,966	3,642	324	15,257*	10,616	4,641	944	860	84

* Includes 460 Andamanese (males 250, females 210) whose ages were not recorded but who are known to have been illiterate.

Locality.	Age.	Persons.	Males.	Females.	Persons.	Males.	Females.	Persons.	Males.	Females.	Persons.	Males.	Females.
Nicobars . .	0—5	1,770	865	905	..	..	..	1,770	865	905	..	..	..
	5—10	1,216	686	530	7	7	..	1,209	679	530	..	..	..
	10—15	951	535	417	7	6	1	944	529	415	..	..	..
	15—20	603	279	324	8	7	1	595	272	323	...	..	..
	20 and over.	4,640	2,512	2,128	161	153	8	4,479	2,359	2,120	17	15	2
Total .		10,240*	5,444	4,796	183	173	10	10,057*	5,271	4,786	17	15	2

* Includes 1,060 persons (567 males and 493 females) whose ages were not recorded but who are confidently presumed to have been illiterate.

TABLE XIII-B.—LITERACY BY RELIGION.

Religion.	Locality.	Population (7 years and over). Total.			Population (7 years and over). Literate.			Population (7 years and over). Illiterate.			Literate in English (7 years and over).		
		Persons.	Males.	Females.	Persons.	Males.	Females.	Persons.	Males.	Females.	Persons.	Males.	Females.
1	2	3	4	5	6	7	8	9	10	11	12	13	14
Hindus . . .	Andamans.	6,607	4,915	1,692	1,390	1,281	109	5,217	3,634	1,583	418	401	17
Brahmanic . .	,,	*6,536*	*4,875*	*1,661*	*1,355*	*1,258*	*97*	*5,181*	*3,617*	*1,564*	*396*	*380*	*16*
Arya . . .	,,	*71*	*40*	*31*	*35*	*23*	*12*	*36*	*17*	*19*	*22*	*21*	*1*
Sikhs . . .	,,	553	448	105	164	154	10	389	294	95	36	35	1
Buddhists . .	,,	2,699	2,394	305	1,008	960	48	1,691	1,434	257	28	28	..
Zoroastrian . .	,,	1	1	..	1	1	..	..	..	..	..	..	..
Muslim . . .	,,	5,581	4,267	1,314	875	819	56	4,706	3,448	1,258	152	148	4
Christians . .	,,	970	727	243	492	391	101	478	336	142	309	247	62
Tribal . . .	,,	474	255	219	..	..	..	474	255	219	..	..	..
Shintoist . .	,,	37	36	1	36	36	..	1	..	1	..	..	..
Total .		16,922	13,043	3,879	3,966	3,642	324	12,956	9,401	3,555	944	860	84
Hindus . . .	Nicobars.	13	12	1	5	5	..	8	7	1	1	1	..
Buddhists . .	,,	10	8	2	6	5	1	4	3	1	1	1	..
Muslims . . .	,,	256	226	30	54	54	..	202	172	30	4	4	..
Christians (Nicobarese)	,,	259	149	110	26	22	4	233	127	106	7	7	..
Christians (Europeans)	,,	2	1	1	2	1	1	..	..	..	2	1	1
Tribal (Nicobarese) .	,,	7,336	3,857	3,479	5	4	1	7,331	3,853	3,478	2	1	1
Confucian . .	,,	107	101	6	85	82	3	22	19	3	..	..	..
Total .		7,983	4,354	3,629	183	173	10	7,800	4,181	3,619	17	15	2

TABLE XV.—LANGUAGE.

Language.	Total Andamans and Nicobars.			Andamans.			Nicobars.		
	Persons.	Males.	Females.	Persons.	Males.	Females.	Persons.	Males.	Females.
1	2	3	4	5	6	7	8	9	10
A.—VERNACULARS OF INDIA	28,833	19,158	9,675	18,706	13,818	4,888	10,127	5,340	4,787
Nicobarese	9,885	5,108	4,777	10	8	2	9,875	5,100	4,775
Munda (unspecified)	73	70	3	73	70	3	..	..	..
Burmese	2,745	2,315	430	2,730	2,304	426	15	11	4
Karen (unspecified)	263	133	130	263	133	130	..	..	..
Tamil	769	535	234	748	520	228	21	15	6
Malayalam	2,073	1,333	740	2,066	1,326	740	7	7	..
Kanarese	178	158	20	178	158	20	..	..	..
Oraon	140	127	13	140	127	13	..	..	..
Telugu	435	309	126	435	309	126	..	..	..
Pashto	441	372	69	441	372	69	..	..	..
Balochi	29	28	1	29	28	1	..	..	..
Sindhi	83	83	..	83	83	..	..	..	..
Marathi	352	283	69	352	283	69	..	..	..
Oriya	191	163	28	191	163	28	..	..	..
Bengali	1,171	969	202	1,151	950	201	20	19	1
Assamese	8	8	..	8	8	..	..	..	..
Hindustani	6,929	,814	2,115	6,908	4,794	2,114	21	20	1
Hindi	*4,618*	*452*	*1,166*	*4,605*	*3,440*	*1,165*	*13*	*12*	*1*
Urdu	*2,341*	*,362*	*949*	*2,303*	*1,354*	*949*	*8*	*8*	..
Gujarati	139	122	17	103	86	17	36	36	..
Panjabi	2,232	,749	483	2,231	1,748	483	1	1	..
Pahari (unspecified)	4	4	.	4	4	..	..	..	..
Naipali	2	2	.	2	2	..	..	..	..
Andamanese	466	251	215	466	251	215	..	..	..
Other languages	225	222	3	94	91	3	131	131	..
B.—VERNACULARS OF OTHER ASIATIC COUNTRIES	329	316	13	218	213	5	111	103	8
Chinese languages (other than Yunnanese)	199	187	12	88	84	4	111	103	8
Arabic	1		1	1	..	1	..	..	..
Japanese	129	129	..	129	129	..	..	..	..
C.—EUROPEAN LANGUAGES	301	228	73	299	227	72	2	1	1
French	1	1	..	1	1	..	..	..	..
English	298	225	73	296	224	72	2	1	1
Swedish	1	1	..	1	1	..	..	..	..
German	1	1	..	1	1	..	..	..	..

TABLE XVI.—Religion.

Locality.	Population.			Hindus. Total Hindus.			Hindus. Brahmanic Hindus.			Hindus. Arya.			Sikhs.			Buddhists.		
	Persons.	Males.	Females.	Persons.	Males.	Females.	*Persons.*	*Males.*	*Females.*	*Persons.*	*Males.*	*Females.*	Persons.	Males.	Females.	Persons.	Males.	Females.
1	2	3	4	5	6	7	8	9	10	11	12	13	14	15	16	17	18	19
Andaman and Nicobar islands .	29,463	19,702	9,761	7,618	5,435	2,163	*7,528*	*5,410*	*2,118*	*90*	*45*	*45*	649	503	146	2,912	2,510	402
Andamans .	19,223	14,258	4,965	7,603	5,442	2,161	*7,513*	*5,397*	*2,116*	*90*	*45*	*45*	649	503	146	2,902	[illegible]	[illegible]
Nicobars .	10,240	5,444	4,796	15	13	2	*15*	*13*	*2*	...	...	...	...	...	...	10	8	2

Locality.	Zoroastrian.			Muslims.			Christians.			Tribal.			Others.		
	Persons.	Males.	Females.	Persons.	Males.	Females.	Persons.	Males.	Females.	Persons.	Males.	Females.	Persons.	Males.	Females.
1	20	21	22	23	24	25	26	27	28	29	30	31	32	33	34
Andaman and Nicobar islands .	1	1	...	6,719	4,966	1,753	1,461	984	477	9,955	5,144	4,811	148	139	9
Andamans .	1	1	...	6,434	4,722	1,712	1,123	797	326	474	255	219	37*	36	1
Nicobars .	...	...	...	285	244	41	338	187	151	9,481	4,889	4,592	111*	103	8

*Others :—Shintoists 37 (males 36, female 1). Confucians 111 (males 103, females 8).

TABLE XVII.—Caste and Religion.

Caste and Religion.	Andaman and Nicobar Islands.			Andamans.			Nicobars.		
	Persons.	Males.	Females.	Persons.	Males.	Females.	Persons.	Males.	Females.
1	2	3	4	5	6	7	8	9	10
TOTAL POPULATION	29,468	19,702	9,761	19,223	14,258	4,965	10,240	5,444	4,796
Hindus :—	*7,618*	*5,455*	*2,163*	*7,603*	*5,442*	*2,161*	*15*	*13*	*2*
Agarwal	29	17	12	29	17	12	..	..	..
Ahir	416	290	126	416	290	126	..	..	..
Asari	8	5	3	8	5	3	..	..	..
Bhangi	29	23	6	29	23	6	..	..	..
Bhisti	4	3	1	4	3	1	..	..	..
Brahman	524	399	125	524	399	125	..	..	..
Chamar	204	139	65	204	139	65	..	..	..
Chetty	23	15	8	23	15	8	..	..	..
Gond	90	66	24	90	66	24	..	..	..
Jat	59	52	7	59	52	7	..	..	..
Kacchi	112	80	32	112	80	32	..	..	..
Kahar	126	79	47	126	79	47	..	..	..
Kayastha	185	118	67	185	118	67	..	..	..
Khasi	65	34	31	65	34	31	..	..	..
Khatri	159	107	52	159	107	52	..	..	..
Kori	47	35	12	47	35	12	..	..	..
Kumbi	66	42	24	66	42	24	..	..	..
Kurmi	491	308	183	491	308	183	..	..	..
Lodha	44	35	9	44	35	9	..	..	..
Mudaliar	122	67	55	122	67	55	..	..	..
Naik	71	42	29	71	42	29	..	..	..
Nayar	29	24	5	29	24	5	..	..	..
Pasi	232	167	65	232	167	65	..	..	..
Rajput	257	212	45	257	212	45	..	..	..
Sunar	28	15	13	28	15	13	..	..	..
Teli	98	57	41	98	57	41	..	..	..
Arya Samajists	90	45	45	90	45	45	..	..	..
Other Hindus	4,010	2,979	1,031	3,995	2,966	1,029	15	13	
Sikhs	649	503	146	649	503	146	..	..	..
Buddhists	2,912	2,510	402	2,902	2,502	400	10	8	[illegible]
Zoroastrian	1	1	..	1	1	..	..	..	..
Muslims :—	6,719	4,966	1,753	6,434	4,722	1,712	285	244	41
Pathan	510	368	142	510	368	142	..	..	..
Mogul	50	33	17	50	33	17	..	..	..
Sheikh	3,272	2,097	1,175	2,987	1,853	1,134	285	244	41
Saiyid	188	126	62	188	126	62	..	..	..
Muslims (unspecified)	2,699	2,342	357	2,699	2,342	357	..	..	..
Christians	1,461	984	477	1,123	797	326	338	187	151
Tribal	9,955	5,144	4,811	474	255	219	9,481	4,889	4,592
Others	148	139	9	37	36	1	111	103	

TABLE XVIII.—Variation of Population of Selected Tribes.

Tribe and Locality.	Persons.				Variation: Increase +, Decrease —.			Net variation 1901 to 1931 Increase + Decrease —.	Males.				Females.			
	1931	1921	1911	1901	1921 to 1931.	1911 to 1921.	1901 to 1911.		1931	1921	1911	1901	1931	1921	1911	1901
1	2	3	4	5	6	7	8	9	10	11	12	13	14	15	16	17
Coast Tribes of Great Andaman	90	209	455	625	—119	—246	—170	—535	38	104	221	335	52	105	234	290
Jarawas	70	114	114	585 (Jarawas and Sentinelese)	—44	..	—354 (Jarawas and Sentinelese)	—465 (Jarawas and Sentinelese)	40	52	52	335 (Jarawas and Sentinelese)	30	62	62	250 (Jarawas and Sentinelese)
Sentinelese	50	117	117		—67	..			25	54	54		25	63	63	
Önges	250	346	631	672	—96	—285	—41	—422	147	204	301	366	103	142	330	306
Total Andamanese	460	786	1,317	1,882	—326	—531	—565	—1,422	250	414	628	1,036	210	372	689	846
Kar Nikobar	7,182	6,087	5,550	3,451	+1,095	+537	+2,099	+3,731	3,708	3,268	2,892	1,830	3,474	2,819	2,658	1,621
Chaura	615	234	348	522	+381	—114	—174	+93	344	141	196	272	271	93	152	250
Teressa and Bompoka	506	640	656	702	—134	—16	—46	—196	263	332	357	382	243	308	299	320
Central Group	1,041	1,071	1,165	1,095	—30	—94	+70	—54	540	591	613	561	501	480	552	534
Southern Group	245	216	272	192	+29	—56	+80	+53	124	94	151	99	121	122	121	93
Shompen	200	375	375	348	—175	..	+27	—148	100	190	190	192	100	185	185	156
Total Nicobarese	9,789	8,623	8,366	6,310	+1,166	+257	+2,056	+3,479	5,079	4,616	4,399	3,336	4,710	4,007	3,967	2,974

TABLE XIX.—European and Allied Races and Anglo-Indians by Race and Age.

Locality.	Total.			A.—European and Allied Races (British subjects).																		B.—Anglo-Indians.																								
				All Ages.			0—13		14—16		17—23		24—33		34—43		44—53		54 and over.		All Ages.			0—3		4—6		7—13		14—16		17—19		20—29		30—39		40—49		50—59		60—69		70 and over.	
	Persons.	Males.	Females.	Persons.	Males.	Females.	Males.	Females.	Males.	Females.	Males.	Females.	Males.	Females.	Males.	Females.	Males.	Females.	Males.	Females.	Persons.	Males.	Females.	Males.	Females.	Males.	Females.	Males.	Females.	Males.	Females.	Males.	Females.	Males.	Females.	Males.	Females.	Males.	Females.	Males.	Females.	Males.	Females.	Males.	Females.
1	2	3	4	5	6	7	8	9	10	11	12	13	14	15	16	17	18	19	20	21	22	23	24	25	26	27	28	29	30	31	32	33	34	35	36	37	38	39	40	41	42	43	44	45	46
Andaman and Nicobar Islands	311	240	71	214	180	34	8	8	8	6	33	4	94	7	17	1	15	5	5	3	97	60	37	3	7	4	2	2	7	4	...	5	1	19	9	8	5	12	2	4	4	1	...	...	...
Andamans	309	239	70	212	179	33	8	8	9	6	33	4	94	7	17	1	14	4	5	3	97	60	37	3	7	4	2	2	7	4	...	5	1	19	9	6	5	12	2	4	4	1	...	...	...
Nicobars	2	1	1	2	1	1	...	...	...	...	...	...	...	...	...	...	1	1	...	...	...	...	...	...	...	...	...	...	...	...	...	...	...	...	...	...	...	...	...	...	...	...	...	...	...

TABLE XX.—Summary Figures for Island Groups.

Island Groups.	Area in square miles.	Population, 1931.			Population, 1921.	Percentage of variation.		Number of persons per square mile.		Distribution by Religion.													
										Hindus.		Sikhs.		Buddhists.		Muslims.		Christians.		Tribal.		Others.	
		Persons.	Males.	Females.		1921—31.	1911—21.	1931.	1921.	Males.	Females.	Males.	Females.	Males.	Females.	Males.	Females.	Males.	Females.	Males.	Females.	Males.	Females.
	2	3	4	5	6	7	8	9	10	11	12	13	14	15	16	17	18	19	20	21	22	23	24
Andamans	2,508	19,223	14,258	4,965	17,814	+7·9	+·98	7·66	7·1	5,442	2,161	503	146	2,502	400	4,722	1,712	797	326	255	219	37	1
Great Andaman	..	*18,923*	*14,086*	*4,837*	*17,351*	*+9·05*	*+2·7*	..	..	*5,442*	*2,161*	*503*	*146*	*2,502*	*400*	*4,722*	*1,712*	*797*	*326*	*83*	*91*	*37*	*1*
Little Andaman	..	*250*	*147*	*103*	*346*	*—27·7*	*—45·16*	..	..	..	..	..	..	..	..	..	..	..	..	*147*	*103*	..	..
North Sentinel Island	..	*50*	*25*	*25*	*117*	*—57·1*	..	..	..	..	..	..	..	..	..	..	..	..	..	*25*	*25*	..	..
Nicobars	635	10,240	5,444	4,796	9,272	+10·44	+5·14	16·12	14·6	13	2	..	..	8	2	244	41	187	151	4,889	4,592	103	8
Kar Nikobar	*49*	*7,492*	*3,950*	*3,542*	*6,352*	*+17·9*	*+60·06*	*153*	*29·6*	*13*	*2*	..	..	*8*	*2*	*221*	*32*	*187*	*151*	*3,521*	*3,355*	..	..
Chaura	*3*	*615*	*344*	*271*	*234*	*+162·8*	*—32·7*	*205*	*78*	..	..	..	..	..	..	..	..	..	..	*344*	*271*	..	..
Central Group	*190*	*1,688*	*927*	*761*	*1,835*	*—8·01*	*—4·0*	*8·8*	*9·6*	..	..	..	..	..	..	*23*	*9*	..	..	*803*	*744*	*101*	*8*
Southern Group	*393*	*445*	*223*	*222*	*851*	*—47·7*	*+11·6*	*1·1*	*2·1*	..	..	..	..	..	..	..	..	..	..	*221*	*222*	*2*	..

PROVINCIAL TABLE.

Territorial Distribution of the Christian Population by Sect and Race.

Locality.	All Denominations.									Anglican Communion.								
	Total.			Distribution by Race.						Total.			Distribution by Race.					
				European and allied Races.		Anglo-Indians.		Indians.					European and allied Races.		Anglo-Indians.		Indians.	
	Persons.	Males.	Females.	Males.	Females.	Males.	Females.	Males.	Females.	Persons.	Males.	Females.	Males	Females.	Males.	Females.	Males.	Females.
1	2	3	4	5	6	7	8	9	10	11	12	13	14	15	16	17	18	19
Andaman and Nicobar Islands	1,461	984	477	180	34	59	37	745	406	591	361	210	143	17	24	16	214	177
Andamans	1,123	797	326	179	33	59	37	559	256	253	194	59	142	16	24	16	28	27
Nicobars	338	187	151	1	1	...	...	186	150	338	187	151	1	1	..	...	186	150

Locality.	Baptist.									Methodists.									Other Protestants.								
	Total.			Distribution by Race.						Total			Distribution by Race.						Total.			Distribution by Race.					
				European and allied Races.		Anglo-Indians.		Indians.					European and allied Races.		Anglo-Indians.		Indians.					European and allied Races.		Anglo-Indians.		Indians.	
	Persons.	Males.	Females.	Males.	Females.	Males.	Females.	Males.	Females.	Persons.	Males.	Females.	Males.	Females.	Males.	Females.	Males.	Females.	Persons.	Males.	Females.	Males.	Females.	Males.	Females.	Males.	Females.
	20	21	22	23	24	25	26	27	28	29	30	31	32	33	34	35	36	37	38	39	40	41	42	43	44	45	46
Andaman and Nicobar Islands	251	132	129	...	2	...	1	122	126	6	6	...	6	...	...	...	...	..	22	11	11	3	...	...	...	8	11
Andamans	251	122	129	...	2	...	1	122	126	6	6	...	6	...	...	...	...	...	22	11	11	3	...	..	...	8	11
Nicobars	...	...	...	...	...	...	...	...	...	...	...	...	...	...	...	...	...	...	...	...	...	...	...	...	...	...	...

Locality.	Roman Catholic.									Salvationists.									Sect Unspecified.								
	Total.			Distribution by Race.						Total.			Distribution by Race.						Total.			Distribution by Race.					
				European and allied Races.		Anglo-Indians.		Indians.					European and allied Races.		Anglo-Indians.		Indians.					European and allied Races.		Anglo-Indians.		Indians.	
	Persons.	Males.	Females.	Males.	Females.	Males.	Females.	Males.	Females.	Persons.	Males.	Females.	Males.	Females.	Males.	Females.	Males.	Females.	Persons.	Males.	Females.	Males.	Females.	Males.	Females.	Males.	Females.
	47	48	49	50	51	52	53	54	55	56	57	58	59	60	61	62	63	64	65	66	67	68	69	70	71	72	73
Andaman and Nicobar Islands	445	378	67	32	13	33	20	323	34	114	62	52	...	...	..	...	62	52	32	24	8	6	2	2	...	16	6
Andamans	445	378	67	22	13	33	20	323	34	114	62	52	...	...	...	...	62	52	32	24	8	6	2	2	...	16	6
Nicobars	...	...	...	...	...	...	...	...	...	...	...	...	...	...	...	...	...	...	...	...	...	...	...	...	...	...	...

GIPD—20Census Commr. for India—22-7-32—550.